They Were Legal:
Balzac y Lopez

They Were Legal: Balzac y Lopez

The History of an Hispanic Family
New York 1901-1960

DIANE FORTUNA

authorHOUSE®

AuthorHouse™
1663 Liberty Drive
Bloomington, IN 47403
www.authorhouse.com
Phone: 1-800-839-8640

First published by AuthorHouse   12/23/2011

ISBN: 978-1-4634-1029-2 (sc)
ISBN: 978-1-4634-1028-5 (hc)
ISBN: 978-1-4634-2641-5 (ebk)

Library of Congress Control Number: 2011962631

Printed in the United States of America

Contents

> So what shall we do for the dead...?
> they cannot see what we hoard–
> photograph, letter, keepsake, muttered or knitted homily—
> as we change flags and houses. We still wish them to serve
> us, expecting from death what we expect of our prayers—
> that their hearts lift like ours with the surge
> of the surf and the cupolas of the sunset, that the kingfisher
> startles their darkness sometimes. But each one prefers
> the silence that was his birthright, and the shore
> where the others wait neither to end nor begin.
> —Derek Walcott, _Midsummer,_

The Balzacs of Puerto Rico

Joseph Balzac + Josephine de Lau
(left Tours, France for Puerto Rico, 1812)

↓

1ˢᵗ gen. P. R.   ### Joseph Balzac + Fidela Dilan

↓

2nd gen. P. R.   ### Genaro Balzac y Dilan
b.ca.1854, d.ca.1922

+	+	+
Marcelina Tizol d.1891	Serafina (Minnan?)	Josefina Velez (Proventud)
↓	↓	↓
Joseph (Pepìn) Balzac b.Apr 10,1882 d.Feb 6,1939	Fidela Balzac y Minnan b.Apr 21,1890 d.Sep 1956	Genaro Balzac y Velez b.Nov 12,1889 d.July1975
	Rosa Balzac y Minnan b.1893 d.1982 P.R.	Irene Balsac y Velez De Vila b.Sep 14,1900
		Alberto Balsac y Velez b.Aug 7,1894 d.Sep 13,1990

3ʳᵈ gen.   ### Joseph (Pepìn) Balzac y Tizol
b.Apr 10,1882, d.Feb 6,1939

+	+
Louise Lopez b.1889,d.Jun 27,1913 NY	Ianthe Eva (Birdie) Lopez b.Apr 17,1887, d.Feb 11,1927
↓	↓
Joseph Henry b.May 17,1910, d.Dec 1984	Mercedes (Nena) b.July 9,1914, d.Feb 5,1960
Fidela (Della) b.July 2,1912, d.Nov 1991	William (Bill) b.Feb 14,1916, d.Apr 20,1956
	Peter (Pete) b.Apr29,1918, d.Nov30,2004
	Frederick (Freddie) b.Sept6,1924, d.Jan19,2000

The Lopez of Kingston, Jamaica, B.W.I.

Christopher Augustus Lopez ll + Eliza Anastasia Kempt

b.Kingston, Ja.ca.1855, d.ca.1920, Ja.   b.Kent, England,ca.1858,

d. 1906, Ja.

m. Dec 21,1875

↓

Christopher Augustus III, dentist,b.1877, m. Eliza Mary.Purcell,b. Ketley,Shropshire,ca.1879. Their four daughters: Signa Elaine,1902; Winnifred,1903; Mingaurette Allison,1904 and Dorothy,1912. Family may have emigrated ca. 1931 to England with

?Charles Cecil or Cecil Charles (Melancholic Uncle Charlie)?

Horace Ivanhoe,b.Sept 27,1880, m. Janet Broderick,Apr.6,1910, d.Nov21,1911, R.I.

Reginald Courtney,b.1882

Vincent,b.July22,1892,d.1956, NY. Son George Vincent,b.1915, lived with his mother Anna (Culo Grande) Oentgen,Sunnyside, Queens

Daisy,b.Jan11,1885,d.Mar27,1911(Triangle Factory Fire),NY

Ianthe Eva (Birdie),b.Apr19,1887,d.Feb 11,1927,NY

Louise Leonora,b.1889,d.June27,1913,NY

Also Harold Lewis,1890;Madeline May,1894; Philip Ernest,1897 and Evangeline Pearl,1901 (Some of these children may have died in infancy).

Christopher Augustus Lopez ll + Adeline Maud Bartlett
(Widower)   nee Campbell, Widow

m. July26,1906

Charles Augustus,b.1909

The Balzac-Lopez in New York:

Children of Pepin and Louise

Joseph Henry Balzac,1910-1982   Della Balzac Redding,1912-1991

↓   ↓

Joseph (Jo Jo) Balzac,1931-   James Redding,1936-

Ross Cook Redding,1942-2005

↓

Garrett (b.ca.1965)

Children of Pepin and Ianthe Eva (Birdie)

↓

Mercedes (Nena) + Mauro   Bill   Pete + Mary   Fred + Ida

↓   no issue   ↓   ↓

Diane, 1936   Lenore (Lenny), 1940   Fred, 1959

↓   Peter, 1944-1945   Billy, 1961

Demi Fortuna,1961   Jeanne Marie,1948

Davin Fortuna,1963

↓

Matthew Fortuna,1985

Introduction
For Demi, Davin and Matthew

You have often asked me to write down what I know about our Caribbean forebears, the Balzacs from Puerto Rico and the Lopez from Jamaica, West Indies. By definition, they were Creoles, peoples of French and Spanish ancestry born in the New World. Since I have been–from the age of four or so–by happenstance and all too voluntary predilection, the awed listener to these sketches and secrets, a memoir seemed a fair way to transmit them.

Many of these tales my mother, Mercedes (Nena) Balzac, told me. Sometimes she related the droll stories of her father, Pepìn, and his sisters from Mayaguez. On her mother's side of the family, she recounted the piteous destinies of the Lopez women in Kingston and New York City. Together with the surmises of aunts, uncles, great aunts and a great uncle, these recollections constituted a Creole chronicle, but my mother did not think of them that way. For her, they were the rich remnants of an exotic romance.

At the turn of the 20th century, as the Balzacs changed houses and the Lopez changed flags, some found themselves in the vortex of an uncommon number of irresistible events. In 1911, Daisy Lopez succumbed in the Triangle Factory Fire; early in World War I, Fidela Balzac lost her fiancé on a poppy-strewn field in France; in 1919, their baby died, a victim of the Great Influenza Epidemic. As best they could, the others went on—chastened—through Prohibition, the Depression, the Great Hurricane of 1938. An allergic reaction to a standard immunization took the life of a second baby in 1944. And because one brother could not serve in World War II, he lapsed into melancholia; because another brother served *semper fi* at Kwajalein, Saipan, Tinian and Iwo Jima, he came home without a scratch, but broken and insane. Silently, the ghosts accumulated.

Until the age of thirteen, I lived much of the time in my maternal grandfather's house in Floral Park, Long Island, New York. The village itself was rural enough to be representative of the American experience, yet close enough to New York to reflect the city's intense political and cultural life. Over the years at various times, 41 Sycamore Avenue housed so many relatives that they seemed more like a federation than a family. At the vital center of all this shared Latin D.N.A. was my grandfather, Pepìn Balzac, a printer and translator; his two daughters, Della and Nena (my mother), their spouses and children; two unmarried sons, Bill and Freddie and a third son, Pete, who married my father's sister, Mary. This union produced my double first cousins, Lenore (Lenny) and Jeanne—by blood as close as sisters.

Growing up under the same roof, I was just old enough never to forget; tender-hearted Lenny, four years younger than I, did not want to remember; and her sister, Jeanne, twelve years my junior, was too young to know.

As a child what I heard and beheld were Balzac-Lopez legends made palpable by hoarded keepsakes, letters, school certificates, and photographs. Now however interesting, legends—especially those of fanciful people from the Islands - - smoothly deviate from historical fact and actual chronology. On one hand, the legendary piece is perfect; its details and intentions are fully explained; nothing jars its symmetry and completeness. On the other hand, history is jagged—time tends to obscure so many facts; motives, much less emotions, are sometimes unclear; participants have died and memories may have faltered. With none from my mother's generation alive, the two-century-old register remains fragmentary. Much has to be inferred, even interpolated—for having drunk of Lethe, the river of oblivion, the spirits speak not a word.

How then to deal with data so diverse that by turns they invoke legend, history, superstition, the real and surreal, the natural and supernatural? How to shape so many complex and alternately comic and forlorn accounts? For the last nine years, I have become a dedicated ghostbuster sifting birth, death and marriage records; sorting Census reports; recording testimonies of second cousins living in Mayaguez and Toronto; avidly combing old newspapers and annals from Jamaica and New York.

Still memory dictates, the shades gather on the shore and I write. What I've collected here, like the shells, pebbles and driftwood that long ago I picked up at the water's edge of the Rockaways or Jones Beach, are the shards of lives that underwent a momentarily lustrous sea change. They are legacies from the littoral drift, caught before the next wave crests, crashes and wipes them away forever.

March 2002 - May 2011

Acknowledgments

This book began with a trip to Europe that I took with my cousin, Fred Balzac in 1983 during which I inundated him with family stories. In turn, he recounted tales that his father had told him. So intrigued were we by the number and variety of these fragmented histories that when we returned to the United States first Freddie, and then my cousin, Lenny, accompanied me to Evergreens Cemetery to find the final resting place of our Jamaican grandmother and her sisters. Having been there as a child, I had a vague recollection of the gravesite.

Searching up and down the paths near the Cooper Street entrance, Freddie found the tombstone that bears only Daisy Lopez' name and the inscription "Greater love hath no man than this: that a man lay down his life for his friends." Seeing the quotation on the headstone for the first time, Freddie was quick to ask, "Had Daisy been heroic in some way?" I discovered the answer to that question some years afterward in Kingston, Jamaica.

Two weeks later, when Lenny and I were able to consult the Evergreens burial records, she exclaimed, "But there's a man in the grave with grandma! Who is Edmundo La Carruba?" And suddenly the floodgates of memory spilled open, and I recalled that when I was five years old, my mother and her Balzac aunts had taken me with them to the cemetery. They sent me to crank water from an old hand pump for the flowers my great aunts had brought for the grave. And they told me that Tia Fidela's baby boy was buried there with the three sisters Lopez.

It was to take another twenty years after Freddie and I found the Lopez grave that I began writing. I had inherited my mother's family photographs, and sometime after I retired from university teaching in December, 1999, I realized that I was the only person left who knew the identities of most of those pictured. And so, in late March 2002, I began a commentary on Balzac-Lopez studio portraits and snapshots.

Along the way, I received early encouragement from Carla Cohen, editor of *The Gateway*, the Floral Park town newspaper, who published three short essays abstracted from the manuscript. James Yin in Suzhou, People's Republic of China, arranged for the publication and translation into Mandarin of a piece in *Translator's Journal*. In their 73rd Annual Writing Competition, October 2004, *Writer's Digest* awarded "A Flower for Daisy" an Honorable Mention and made me believe that a wider audience than my family might be interested in this memoir.

I owe special thanks to New York Senator Serphin R. Maltese who brought my essay about Daisy Lopez to the attention of the then State Commissioner of Labor, Linda Angello. She and her able staff, headed by Francina Kitchen, printed it and showcased Daisy's portrait for the 94th Triangle Fire Commemoration, March 2005 in Albany. A month later, Senator Maltese, whose family suffered the loss of a grandmother and two great aunts in the fire, graciously invited me to join him on his weekly TV program to talk about the tragic death of Daisy Lopez.

For help with research, my gratitude goes to the reference staffs at The Emma Clark Library in East Setauket, the Floral Park Library and the New York Public Library. With great care, Jennifer Huynh reproduced a rare copy of a Red Cross document at the University of California at Berkeley and sent it to me. In Kingston, Jamaica, I was able to access the 1911 archives of *The Gleaner* with Michele Anderson's kind assistance.

Any author writing a memoir recognizes the collaborative nature of the task. I wish to thank Fred Balzac and Lenore Balzac Goebel for their caring and provocative interest and my sons, Demi and Davin Fortuna, for their continuous attention and unfailing editorial assistance as this project gradually evolved.

In addition, I am grateful to all those who so abundantly shared anecdotes and answered repeated questions: my aunt and uncle, the late Mary and Peter Balzac; their daughter, Jeanne Balzac Kane; my cousin, Joe and his wife, the late Dotty Balzac. My Aunt Ida and Cousin Bill Balzac also contributed recollections, and Bill went out of his way to provide me with copies of our grandfather's journal and his father's photographs.

Above all, for indispensable listening, discussion and readership of the work in progress, I am most indebted and sincerely grateful to Rebekah Ackerman, Dorothy Hoffmann and Marilyn Lombardo. Without their constancy and criticism, this project would never have been completed.

Pencil in hand, Marilyn read whole chapters for hours on end as we met for breakfast at the Millennium Diner in Smithtown. As a final acknowledgment, I wish to thank the diner's genial waiters and waitresses for their extraordinary patience despite our lengthy stays.

Part 1: The Book of Pepìn

Pepìn Balzac 1922

Part 1, Chapter 1
The Balzacs of Puerto Rico: 1812-1901

Adios, adios, que me marcho   (Goodbye, goodbye, I'm off
Confiado en que mi destino   Hoping that my destiny
Quizás no me sea adverso;   Will not be adverse;
Adios, adios, me despido!   Goodbye, goodbye and farewell!)

—José Balzac, "Adios" unpublished poem, July 5, 1900

In the late 1930s on weekdays at 5:30 a.m., my father would quietly enter the bathroom at the end of the hall, run the water very slowly and then go downstairs carefully avoiding the squeaky fourth step from the top. Sitting up in my high bed, I would strain, listening for his slow shuffling in the kitchen, and then wait for the click of the cellar door, the rumble of his old car.

He didn't like me to awaken my mother, but as soon as he left for work, I would get up and walk across the bare waxed pine floor to the hall. Quietly, I'd call at my mother's door. "Mama, can I come in and sleep with you?" The merest grunt I took as permission to climb into my mother's body-warmed bed. Nena Balzac lay ladled on her side, both hands cupped beneath her head, the scent of her *Nights in Paris* talc mingling with the faint smell of the outdoors coming from the crisp, ironed sheets.

Blue-flowered paper decorated the walls of Mama's room as well as the small alcove where my crib had stood when I was an infant. Just beyond its big windows were three great Norway maples that my grandmother, Ianthe Eva (Birdie), had planted when she and my grandfather, Joseph (Pepìn) Balzac bought the four bedroom Dutch colonial in 1915 on Sycamore Avenue in Floral Park, New York.

On windy Long Island mornings, the boughs whistled, and the smaller branches tapped the windows mournfully. Just beyond them, I could see the steeple of St. Hedwig's, the Roman Catholic Polish Church, two blocks away. If my mother wanted to sleep a bit longer, I would try to stay very still amusing myself by closing one eye and then the other, making the steeple move back and forth. I knew that it didn't really move, but why did it seem to? I couldn't account for it.

Sometimes I would play, tracing—ever so lightly—the prominent veins on the back of my sleeping mother's hand. I used to call them her "spaghetti" and wonder if my hands would come to look like that.

Snuggling next to her, I tried to understand why she seemed so often preoccupied, always clutching her pocketbook tightly when we went shopping along Jericho Turnpike. Times must have been hard just before World War II. As a 4-year-old, I knew that my mother worried about money. I remember being puzzled when we went to Mr. Porrelo's greengrocer's shop for salad or soup fixings. Why did she have to give him dollars? Shouldn't he pay us for taking the vegetables and fruit away before they rotted?

Finally, having exhausted myself with questions of optics, anatomy and high finance, I would begin to fidget, and Mommy would reluctantly wake up. Sometimes she sang to me in a breathy voice or told me children's stories or taught me poems and prayers.

Best of all, she would open the bottom drawer of the high bureau that had belonged to her father and get out the inlaid mahogany box that contained generations-old pictures, class photos of her sister and four brothers and school records back to 1928.

> *Did I ever tell you that in 1812 my great, great grandmother, Josephine de Lau Balzac, a Frenchwoman out of Tours, vowed to give all her jewels to the Church if only she and her husband could get to the New World in safety?*

Josephine de Lau's husband, the first Joseph Balzac, was one of two brothers, well-to-do French merchants on the verge of being ruined by the Napoleonic Continental Wars. Both left Tours bound for Port au Prince, Haiti. Eventually, Brother Henri went to San Domingo (now the Dominican Republic). Joseph and his wife ended up in Puerto Rico where in time he became one of the largest exporters of sugar and coffee on the island. They were prominent members of the merchant class and proud of their elevated social position. One of his sons was named for him, and at least one Joseph (Sp. José) occurs in each succeeding generation.

In the beginning, Balzac operated out of San Juan; later he kept an office in the capital and a huge warehouse in Mayagüez. Closed since the 1970s, the faded blue building near the waterfront still bears the name Balzac & Sons. Preferring the sleepy provincial town on the West Coast to the capital, Balzac bought land on a high hill in Mayagüez and built a huge hacienda with many porches to catch the tropical breezes. At one point, 35 Balzacs lived there together.[1]

My grandfather, Joseph (Pepìn) Balzac was born in 1882, a third generation Puerto Rican (though that term did not indicate an ethnicity until the late 1940s). In addition, he was doubly a Creole in the sense that he was of both French and Spanish ancestry born in the Americas. Neither he nor the family ever used these proper nouns—Puerto Rican or Creole—to describe themselves. As far as the Balzacs were concerned, they were French and Spanish with a name obviously allied to that of Honoré de Balzac, the great French writer and father of the novel. Was Honoré not originally from Tours like Josephine de Lau and Balzac Premier? Did Honoré not have a half-brother named Henri, and hence, all the Genas and Genaros in the Puerto Rican branch? How else to account for the literary and linguistic talents of the entire family?[2]

Pepìn was the eldest of six children. An early—and by virtue of the American victory over Spain in 1898—a legal colonial immigrant, he arrived in New York City in 1901 at the age of 19. The next child to emigrate was Fidela, who left Mayagüez for the United States to join her brother.in 1914. Rosa came in 1922 living in New York eventually with and in the shadow of gentle Fidela. Gena, Jr., Irene and Alberto were the children of Genaro Balzac and his second wife, Josefina Velez Proventud. They remained in Puerto Rico.

When Pepìn was a boy, the children had a French governess, and all of them were bi-lingual in keeping with their heritage. Pepìn claimed that he first heard English in the summer of 1898 when American soldiers occupied Ponce and Mayagüez. To his last days when on rare occasions he lost his temper (having been provoked beyond human endurance), he would bellow, "Suleiman bitch," the curse that he had learned from Yankee soldiers. (As a youth, he thought they were cursing in the name of Roxelana, the evil wife of Suleiman the Magnificent, the great 16th century Ottoman emperor). Of course, they had said "son of a bitch," but in the heat of their father's anger, none of his children dared suggest that he correct his pronunciation or cultural misapprehension.

Pepìn was the only child of Marcelina Tizol, to whom he was devoted, and Genaro Balzac, a bull-necked, mustachioed grandee who must have expected his oldest son to take over the business. Marcelina died in 1891, possibly of diabetes, when Pepìn was 9 years old. Her family came from Madrid, and she clearly was of mixed Spanish and Moorish lineage.

Peter Balzac

His grandmother
Marcelina Tizol y Balzac

Not only her surname attests to this fact, but her photograph (ca. 1885) shows her to be *una tipa arabe*. She has thin hair, probably graying, a high forehead, slanted eyes, an aquiline nose and thin lips, features strikingly like those of her grandson, Pete.

Two pictures of Genaro are also extant: one, a studio portrait, taken in his thirties; the other, a photo postcard, of much interest, sent to Pepìn

from Mayagüez some forty years later when Genaro was in his sixties. On the back of the card, Genaro wrote:

Apreciado hijo: Recibe este retrato; como obsequio que te dedica tu padre, que mucho te quiere.
(Valued son: Receive this portrait; your father, who loves you very much, inscribes it as a gift to you).

Genaro Balzac, 1917

He signed it, Genaro Balsac, January 2, 1917, using an "s" in the last name rather than the "z" that Pepìn eventually adopted. White haired with a bushy mustache, he looks slimmer than in an earlier photo, but the large and intensely dark eyes, bullet head, round face and somewhat bulbous nose are the same. Both Pepìn and Gena Jr. resembled him, but they had finer features.

Pepìn's beloved sister, Fidela, was born in 1890. Only upon her death did the family discover a decades old secret. In 1956, while making funeral arrangements for Fidela's burial, in her grief, Aunt Rosa slipped up. When the funeral director asked for their mother's name for the record, Aunt Rosa tearfully replied, "Serafina." Shocked, my mother, Nena blurted out, "But Dad's mother was Marcelina Tizol!" Aunt Rosa immediately clammed up. Unabashed, Nena asked a friend who was going to Puerto Rico to make inquiries.

Gossip dies slowly in sleepy provincial towns. More than fifty years after the fact, someone remembered that for at least two decades Genaro had had a mistress, Serafina Minnan, who was the mother of his two elder daughters. Pepìn, nevertheless, always called Fidela and Rosa his sisters and treated them as such. He never indicated to any of his children that he and they had had different mothers.

What of Marcelina? Was she ill, or had she stopped caring? Fidela was born the year before she died. Did Serafina live in the great house too? Was she a servant? Even more to the point, what was her relationship to Genaro's volatile second wife, Josefina Velez Proventud, a startling, gaunt Spanish and Indian widow whom everyone called Mama Pepe? She was the mother of Gena Jr., Alberto and Irene. Nor did Genaro Père discard Serafina once he remarried. Nor did Genaro Père discard Serafina and her children once he remarried. Fidela and Rosa were raised in the Mayagüez hacienda with all the other Balzac offspring.[3]

By the time Pepìn was a teenager, he and Mama Pepe were not getting along. Having no interest in the family business, in the spring of 1898 Pepìn apprenticed himself to Manuel Lopez, a printer in Ponce. More than anything else, he wanted to be learned, and he needed a trade to fall back on if he were going to become a poet and writer. No doubt he also wanted to get away from home and his stepmother, though his affection for his father and little grandmother (*abuelita*) remained undiminished. Throughout the printing apprenticeship, he wrote in a red cloth-covered journal produced and printed in the shop where he worked. It bore the elaborately decorated flyleaf of Manuel Lopez, and on it appears Pepìn's signature at the time, José Balsac y Tizol, Marzo (March) 1898.[4]

Pepìn reserved thirty-odd pages, the first half of the book, for a series of poems and sketches in Spanish to his father, dear grandmother and friends. They include sonnets, light commentaries, epistles, epigrams and jingles dating from June 1900 to February 1901. In almost all of them, Pepìn expresses his misery. He complains that the nine-hour workday that includes holidays, the meager salary of an apprentice ($5 per week) and the lack of opportunity in Puerto Rico are crushing his spirit. Each time he goes home and sees Mayagüez, the city makes him sadder. He seems to have aspirations that his friends (and possibly his family) neither share nor appreciate.

By July 1900 in the second poem of the journal, a verse entitled "Adios!" Pepìn is writing about leaving home and breaking off relationships with all who know him, including his sweetheart. He's ready to go, ready "to march off to distant lands and dauntlessly confront whatever dangers lie ahead on this long road." Already he's anticipating immigrating to the United States whose history and freedom have fascinated him from childhood.

Of all these youthful effusions, the most troubling is a long poem written to his father. Pepìn loves and will always love his dad without reservation, but his father doesn't seem to recognize him or his privations. Away from home, Pepìn "lives without joy" in Ponce. A forgotten son, he has little hope and cannot understand his father's profound silence and indifference to him.

The poems are sophisticated using intricate rhyme schemes, a variety of genres and elevated, sometimes archaic, diction. At eighteen, Pepìn was a budding and witty poet, but Balzac Père probably considered writing as a career absurdly impractical.

Thinking that knowing yet another language would be helpful in business and utterly necessary should he go to the States, Pepìn began to take English lessons at a night school near work. He paid "his kind tutor," Mr. Boerman, $2 a month from his scanty salary writing out thirty exercises in both Spanish and English. He carefully inscribed this schoolwork in the second half of his chapbook after a page that he decorated with a log-shaped design labeled "1900."

From the very first exercise, Pepìn tells his teacher that he intends to come to the United States. Pepìn does not date his essays more specifically, but in Exercise 25, he mentions that Boerman has taught him for five months. When he visits Mayagüez, his family is astounded at his progress in the language, but he will not be satisfied until he speaks English as well as he speaks Spanish. Then his father will understand that his son is not "losing" his time.

Pepìn also writes in his journal about his girlfriend, but his poverty is affecting their relationship:

> My poor being loves a young lady and she loves my poor being; but I am not happy. I cannot be so because my poverty does not permit me to be as I wish.

> Yesterday I walked much, but I was rather sad, because my sweetheart was not in her house, and she was walking without having my leave.

Eventually, Genaro came to Ponce to see his son. Pepìn was overjoyed. In turn, Genaro promised to help his son financially.

In Exercise 29, Pepìn writes:

> My desire to sail is greater every day, but I am very patient and though all things which are said to me are good, I shall be in this city [Ponce] as much time as God may like. As I have been learning the English language, when I may go to New York or Philadelphia, I shall then speak well English.
>
> I don't see the moment come, in which I may be in those great States which are called United and where a young man who works can live in plenty, for there a workman is very respected.

Genaro approved of his son's learning English, but he certainly did not want his teenager to go away. At work, Pepìn had met a ship captain who was willing to take him to New York or Philadelphia, but he wanted his father's permission.

Within weeks after his father's visit, Pepìn records a final essay and the title of the next. His English lessons abruptly come to an end on February 15, 1901, and the notebook seems to indicate why.

From Exercise 24 on, Pepìn has crossed out all but one reference to "mother" or "mama." Apocrypha has it that stepson and stepmother clashed frequently and with increasing bitterness. During one particularly acrid exchange, Genaro sided with Mama Pepe.

Defiant and hurt, Pepìn left Puerto Rico working as a deckhand in return for his passage to the Port of Philadelphia. As a citizen of Puerto Rico and a U.S. national from an American territory, he didn't need a visa. He departed immediately. From Philadelphia, he took the train to New York where the offer of a job as an assistant compositor on a Spanish newspaper awaited him. It was 1901; in April, he would be 19.

Some sixteen years later, the affectionate and regretful note on the back of Genaro's postcard indicates that by 1917, father and son had reconciled. In that same year, Congress granted United States citizenship to all those born in the Territory of Puerto Rico. By that time, Pepìn had already buried one wife, taken another and was the father of four children. "Knowledged with responsibility," he never returned to Mayagüez.

The Lopez of Kingston, Jamaica: ca. 1817-1907

A hundred midsummers gone, with the rippling accordion,
Bustled skirts, boating parties, zinc-white strokes on water,
Girls whose flushed cheeks wouldn't outlast their roses.
—Derek Walcott, Midsummer,

On other mornings as dust motes floated on the brilliant rays of light streaming in from the windows, my mother would get out the studio portraits of the Lopez of Kingston, Jamaica. Her low and breathy voice transported me into another time and place. It was made up of lush tropical plants, rain forests and ornate Victorian houses; of men who parted their hair in the middle and sported handle-bar mustaches; of women in flowing ball gowns and bustles and of children dressed in white eyelet and high laced shoes.

My mother began by showing me a sepia studio picture of her grandmother, Eliza Anastasia Kempf, an Englishwoman originally from Kent, England. Signed by A. Duperly and Sons, it dates from the 1890s as indicated by the furnishings of the room and the furbelows of her gown.

Adolphe Duperly was a famous daguerreotypist and photographer noted for early studies of the Jamaican landscape. His son, Armand John Lewis, carried on the family business and may have taken the original photo of Eliza that became the basis for a large, hand-tinted portrait. In the small photograph, a full-length pose, Eliza stands with her hand slightly folded on the back of an elaborate faux bamboo, straight-backed chair. Fashionably turned out in Victorian attire, she wears a light-colored long dress with a lace bib that extends from her neck to her bosom and forms a high ruche under her chin. A dark-rimmed straw sailor hat, topped by a white feather and large bow, perches on an angle over her swept back, auburn hair. Despite multiple childbirths, she has only a slightly thickened figure. A petite woman in her thirties, she is attractive despite a wide mouth and prominent jaw.

Eliza Anastasia Kempf Lopez, ca. 1890

Written on the back of the photograph are the name Lopez, and her son Vincent's Manhattan address, 414 E. 89th Street. He gave both the photo and the large oval portrait, a colored bust of their mother, to his sister, Ianthe for safekeeping.

The portrait is a blow-up duplicate of the smaller study. Eliza, sans hat, has a high forehead, dark eyes and a finely chiseled nose. The photographer has carefully painted in her wavy, reddish brown hair and tinted her afternoon dress a pale green.

When and why Eliza came to Jamaica from England and met and married Christopher Augustus Lopez II is unknown. Born in Kent in 1858, she was 17 when she married Christopher Augustus Lopez II on December 18, 1875. The ceremony was performed by the Rev. Charles Weskey of the North Street Congregational Chapel and reported in the *Daily Gleaner* on December 21.

Wed at 20 (b. 1855), Christopher Augustus II came from an established Kingston family dating back to 1817. His father, Christopher I wrote an extensive account of his forebears and life in 19th century Jamaica in a two volume journal now in the Jamaica National Library.[5]

The line begins with the first Christopher's grandfather—Don Eduardo Augusta Lopez, a Spanish general stationed in Cuba who may have been killed by his own men (ca. 1790s).

The general's son, Eduardo Augusta Lopez married Mary Lewis Grant, daughter of Isaac Lewis, a merchant and large slave owner in Charleston, South Carolina. They arrived in Jamaica from Charleston in 1817. Fluent in Spanish and English, Eduardo earned his living as a scholar and legal scribe composing letters from petitioners to the government—the Common Council Board, the Aldermen's Board and the House of Assembly.

Christopher Augustus I was born July 15, 1829. He briefly records having a brother and two sisters. After the death of his father in 1843, he apprenticed as a tailor. In 1851 when he was 22, Christopher I married Sarah Celestine Melvin. She was 16. Over the years, she bore him twelve children and lived to age 68. Seven siblings were still living when their father, Christopher Augustus I wrote his memoir in 1905. One of their twelve offspring was named Christopher Augustus II for his father, and he also became a Master Tailor.

Further information about the Lopez appears in the 1878 Business Directory of Jamaica. It lists a family of tailors, Christopher I, Master Tailor and a nephew, Louis Lopez who lived at 39 Charles Street and worked together at 147 Harbour. After their establishment suffered two fires, in 1875 and again in 1882, Christopher I gave up keeping a shop, but he continued making uniforms for members of the Army, Prison and Fire Department. According to the 1878 Directory, Eliza Kempf's husband, Christopher A. Lopez II maintained a nearby outfitter's store at 141 Harbour. At that time his home address was 52 Beeston.

Thirteen years later, C. A. Lopez II, adding "Jnr." to his name, took out an ad in the 1891 Business Directory as a Merchant Tailor and General Outfitter now situated at No. 121 Water Lane. Though no picture of Christopher Augustus II seems to exist, his daughter Ianthe Eva described him as a drunken, violent monster with flaring nostrils and a cruel sensual mouth. Whatever his behavior at home, he managed to stay sober at work passing as a model of respectability. Lopez' business prospered. A pillar of the community, he provided amply for his wife and burgeoning family proudly settling them in a fancy Victorian house with a wrapped-around sun porch.

Eliza may have given birth to eleven or twelve children, but some died in infancy. Between 1878-1892, the Lopez had four or five boys and three daughters. The sons were Christopher Augustus III, Horace Ivanhoe, Reginald Courtney, Charles Cecil and Vincent Conroy.

The eldest son, Christopher Augustus III studied for his dental degree in England and became a well-known dental surgeon with a beautiful English wife, Eliza Mary Purcell Lopez. They had four lovely daughters. A 1910 List of Residents of Kingston names him as C. A. Lopez, Dr., a dentist, living at 3 Rosedale Avenue.

Ivanhoe and Reginald Courtney were the first to emigrate, ca. 1900, settling initially in New York City. Ivanhoe later moved to Rhode Island where he was involved in a rubber business.

A fourth son whom everyone called Melancholic Uncle Charlie came to Floral Park on brief visits when my mother was a child. Though records of the birth and/or death of all the other Lopez offspring are extant, to date no documentation concerning Charles has surfaced; nevertheless, my mother recalled him vividly and treasured a photo of his high school graduation.

The fairest of the Lopez was Vincent, who even as an older man was proud of his milk-white skin and blond hair. Like Charlie, he was devoted to his sister, Ianthe Eva.

Lovely, tragic Daisy was the eldest of the three daughters; next, my grandmother, Ianthe Eva, affectionately called Birdie because she was slim and petite; and then thoughtful Louise.

As if looking through a keyhole, my mother remembered tiny, languid details of life in Jamaica that on quiet mornings Birdie had shared with her children. The way that Birdie described it, the island seemed like a tropical Eden with tall coconut palms, dark green banana plants, silver sands, coral reefs and an indigo and turquoise sea.

The Lopez household had black servants, and at least one maid practiced voodoo. As she deftly rolled the dough for meat pies or pared papayas and mangoes for fruit salad, she both terrified and fascinated the Lopez children with her tales of Obeah rituals, spells, charms and animal sacrifice.

On weekend mornings, the maid would prepare *ackee* for herself, a dish tasting like scrambled eggs made from the black, button-sized fruit of a native tree. Mixed with salted codfish, it served as her breakfast. If the children had behaved all week, she would let them have a taste. "It's good for your wombs," she'd say with a laugh, no matter whether the recipients of the treat were girls or boys. Until he was nine or ten, Vincent, the baby of the family, thought a "womb" was another word for "stomach."

On sultry summer days as the girls got older, Eliza and her daughters took siestas mid-afternoon. Unmarried young women in the tropics wore white dresses in the summer. Before lying down, they carefully placed their starched organdy, batiste or dimity frocks over the backs of chairs. The older boys were allowed to stay up if they wished, but they had to be quiet while their mother, sisters and the baby rested.

Crustless bread and butter sandwiches accompanied the everyday High Tea at four o'clock. On special occasions or if the children had school friends over for a visit, Eliza had the cook make little poppy seed cakes and biscuits or scones served with Eliza's own quince jam. In good weather, she had a mahogany and cane cart wheeled out onto the wrapped-around porch where she poured the hot amber liquid from an ornate silver teapot. She enjoyed fussing for her children's sake and set out her best Coalport cups and saucers and an elegant Staffordshire Rose vase full of seasonal flowers. "She was such a gracious hostess," Birdie recalled.

When the family went downtown to shop, the girls were obliged to carry parasols to protect them from the sun. Young men, their mother reminded them, found young ladies with delicate, fair skin highly desirable.

Despite Eliza's warning about the effects of sunlight, as teenagers all of the girls enjoyed playing croquet on the Bermuda-grass lawn at home or at friends' houses. Dressed in long white skirts and cotton blouses with leg-of-mutton sleeves, they were also supposed to wear broad-brimmed straw hats. More often than not, Daisy, the most athletic of the girls, played bareheaded, coming indoors flushed from the exercise and slightly tanned.

Eliza did not approve. "Keep that up," she scolded her eldest daughter, "and you will have freckles for your 'coming out.'" In Jamaica, girls of marriageable age were introduced into society at a 'coming out' party or dance. Allowed to put their hair up for the first time and to wear a fancy ball gown, the Lopez girls and their friends looked forward to this first public rite of passage to womanhood. But by the time Daisy and Ianthe were old enough, they weren't concerned with facial blemishes. Neither of them 'came out'. Their beloved mother Eliza was terminally ill.

By all accounts, Eliza was genteel and loving. Had she not contracted cancer in her early forties, her daughters contended, she would have been driven to an early death by the repeated cruelties and indifference of her husband. She suffered in the upstairs master bedroom, the girls taking turns caring for her, the older boys no longer living at home.

Christopher Lopez, Sr. didn't even wait for his wife's demise before installing his mistress in the house. As she lay dying, Eliza could hear the upstart woman lording it over her daughters and little boy. Ianthe never forgave Christopher Lopez for this final affront to her mother.

According to Nena Balzac, the story of how the Lopez girls came to America is one for the annals of N.O.W. Daisy, Ianthe and Louise bided their time until after their mother's funeral. Then one morning when their unsuspecting father had gone to work, the three of them beat up the mistress and threw her out of doors. They had arranged in advance for a local dealer to buy and remove their mother's furniture from the house. When Lopez returned later that day, he found his daughters missing, his house empty and his mauled doxy crying in the yard. With the money gleaned from the sale of the furnishings, the girls booked passage to New York. Encouraged and apprehensive in turn, Daisy, Ianthe and Louise fled Jamaica and never looked back.

As a child, I admired the audacity shown by my grandmother and great aunts. They were clever and undaunted. Only later did I realize that this was the stuff of legend. The story of the girls' flight was worthy of a screenplay for one of the Saturday matinee serials that I rapturously watched at the Floral Movie Theater. Its perfectly transparent moral could have served as a sub-title for a melodramatic episode: "Virtuous daughters avenge the insult to their dead mother and sail to America triumphant." The tale is too pat, its timeline too continuous; it proceeds without a single hesitation on the part of the Lopez women.

I do not believe that Nena Balzac, storyteller *par excellence*, deliberately distorted the facts. Over the years, as the parlor game "Telephone" so clearly demonstrates, the rough edges had become rounded, actions and reactions, simplified. Had Nena been confronted with the facts available in the Ellis Island Records of Immigration, she still would have claimed that her version made a great story even if tiny details were incorrect.

In point of fact, the situation in the Kingston house leading up to the death of Eliza Kempf Lopez was appalling. By all accounts, she died screaming in agony either in late 1905 or in early 1906.

Whatever the date, the bereavement of Christopher Augustus II was of short duration. On July 26, 1906, he married a widow, Mrs. Adeline Maud Bartlett, née Campbell. Serving as witnesses were Fred A. O'Sullivan and John Campbell, Adeline's father. The ceremony took place at 13 Bray St., Browns Town, 1906, Christopher's residence at least since 1901.

Within three months after the wedding, the two youngest children—Louise, 17, and Vincent, 14 accompanied by their new step-mother–left for New York. According to the Ellis Island Immigration Records, the youngsters sailed from Kingston on the *Sibiria*, a Hamburg-American liner, October 10 and arrived October 18, 1906. The ship's manifest lists Louise as a 5'4" brunette and Master Vincent Lopez, 4'10", as a blonde with brown eyes, both of Spanish-American (sic) ancestry. It also records Vincent's age as 10 (he was 14) and Louise's age as "12," the "7" possibly misread as a 2.

Accompanying her youngest step-children on their trip to New York and using her maiden name, Mrs. Adella Campbell, 53, was herself in transit to Toronto, Canada to visit her father. She may have deliberately given the Purser incorrect information about the ages of her two charges. As children 12 and under, they would have qualified for reduced fares. As their sponsor, they list their brother, R. (Reginald Courtney) Lopez at 222 W. 35th Street in New York City.

However precipitous, the departure of Louise and Vincent was fortunate. Three months after they sailed, on January 14, 1907, a catastrophic earthquake hit Kingston and an area radiating 12 miles from the city. The shock from the west (magnitude 6.5) lasted only 36 seconds, but as cement and brick walls collapsed throughout the harbor front leaving not one sound building, shop owners and customers ran north toward the racecourse. Within a half-hour, a raging fire wiped out the entire business district. It took almost a full day to put out the flames, but by that time, over 1000 people had died.

Whether downtown working or shopping at 3:30 p.m. that calamitous Monday afternoon, among the injured was Daisy Lopez. In reporting the event later, the Red Cross noted that her wounds were severe enough to qualify her for disaster relief.

With this award (and possibly the money received from the sale of their mother's furniture), Daisy and Ianthe Eva bought steamship tickets on the *R.M.S. Trent*, Thomas R. Pearce, Master. The Ellis Island Immigration Record shows that they arrived in New York nine months after their younger siblings. On the ship's manifest, they list Browns Town, east of Kingston and north of Mt. View Road, as their former residence. Both young women name C. A. Lopez as their closest Jamaican relative.

Unfortunately, the manifest raises as many questions as it answers. The earthquake in January, 1907 certainly destroyed Christopher's outfitters store situated on Water Street in the harbor area. Like Daisy, had he also been hurt and unable to work? Did the girls grit their teeth and stay at the Browns Town rental only as long as it took Daisy to recover from her injuries? Almost a year after their father's second marriage, did they no longer feel welcome in the home now occupied by their new step-mother?

By 1910, according to the Jamaica Directory, Christopher Augustus Lopez had bought a bookstore and stationer's shop. How did their father fare in his new business? Within a few years after landing in New York, Daisy was sending him money on a regular basis. Was she helping him through a hard time or investing in the bookstore or repaying monies he had loaned her to make her way in New York?

Like Louise and Vincent, under the rubric "destination," the sisters name their brother, R. C. Lopez (adding a middle initial) as their relative in America, but Reginald Courtney Lopez' address has changed to 537 Broom (sic) Street.

In 1907, the peak year for European immigration, 1,285,349 persons entered the United States. Among them were the two oldest Lopez daughters, Daisy, 22 and Ianthe Eva, 20. Both girls carried English passports and had legal resident visas. They were joining a relative already in the States, and because of the devastating Kingston earthquake, they may have received expedited permission to emigrate as environmentally displaced persons. The historical record shows that they arrived in New York on July 25, 1907, all thoughts of fire, death and destruction left behind.

[1] The wooden framed hacienda was replaced in the 1960s by a four-story cement-block building. When my son, Davin, and I went to Puerto Rico in 1991, both Uncle Gena and his son, Pepìn had died, but Gena's daughter,

Alicia entertained us. She told essentially the same story about 1812, Joseph Balzac from Tours and his wife, Josephine de Lau and showed me her family album that contained an arresting photograph of her grandmother, Mama Pepe. When I mentioned Serafina, Alicia began laughing: "So you know all my grandfather's sins."

[2] The family's relationship to Honoré de Balzac is, unfortunately, pure myth. The writer's father, Bernard-François, originally came from Tarn in the Cevennes and changed his name from Balssa to Balzac, the name of a noble family from Entragues. After the birth of his third child, Bernard-François sometimes added the particle "de" to his surname, a practice that Honoré consistently adopted. Henri Balzac was the writer's half-brother, the child of Mme. Balzac and a lover and therefore not a Balzac at all. As for Honoré himself, though he married late in life, he had no legitimate children. See André Maurois, *Prometheus, The Life of Balzac* (New York: Harper Row, 1956), 1928.

[3] The children of three different mothers were all raised together. They were Balzacs—no distinctions were made among them. Josefina, maiden name Velez, was the widow of Proventud when she married Genaro, Sr. With Pepìn, Fidela and Rosa in New York when their father died, ca. 1922, Mama Pepe secured the inheritance for her children, and Gena, Jr. took over the business of Balzac & Sons.

In the 1950s, two of Mama Pepe's grandchildren from her first marriage, Elena and Aida Proventud visited my aunt and uncle, Mary and Pete Balzac in Floral Park and my mother in New Jersey. A successful real estate broker in Puerto Rico, Elena called herself Madame de Balzac.

[4] I had the chapbook from my mother for many years and finally gave it to her brother, Fred, as a memento of his father. After Fred's death, the journal passed to his son, Bill Balzac, who kindly provided me with a copy.

[5] "The Reminiscences of Christopher Augustus Lopez, 1829-1905", a two volume manuscript now in the Jamaica National Library, documents the history of the Lopez family in Jamaica. Glory Robertson summarized this memoir in the Jamaica Historical Bulletin [vol. 10, no. 13, n.d.] Since men in three successive generations bear the same given name, I will refer to the journal writer as Christopher Augustus I; his son—Eliza Kempf's husband—as Christopher Augustus II and the writer's grandson, my grandmother's brother, as Christopher Augustus III.

In documenting the Jamaican Lopez, I am indebted to information supplied in part by Michele Laing and especially by John and Greg Lopez, my cousins, all of Toronto, Canada. Michele is the great granddaughter of Desmerara Virginia Lopez; John and Greg Lopez, the grandsons of Isaac Cecil Lopez. Desmerara and Isaac were siblings of Christopher Augustus Lopez II, my great grandfather.

Counting Charles Cecil, Eliza Kempf Lopez had twelve children. In addition, John Lopez has found records for Harold Lewis, born 1890; Madeline May, born 1894; Philip Ernest, born 1897, and Evangeline Pearl, born 1901. (Some of these children may have died in infancy).

Part 1, Chapter 2
New York, 1901

O my America! my new-found-land,
My mine of precious stones, my empery,
How blest am I in this discovering thee!
—John Donne, *Elegy XIX.*

As he strolled across town on 23rd Street in the late summer of 1901, 19-year-old Pepìn Balzac admired the wasp-waisted young working women who passed by. "Gibson girls" the newspapers were calling them after Charles Dana Gibson's wildly popular drawings of delicate American beauties dressed in long dark skirts and crisp shirtwaist blouses, their hair piled up in pompadours or deftly wrapped around chignons.

Turning to look after one lovely blonde, Pepìn wondered if he could pass for a "Gibson man" in his new blue and white striped seersucker suit. When he bought the moderately priced jacket and trousers at Ohrbach's on 14th Street, he also treated himself to a Panama hat and a walking stick. Pepìn was feeling jaunty, even debonair, a far cry from his hopelessness the year before in Puerto Rico where young men had few prospects for the future.

Self-consciously, he patted his pants pocket. Coins jingled in it, and he could feel a snug little wad of paper money. For the first time, he had extra dollars to save or spend as he saw fit. Despite all familial warnings to the contrary, he had blown into New York on a tropical wind and landed squarely on his feet.

Pepìn worked setting type in the office of *El Diario de las Novedades*. The business manager of the newspaper had found Pepìn a room nearby in a French lady's apartment off 7th Avenue. Pepìn spoke to her in French, pleasing Madame Bonnet no end, but when he told her his name, at first she didn't believe him. *"Alors avec ce nom, vous êtes écrivain, n'est-ce pas?"* "With that name, you are a writer, of course," she responded gaily. He blushed. *"Non, Madame, seulement compositeur."* "No, Madame, I am just a printer". Demi-pension at $5.00 per week, she continued, would include his room rent, coffee and rolls for breakfast and a simple but ample dinner Monday through Friday. Madame did not cook for boarders on Saturday and Sunday, she said.

New York, he could see, was going to be expensive—in Ponce, he had paid $3.50 for room and board including meals on the weekend. But Pepìn agreed to Madame Bonnet's terms when he saw the room. It was large, immaculate and bright, the bedspread and matching draperies done up in a cheerful chintz print. She had placed a huge desk and swivel chair in front of two large windows overlooking 28th Street. A mahogany chiffonier and bookcase completed the furnishings.

On the weekend, Madame suggested that he try any one of a number of small inexpensive cafés in the area. From 28th to 40th Streets on Seventh Avenue, there was a small French community bordered on the south by Italians and on the east by Greeks, Syrians and Turks. In these areas, he soon learned, restaurants catered largely to neighborhood families with ethnic dishes that were authentic, well prepared, filling and cheap. On the west lay the notorious Hell's Kitchen. Madame warned him to stay away. Only a year before, race riots had broken out there between the Irish and the Blacks.

As the days passed, he found that he liked both his living arrangements and his job—salary $12 dollars a week to start, more than double what he had been earning in Ponce. Pepìn calculated: room and board, meals on the weekends and laundry should cost him no more than $7 week if he were careful. He would have $5 to spare, a veritable fortune.

And working conditions were excellent—an eight-hour day, no holidays and the weekends free. A couple of times when a deadline loomed, the editor of *El Diario* had asked Pepìn to stay an hour or so later than quitting time. The young man had assumed he wouldn't be paid but acquiesced graciously nonetheless. To his surprise and delight, Pepìn found one and one-half times the extra hours' wages in his paycheck at the end of the week.

The editor, business manager and staff seemed to like the youngster. They even laughed at Pepìn's jokes. He was punctual, courteous, good humored and, above all, quick and accurate at typesetting. The head compositor, Eduardo Morales, was an older man who had a son Pepìn's age. Though Lalo, as he was called, might refer to Pepìn as a kid, Manuel Lopez of Ponce had trained Pepìn well. As a printer, Pepìn knew his job.

While Pepìn was eating lunch, he read his English dictionary, writing down all new words and trying to use them three times in a sentence in order to set them, like type, in his memory. After work, he scanned the newspaper, usually *The New York Times*, from cover to cover, to improve his vocabulary and to be informed about world affairs. At his desk in the evening he studied Italian so that he might read the cantos of the great Romantic poet, Giacomo Leopardi in the original.

Eventually, he hoped to be learned enough to read Dante. When he wearied of studying Italian, he read one of Shakespeare's *Selected Plays* picked up from a bookseller's bin on Fourth Avenue.

On weekends, Pepìn took long walks. He examined the faces of the people hurrying by with the studied concentration of a scientist looking through a magnifying glass at rare butterflies. New York wasn't a city, he immediately decided—it was a polyglot universe unto itself. He took a ride on the 9th Avenue elevated railway, commonly known as the "el", to the end of the line at 155th Street just to observe the passengers—their variously shaped noses and eyes, their skin tones, garbs and accents.

"O, brave new world that has such people in't!" he said to himself, quoting Shakespeare's *The Tempest*. Had someone told him that he had entered the confines of Babel on the border between Odessa and Timbuktu, he would have believed it and cried, "All hail!"

He tried to identify the sometimes guttural, sometimes mellifluous languages the passengers spoke. Someday, he promised himself, he would know those languages and be able to converse with the most interesting of the faces. In contrast to Mayagüez and Ponce, those indolent little sun-baked towns, here nothing seemed to be still or quiet. Everyone and everything seemed to be in constant, restless motion. Once on the street, he found that his pace automatically picked up to match the scurrying, elbowing, noisy crowds. Contributing to the din were trolleys, carriages, electric buses, pushcarts, horse-drawn wagons, hucksters hawking their wares and, above one's head on 9th,

6th, 3rd and 2nd Avenues, the careening rumblings and screechings of the "els" taking thousands to work and home again.

The first thing Pepìn wanted to see was the great statue that Frederic Auguste Bartholdi had designed as a gift to the United States on the 100th anniversary of the American Revolution. He had shipped it piece by piece from France and, serving as structural engineer for the project, Gustave Eiffel had reassembled all 350 sections of the sculpture on Bedloe's Island in New York Harbor. Liberty Enlightening the World, Bartholdi had named it in 1886, but almost immediately, everyone called it the Statue of Liberty.

Pepìn took the 6th Avenue "el" to Rector Street, then strolled to the Battery where he boarded a ferry. The mini-voyage was bracing. A stiff breeze whipped the surface of the water creating a fine salt spray while a score of shrieking gulls circled overhead. Landing on the island, he took his place on line behind other tourists and a group of chattering and excited school children waiting to enter the statue. Pepìn gazed upward at the great copper lady. In her left hand, she held a tablet inscribed with the date July 4 and the year 1776; in the other, she held a torch aloft as if she were lighting the way far into the heartland of the vast continent. From the ground to the tip of the flame, pedestal and statue stood 305 feet. She was magnificent.

Pepìn decided to ascend to the first observation platform within the top of the 150-foot pedestal. He could have gone higher to a viewing stage in the statue's crown or even beyond that up a wooden ladder into the torch. A few intrepid souls made the full climb, but neither a lover of heights nor enclosed places, Pepìn was satisfied to look out at the city from the monument's first vantage point.

To the east, he could just see the Brooklyn Bridge, no longer referred to by its original name, the Great East River Bridge. Its delicate cables sloped downward from twin Gothic towers like a fantastic spider web connecting Manhattan to Brooklyn. In 1901, it was the largest suspension bridge in the world.

Innumerable wharves jutted out into the harbor, and sprinkled on the blue expanse were sailboats, tugs and barges reduced by the distance to the size of toys. Beyond the green of the Battery stood the impassive gray facades of Wall Street. To their west rose the spire of Trinity Church, at one time the highest structure in the city, and behind it, the soaring skyscrapers of Park Place. A crazy-quilt grid of streets heaped with great piles of brownstone, brick and granite reached as far as the eye could see.

In the late afternoon sun, New York City gleamed like a gigantic behemoth basking on the bedrock between two great rivers. Dazzled, Pepìn tried to take it all in, but so packed with buildings was the vista before him that it was impossible to identify any but the closest structures. He stood gazing out for at least fifteen minutes before he descended slowly to ground level for the return trip on the ferry. Once aboard, he watched through the cabin window as the great monument slowly receded into the distance.

How many immigrants had wept seeing the Statue of Liberty for the first time as they sailed into New York harbor? Thousands upon thousands, Pepìn thought to himself. Thousands of exiles had endured an arduous, steerage-class voyage not knowing what fate awaited them at journey's end. Some had naively believed that American streets were paved with gold; others had come more realistically to work hard, put aside a bit of money and be their own boss; many more sailed as a last recourse to evade starvation, persecution and injustice.

Overcome by a new sense of compassion for their collective sufferings, Pepìn empathized with them all. He was glad that he had come to Bedloe's Island.

After this experience, Pepìn wanted to walk through the neighborhoods of New York. He had explored the area around his rooming house; he was ready to venture further. Choosing a different section of the city on subsequent weekend outings, Pepìn visited places that he had only heard or read about: Chinatown, Little Italy, Yorktown and Kleindeutschland, the Lower East Side. His Sunday evening meals thereafter consisted of inexpensive ethnic samplings: pork fried rice and black tea; pasta e fagioli and espresso; bratwurst on pumpernickel and a lager; blintzes and sour cream finished off with celery tonic. Sometimes at noon, he stopped at an Irish saloon. For the price of an ice-cold draft on tap, he helped himself to a free lunch—fixings spread out on the bar. He enjoyed listening to the banter of the barkeep and his patrons, many of whom spoke with thick brogues. The smells, the tastes, the accents, the checkered tablecloths, the sawdust on the floor, the overcrowded tenements, the laundry waving on clotheslines strung across the streets, the open air markets—he ingested the myriad impressions of all these locales as avidly as the food.

Today Pepìn proposed to cross over on 23rd Street to 5th Avenue and walk uptown to Central Park. As he approached the sharply angular intersection of Broadway and 5th, Pepìn checked on the progress of a new skyscraper, the Fuller Building, still under construction. Even with scaffolding around it, its great frame dwarfed all the surrounding buildings. Situated on a narrow plot, the rising steel trellis was triangular, like no building Pepìn had ever seen. When completed, the V-shaped structure would not come to an exact point; at its tip, it would measure a mere six feet wide.

Scanning the 20 or so stories, Pepìn thought the completed 285-foot skyscraper would look like a huge wedge cleaving the busy intersection. He corrected himself. No, it would look more like a ship's prow. They should call it "The Ship of Commerce Building," he decided. But New Yorkers thought otherwise: they affectionately dubbed it the Flatiron Building. The architect of the Chicago Colombian Exposition of 1893, Daniel H. Burnham had designed it. No doubt he was challenged by the novelty of the property's shape to create something soaring and beautiful in keeping with his Beaux-Arts background.

"Novelty," Pepìn mused, derived from the Latin, *novellitas*, and *novus* for new. Yes, that was the meaning of the "New" in New York. Everything was novel, new, fresh and over-sized—so many unique and huge constructions still half on the blueprints. In addition to the Fuller Building, the designs for the New York Public Library, begun in 1897 and only in the initial stages of construction, gave assurance of a stately and magnificent edifice. The city was already advertising the library as the People's University. And the unfinished Rowland H. Macy store on Herald Square was going to occupy the inconceivable expanse of half a city block. With so many late 19th century innovations—the trans-Atlantic cable, telegraph, linotype, telephone, talking machine, electric buses at 5 cents a ride, streetlights so bright that a stretch of Broadway was called the Gay White Way, the city, nay the century itself, was new, full of promise and high hopes.

Pepìn turned north on 5th Avenue. Having seen the warrens of the poor, he wanted to behold the mansions of the rich. 5th Avenue began in the heart of Greenwich Village. From the triumphal, yet somehow modest Washington Square Memorial Arch, a tree-lined thoroughfare unfolded northward. Perhaps in the early 1800s, Pepìn speculated, the well to do residents had thought to create a more tasteful and decidedly American Champs Elyssée. Along it stood comfortable Greek revival brownstones, the refined Brevoort Hotel and genteel cultural and literary organizations like the Union League Club and the Athenaeum.

But since the 1860s, a new breed of the fabulously wealthy had fabricated an enclave of unbelievable luxury from 23rd Street north, some of the dwellings as ornate as Renaissance palaces; some, marble-faced and colonnaded, looking as if they had lately been transported from ancient Athens. Here, more spendthrift than Eastern potentates, lived the captains of industry, the directors of great banks and trusts, the entrepreneurs who propelled the economic growth of the nation. Here the Stewarts, Vanderbilts, Astors, Goulds, Jeromes, Townsends and Morgans outdid each other in splendor. On 5th Avenue in 1864, A. T. Stewart, the department store magnate, built the most expensive private home in North America. Its $2 million price tag, however, was dwarfed some twenty years later by the Vanderbilts' four ostentatious townhouses reputedly costing in total $12 million dollars to construct and furnish. Interspersed between these alabaster shrines stood grand hotels and exclusive clubs. Pepìn made a mental note of the 5th Avenue Hotel, the Holland House, the Savoy, the University and Metropolitan Clubs, Delmonico's at 44th Street. Aside from these public and private bastions of elegance, on the Avenue stood fashionable houses of worship, Protestant, Catholic and Jewish, where the moguls and their families prayed. Yes, Pepìn grimaced, no doubt they prayed for more money.

As he crossed 59th Street to enter Central Park, Pepìn was still shaking his head in disapproval. Theodore Veblen was right: these displays of wealth constituted "conspicuous consumption," especially when only a few miles south, the masses, struggling to survive, lived in squalor.

Pepìn dismissed these serious questionings of class and privilege with some difficulty, but his mood began to change for the better when he recalled his destination. On this bright temperate afternoon, he headed toward the ornate, wrought iron Music Pavilion on the northwest side of the Mall for a free concert. In 1901, John Philip Sousa, the great master of the march, was touring Europe, but he had often conducted his band at the Pavilion. As Pepìn approached it, hundreds of people had already gathered and were seated on blankets on the green.

This scene was more to Pepìn's liking: here in an urban community, all differences of rank and race disappeared just as the creators of the park, Frederick Law Olmstead and Calvert Vaux, had envisioned. A People's Park and soon a People's Library open to one and all—along with the Statue of Liberty, these were the great monuments of American democracy. Comforted by this thought, he enjoyed the concert enormously, tapping his foot in time to the last selection on the programme that all New York was whistling, Scott Joplin's "The Maple Leaf Rag."[6]

* * *

On September 6, 1901 the nation's self-congratulatory complacency suddenly shattered. A lone gunman shot the President of the United States, William McKinley, at the Pan-American Exposition in Buffalo, New York.[7] The terrible news came in over the wire at the office of *El Diario* just after 4 p.m. as Pepìn was finishing up for the day.

The President had been greeting a crowd of well-wishers on the stage of the Temple of Music exposition hall when a young man approached, his hand wrapped in a handkerchief concealing a gun. It had been a hot day; a number of people were fanning themselves and wiping their brows as they waited to see President McKinley. Someone approaching the dais with a handkerchief in his hand did not, therefore, alert the honor guard of soldiers and Marines, nor the members of the Exposition and Buffalo police forces, nor the Secret Service men assigned to protect the President. At point blank range, a 28-year-old professed anarchist, Leon F. Czolgosz fired twice—hitting McKinley in the abdomen and gravely wounding him. Outraged, the President's guard nearly tore Czolgosz apart knocking him to the floor and furiously pummeling him. Lying on the ground and bleeding, McKinley, a devout Christian, told the members of his retinue not to let anything happen to the young man.

McKinley's stomach wound proved to be inoperable. His doctors could not find the bullet lodged near his spinal column. On September 14 at 2 a.m., eight days after the attack, he died of gangrene. That afternoon, Theodore Roosevelt was hastily sworn in as 26th President of the United States.

Just as pandemonium broke out at the scene of the crime, so it broke out at the sites of Czolgosz' incarceration and trial: city police barely managed to restrain violent mobs gathered at the Buffalo jail where the assassin was first held and at the courthouse where he was tried. Officers with billy clubs had to beat back hysterical crowds screaming "Lynch him! Lynch him!"

The trial itself took less than a month, the verdict a foregone conclusion. Though Czolgosz was more than likely deranged, his lawyer didn't even bother to enter a plea of insanity. Rushing to judgment, the jury found the silent and confused assailant guilty of premeditated murder. On October 29, seven weeks after the shooting, Leon Czolgosz died in the electric chair—yet another new and most sinister invention of the age.

Just three years before the assassination, an upsurge of nationalism had attended the Spanish-American War. By vanquishing Spain, the United States seemed to have come of age and taken its rightful place in the world as a great power. For many Americans, it had been a holy war that liberated peoples fearfully oppressed from a cruel government. Political generalities and bandwagon rhetoric proudly noted that under McKinley America had entered the 20th century as an empire with important overseas possessions. After the death of the President, however, this glad flag waving gave way to raging chauvinism. The assassination seemed to have brought an abrupt halt to the advance of the country itself. The reaction to this intolerable injury was immediate and widespread; hatred directed against anarchist organizations infected the entire nation.

There was some justification for fear: three of the last seven elected presidents—Lincoln, Garfield and now McKinley—had died at the hands of an assassin. At least four European heads of state, all victims of anarchist plots, had been murdered in the recent past, including King Umberto I of Italy only the summer before in 1900.

The most prominent proponent of anarchism in America, Emma Goldman was immediately interrogated. Though Czolgosz had attended one of her meetings, she had had nothing to do with his desperate act. She was jailed for fifteen days in Chicago, nevertheless, on record as having proclaimed that "all forms of government rest on violence and are therefore wrong and harmful, as well as unnecessary."

Pepìn did not sympathize with anarchists, but their contention that governments derived their power from violence seemed irrefutable. As far as Pepìn was concerned, nothing could justify what the State did to Czolgosz. After 1,700 volts of electricity coursed through his body not once but three separate times, the top of his head was sawed off to see if his brain showed any noticeable deformities and then sulfuric acid was poured on his body as it lay in the grave. Ever afterwards, Pepìn Balzac would be an opponent of capital punishment. When the State carries out the sentence of death, he firmly believed, it is as much an assassin as the criminal.

Pepìn had been horrified at the news of the President's death on September 14, notwithstanding that he hadn't been a supporter of McKinley's bid for re-election in 1900. As a teenager in Mayagüez, Pepìn had ardently championed the Americans during the four month long Spanish-American War of 1898. He was all for the annexation of Puerto Rico—anything to be rid of Spain. When, in Secretary of State Hay's phrase, the "splendid little war" was over, Pepìn and his father had applauded the United States for guaranteeing Cuban independence. All Latin America was joyously chanting *"Cuba libre, sí!"*

By 1900, however, the U.S. had done little to improve Puerto Rican affairs, and Pepìn had written in his Ponce journal that the Americans were as bad administrators as the Spanish had ever been. More than anything, Pepìn deplored the betrayal of Émilio Aguinaldo, the Filipino guerilla leader whom the Americans had supported in his fight against unjust Spanish rule. Once the combined native and American forces had defeated the Spanish, the American government reneged on its promise of independence for the islands and jailed Aguinaldo until he foreswore all resistance to United States' suzerainty.

In a widely publicized speech delivered in the Methodist Church, McKinley explained why the United States had annexed the Phillipines:

> I walked the floor of the White House night after night until midnight; and I am not ashamed to tell you, gentlemen, that I went down on my knees and prayed Almighty God for light and guidance more than one night. And one night it came to me this way—I don't know how it was, but it came: 1)

that we couldn't give them back to Spain—that would be cowardly and dishonorable; 2) that we could not turn them over to France or Germany—our commercial rivals in the Orient—that would be bad business and discreditable; 3) that we couldn't leave them to themselves—they were unfit for self-government—and they would soon have anarchy and misrule worse than Spain was; and 4) that there was nothing left to do but take them all, and educate the Filipinos, and uplift and civilize them, and by God's grace do the very best by them as our fellow-men for whom Christ also died. And then I went to bed, and went to sleep and slept soundly.

Pepìn had all but exploded when he read this address. Never in the history of man, he sputtered, had such a pietistic, self-serving imperialism so blatantly justified an illegal and immoral action. *Pobre Jesucristo!* Poor Jesus Christ! The terrible things that are done in his name!

Nor in 1900, did Pepìn particularly admire Theodore Roosevelt, McKinley's Vice President and former Governor of the State of New York. Roosevelt had become a national hero as a result of his exploits as Lt. Colonel (later Colonel) of the 1st U.S. Volunteer Calvary Regiment, the Rough Riders, during the Spanish-American War. Somewhere Pepìn had read that the famous charge up Kettle Hill near Santiago de Cuba had been reckless, the Rough Riders sustaining, in Roosevelt's own words, "the heaviest loss suffered by any regiment in the cavalry division." Although in making the statement Roosevelt had intended to praise the heroism of his troops, Pepìn saw the quotation as proof of their commander's heedless disregard for the lives of his men.

As Vice President, T. R. had advocated extending the United States' sphere of influence to Asia. An outspoken expansionist, he had argued for the annexation of the Hawaiian Islands and Guam as well as the Philippines. The country needed coaling stations in the Pacific from which to conduct trade. Despite the short-lived Boxer Rebellion of 1900, the Open Door policy with China provided for a vast influx of cheap and exotic imports, a lucrative new market. For the first time America had spread far beyond its continental borders: it was *ipso facto* an empire, and Roosevelt made no apologies about it.

Despite severe reservations concerning the new President, even Pepìn had to admit that Roosevelt's first months in office were astounding for their honest and strenuous pursuit of American interests at home and abroad. At the end of his first month in office on October 17, the new President scandalized politicians in the Capitol and constituents throughout the South by inviting Booker T. Washington to dinner at the White House, the first time a black man had been so honored. Roosevelt was acknowledging Washington as a spokesman for his race, since in 1900 the last black Congressman elected during Reconstruction, George White, had given up his seat in the House of Representatives.

On December 3 just six weeks after Mc Kinley's death, President Roosevelt delivered the State of the Union Address outlining one of the toughest and most ambitious plans of any Chief Executive in American history. Along with a number of other important concerns, he proposed four major initiatives. First, he would ask Congress to use deportation and "rigorous punishment" to stamp out anarchism "as an offense against the law of nations."[8] Second, he would promote legislation to supervise, "and within reasonable limits," regulate corporate trusts involved in interstate commerce. Third, his administration would create a canal across the Isthmus connecting North and South America to augment national and international trade. Fourth, the federal government would protect America's abundant natural resources and establish national parks.

And Roosevelt managed to get his entire agenda enacted.

* * *

At Christmastide, Pepìn went shopping along Broadway. In November, he had thought he could get away with a heavy sweater underneath his jacket, but by mid-December, at every corner as he walked to work, he winced at the wet blasts of wind coming from the harbor. He had never felt such cold. In a men's store on 16th Street, he found a serviceable, heavy tweed overcoat and amused the shopkeeper by removing the price ticket and immediately wearing it on top of what he had on.

Once outfitted properly, Pepìn began to enjoy the spirit of the season. Though some stores had moved further uptown, the entire shopping area from 10th to 23rd Streets on Broadway and 6th Avenue, once referred to as the Ladies' Mile, was festooned with lights and red and green holiday decorations. Individual shops featured Christmas displays of dolls and mechanical toys in their windows, and a bonneted Sister of the Salvation Army rang a bell soliciting donations in front of B. Altman's. On the corner of 20th Street, a group of carolers sang *a cappella*, "We Three Kings of Orient Are." Reminded of *El Dia de los Tres Reyes*, Three Kings' Day when presents were exchanged at home, Pepìn bought small gifts for his brothers and sisters, cherry-flavored tobacco for his father, pretty scarves for his grandmother and Mama Pepe. If he mailed them before Christmas, they would be sure to arrive by January 6. Buoyed by the festive atmosphere, he hurried homeward loaded down with parcels. The sky looked like a leaden bowl. At work, Lalo Morales had said it might snow.

Pepìn had never seen snow before. Seated at his desk later that night, he watched as large flakes lazily floated down, first covering the sidewalks, then the streets. Few and fewer carriages passed by, foot traffic gradually subsided and still the virtually windless snowstorm continued blanching and muting everything. Had he not worked all day, then gone shopping, he would have loved to walk up to Central Park to see the trees and lakes blurring like a black and white Steiglitz photograph. Instead he opened the window, put his hand out into the bracing air and caught a few flakes. He watched in fascination as each uniquely shaped crystal melted almost on contact. He looked up and down the empty street. How shining and silent his white city had become!

At work on the Friday before Christmas, Pepìn received a long awaited raise and an unexpected holiday bonus. Lalo had put in a good word for him, he was sure. "You don't have to thank me," the older man replied. "Come have dinner with us next Wednesday, kid. No one should be alone on Christmas Day. And my wife cooks good Spanish food," Lalo said putting on his coat. Adjusting the fit of his gloves, he repeatedly tapped between the fingers on one hand with the index finger of the other. "Besides," he whispered mysteriously, "I've got a business deal to discuss with you."

Lalo hadn't exaggerated—Delia Morales was a fine cook, and Pepìn thoroughly enjoyed everything she put before him. All through the meal, Lalo was talking about opening a budget print store with typesetting on site, not immediately, but sometime in the next year or two. He wanted Pepìn to join him—they worked well together. It was too early to accept such a proposition, Pepìn told Lalo, but working as a partner in a New York City print shop was an enticing possibility. He certainly would give it some thought. He walked home, completely unmindful of the cold, quite happy with his new prospects. Or was his euphoria a function of all the wine he had drunk?

As was his wont after Christmas, Pepìn took stock of the past year. Though he missed his father, grandmother and 11-year-old Fidela, he had no regrets. He had forsaken everything—home, family, friends, sweetheart, his native tongue—and left Puerto Rico. The stultifying sameness of experience there would have destroyed him. Never even realizing it, his friends were content to sleepwalk through their lives. Unlike them, he was restless; he wanted to see something of the world, and he loved the challenge of an adventure. New York City had fulfilled, even exceeded, his expectations in that regard.

He reread his Ponce chapbook and dismissed most of it as immature—the outpourings of a mewling boy who had dreamed of becoming a poet. Soon he would be twenty, and it was time to put away childish things. Though he had complained about his salary in Ponce, he understood now that he had never been poor. He came from a comfortable upper middle-class family and had received a good foundation in Spanish, French and Latin. Clearly, his gift was linguistic, not imaginative, and with that gift and his trade, he would never want. With a little effort, he could teach himself. And New York would provide the rest of his higher education: its newspapers, museums, libraries, concerts and opera would help him to become learned.

Alone in the United States for less than a year, Pepìn felt that he had witnessed first-hand the underlying contradictions of American experience. He could give testimony to the poverty of the many, the wealth of the few; the ugliness of the tenements, the beauty of the new buildings; the violence and purblind nationalism of its common people and leaders as well as their creativity and unstoppable energy.

Thinking of the country as a whole, Pepìn suddenly remembered some lines from a verse: "O my America! my new-found-land... How blest am I in this discovering thee!" But try as he might, he couldn't recall the context or the title and author. For a moment he was puzzled. He didn't think he knew any patriotic poems.

Then Pepìn began to laugh. In "Elegy XIX Going to Bed," John Donne addresses his lady and equates making love to her to exploring the New World:

> *License my roving hands, and let them go*
> *Before, behind, between, above, below.*
> *O my America! my new-found-land,*
> *My kingdom, safeliest when with one man manned,*
> *My mine of precious stones, my empery,*
> *How blest am I in this discovering thee!*
> *To enter in these bonds is to be free;*
> *There where my hand is set, my seal shall be.*

Ah, that's what's missing, Pepìn chuckled. If only he had a sweetheart!

[6] Facts about New York City, circa 1901, are taken from Eric Homberger, *The Historical Atlas of New York City* (New York: Henry Holt and Company, Owl Books, 1998). The phrase, "conspicuous consumption," comes from Veblen's *Theory of the Leisure Class* (1897). "The Maple Leaf Rag" published in 1899 was Scott Joplin's first big hit.

[7] For the rise of nationalism and anarchism, the circumstances of McKinley's assassination, the subsequent death of Czolgosz and the early months of Theodore Roosevelt's Presidency see Richard Drinnon, *Rebel in Paradise: A Biography of Emma Goldman* (Boston, Massachusetts: Beacon Press, 1970); Larzer Ziff, *The American 1890s: Life and Times of a Lost Generation* (New York: Viking Press, 1968); and Howard Mumford Jones, *The Age of Energy: Varieties of American Experience, 1865-1915* (New York: Viking Press, 1971). The quotation from McKinley's Address to his Brethren of the Methodist Church comes from James Ford Rhodes, *The McKinley and Roosevelt Administrations, 1897-1909* (New York, 1923), 106-107 as quoted by Ziff, 221.

[8] The parallels between September 6, 1901 and September 11, 2001 are striking: for "anarchism" read "terrorism." Roosevelt initiated a crackdown on immigration, an increase in deportations. He also called for new legislation and international treaties to suppress anarchism. President George W. Bush took the same measures (largely against Moslems) in 2001 and implemented the Patriot Act.

Part 1, Chapter 3
A Flower for Daisy

...naked they shall be one
With the man in the wind and the west moon
When their bones are picked clean and the clean bones gone,
They shall have stars at elbow and foot...
Though lovers be lost love shall not;
And death shall have no dominion.
—Dylan Thomas

We have wonderful pictures of the Lopez offspring, but the most charming is a studio portrait of Daisy in formal dress taken in New York, ca. 1909. It may well be an engagement picture. Her wavy upswept brown hair frames her round face. Her ample shoulders are bare, and a tulle scarf, held in place by two large silk roses, softens the décolletage of her gown. Her eyes are dark and serene, her mouth wide and generous.

Engagement Photo Daisy Lopez

Soon after she came to New York, Daisy took a job as a practical nurse in Long Beach on the Jersey shore. In the only other photograph of her—taken at a convalescent home—she stands to the right of a group of co-workers in striped shirtwaists, white lace collars and long white skirts, some sitting on the sand in front of a columned courtyard. Like Louise, Daisy has a dimpled chin, but unlike either of her sisters, she is stocky and buxom.

According to the 1910 Census taken in April of that year, Daisy was living in a boarding house at 13 Charlton Street south of Greenwich Village and working as a stenographer in an insurance office. Her sweetness attracted the attention of another boarder, a young Swiss hotel tradesman and bartender, Henry Bertram Fitze. They fell in love and, after a brief courtship, married at the Spring Street Presbyterian Church on January 15, 1911.

For years, Fitze had dreamed of buying and managing his own inn, and like many immigrants, he wanted to return to his native land and buy property there. Soon after they married, Daisy and he agreed that he should go to Switzerland alone, roughing it to save money until he found the right place. Once Henry accomplished that, he would send for her. At most, they would be separated for a few months. He sailed at the beginning of March. By May, at the latest, they would be together again.[9]

Though her husband had left her with sufficient money, Daisy felt lonely with him gone and, having time on her hands, decided to earn a few extra dollars. Thrifty and conscientious, Daisy planned on living on her salary, thereby keeping her small nest egg intact for their future needs. She saw an ad calling for garment workers at a downtown factory. Like all the Lopez girls, she sewed proficiently and had no difficulty landing the job near Washington Square. The factory occupied the top three floors of the Asch Building (now owned by New York University). She could easily walk from Charlton Street, just south of Houston Street, to work.

One Saturday in early spring—it was March 25, 1911—Daisy left for work hopefully. She was young and pretty. A bride of almost ten weeks, she loved and was loved in return. Soon she would be sailing to Europe to start a new life. The world lay all before her.

Daisy Lopez Fitze never came home from the Triangle Shirtwaist Factory. When the fire broke out on the eighth floor of the Asch Building shortly before quitting time, she had just picked up her paycheck. Within minutes, the ninth floor where new hires worked was also engulfed in flames. The windows shattered and blew out from the heat. Panic ensued. There seemed to be nowhere to go: the elevators jammed, at least one of the doors to the narrow stairwells was locked and the inadequate iron fire escape literally melted.[10] In desperation, workers perched on the window ledges high above the street. As the flames and smoke swiftly and relentlessly advanced toward them, girls began hurling themselves off the sills.

Appalled spectators witnessed one woman lifting up her arms and eyes to the indifferent sky, seemingly mouthing a silent prayer before she threw herself down to the street below. Many workers fell and piled on top of one another, the weight of their bodies rendering useless the safety nets held by firemen. Some victims smashed through the glass-block vault lights in the sidewalk making a hole five feet in diameter. Their mangled corpses were later found in the basement.

Rather than burn to death, Daisy and her friend, Freda Velakowsky jumped hand in hand. Amazingly, they both survived the plunge from the ninth floor. A rescue van transported them to New York Hospital where Daisy lingered for two days and Freda for three, both finally dying of shock and internal injuries.[11]

When the worst fire in New York history was over, one hundred and forty-six workers, most of them immigrant girls, had perished. The hospital and municipal morgues overflowed with the bodies of the dead. Victims for whom there was no space were laid out side by side on the Twenty Sixth Street pier. Some were so badly burned that stricken family members could make positive identification only by recognizing an article of jewelry or, in one case, the remains of a single repaired shoe.

Some bodies could not be identified. They were buried in a mass grave at the Evergreens Cemetery, Brooklyn. With profound and public grief, the officials of the City of New York erected an imposing granite tablet that for many years stood alone in an empty field at the site. Now there are other graves around the memorial, but at the time, the desolation of the scene was itself profoundly moving. Cut deeply into the stone is the figure of a classically draped woman resting her head on an urn, one knee bent, in an attitude of prayer or resignation. An inscription beneath the relief reads:

> In sympathy and sorrow the Citizens of New
> York raise this monument over the graves of
> unidentified women and children who with one
> hundred and thirty others perished by fire in the
> Triangle Shirtwaist Factory, Washington Place,
> March 25, 1911.

Horrified by the tragedy, the State legislature enacted strict safety standards for garment factories as well as for other businesses, rules that still are in force today. Testifying to these efforts, the International Ladies' Garment Workers Union had a brass plaque installed on the façade of the Asch Building:

> On this site, 146 workers lost their lives in the
> Triangle Shirtwaist Company fire on March 25,
> 1911. Out of their martyrdom came new concepts
> of social responsibility and labor legislation that
> have helped make American working conditions
> the finest in the world.

In 1991, a second plaque placed beneath the first declared "The Triangle Shirtwaist Factory (Asch Building) a National Historical Landmark."

In response to the disaster, New Yorkers donated generously to a subscription that raised more than $120,000 for the families of those lost or injured in the fire. The Red Cross dispensed the funds here and abroad. The Emergency Relief Committee published a pamphlet documenting its disbursement of the monies. It supplies some arresting details concerning Daisy's case:

No. 21 (English). A young married woman of 26 died from the effect of injuries received in jumping from a ninth-story window... She had a father in Jamaica to whom she had been accustomed to send money. She and a sister had come to New York after the Kingston earthquake a few years ago, with the assistance of the relief fund. The younger girl is taking nurse's training in a New York hospital, and looked to her married sister for help in case of emergency. There is a married sister in New York who is in poor circumstances, and brothers in Providence and in Jamaica who are said to be prosperous, but who seem to do nothing for their relatives. $100.00 was given to the sister for a reserve fund, and £72 in all ($349.50) was sent to the father. The husband has not been heard from in any way.

Emergency Relief after the Washington Place Fire, New York, March 1911: Report of the Red Cross Emergency Relief Committee of the Charity Organization Society of the City of New York, 1912, 35.

In Switzerland, Daisy's stunned young husband grieved privately. The Red Cross tried to compensate him for his loss, but he never contacted its representative.

Surprisingly, the major recipient of relief was Christopher Lopez, Sr. of Kingston, Jamaica. Sometime during the four years after Daisy reached New York, she and her father must have settled their differences.

What had happened that he needed Daisy's financial support? Had the 1907 earthquake and subsequent fire effectively wiped out his business? Did Christopher, Jr. and Charlie also help him? As for the brothers in America, when Daisy died Vincent was 17, living in Providence with Ivanhoe Lopez. Described as prosperous, why didn't Ivanhoe or Reginald Courtney come to their father's aid?

By 1911, Daisy may have forgiven her father, but Ianthe, the nursing student, never did. (She was a hard woman who whenever the topic of her father came up declared bitterly that "Spaniards and elephants never forget!") As far as I know, Birdie never mentioned that as a result of Daisy's death she received compensation to finish her nurse's training possibly at the Sea Breeze Hospital in Coney Island.

By the time of the Red Cross report, April 10, 1912, the sister "in poor circumstances," Louise Lopez had married Pepìn Balzac, had a toddler and was pregnant again. The Balzac's affairs did not ameliorate until Pepìn took a job with Sidney Ross Pharmaceuticals later in the year.

Red Cross funds not only provided relief to two members of Daisy's family but also paid for the large Evergreens grave plot where she was buried and for the gray marble headstone there that marks her resting place. Engraved on the stone are the words, "Daisy Lopez Fitzi. Greater love hath no man than this: that a man lay down his life for his friends."

What could Daisy have done to merit such an inscription? Had she been heroic in some way? Had she saved others and sacrificed her own life?

The archives of the Kingston, Jamaica newspaper, *The Gleaner,* provide the answers to these questions. In early April 1911, the daily carried the notice of Daisy's death relying on information supplied by her brother, Christopher.

A Jamaican's Death

Dr. Lopez, the dentist, yesterday received a letter from New York telling of the death of his sister, Miss Daisy Lopez, in the great fire. She jumped from the ninth floor and was injured. She was removed to a hospital in New York, where she died on the 27th ult. Miss Lopez was injured in the 1907 earthquake in Kingston, and left afterwards for New York, where she joined her brothers and sisters.

"Great Horror: Details of New York's Terrible Blaze," *The Gleaner,* 5 April, 1911, 14.

In a story five days later, the newspaper added her married name and the justification for the quotation on her tombstone.

A Jamaican's Heroism

The funeral of Mrs. Daisy Fitze, one of the two young women who were found alive after jumping from the ninth story of the Asch building, in Washington place last Saturday, was held last night from the Spring Street Methodist Church.

Mrs. Fitze, who died at New York Hospital, was declared by the Rev. Roswell Bates, pastor of the church, in his funeral sermon, to have sacrificed her life in saving others. He declared that she had told him before her death that she had directed more than fifty girls to a stairway, and had jumped to the street only after she found that escape was impossible for her.

"Terrible New York Fire," *The Gleaner*, 10 April, 1911, 14.[12]

Perhaps the knowledge that she had saved so many eased Daisy's final hours. To her sisters, Ianthe and Louise, and to her brother-in-law, Pepìn Balzac, it seemed a terrible irony that having narrowly survived the 1907 Kingston conflagration, she had delivered herself all unknowingly to the fire next time in New York City.

* * *

Young woman, eyes swollen shut. Jumped from ninth floor to avoid factory fire. Brought to hospital in semi-conscious condition. Broken left iliac crest of pelvis, considerable hemorrhage, broken right humerus. Contusions and abrasions on face, head. Patient rallied from primary shock, but secondary shock followed, and

> *condition rapidly became worse. Died sometime after*
> *2a.m. 3/27/1911.*
> —*New York Hospital* medical records of Daisy Lopez
> Fitze, victim of Triangle Waist Company Fire

City officials called for a day of mourning and announced a public funeral parade to take place twelve days after the Fire. By then, all but the unidentified dead had been buried. As part of the procession, eight flower bedecked coffins carrying their remains would be accompanied via ferry to the Evergreens Cemetery.

On April 6, the weather was terrible. Because of the driving rain, Pepìn had talked Louise into staying home with 10-month-old baby Joey at their 16th Street apartment. She had wanted to pay her last respects to her sister but had been close to emotional collapse since the burial service for Daisy on March 30.

Around 1p.m. Pepìn closed his printing shop and strode east on Sixteenth Street to Fourth Avenue to stand silently with hundreds of other onlookers, watching the procession from under big, black umbrellas. Drenched, those without umbrellas marched solemnly in the pouring rain. Many were hatless. Almost all of the mourners carried small American flags draped in black crepe. As the parade progressed, one saw a few banners reading "We Mourn Our Dead." From uptown and downtown, thousands walked silently in memory of the victims. Tens of thousands lined the long, sodden routes converging on Waverly Place, around the corner from the Asch Building.

Public outrage against the company's owners, Max Blanck and Isaac Harris was so formidable that by mid-April they were arrested for manslaughter in the first and the second degree, charged in particular with the death of Margaret Schwartz. Both men immediately made bail.

Their trial didn't begin until early December. During it, Max Steuer, counsel for the defendants, managed to destroy the credibility of one of the survivors, Kate Alterman, by asking her to repeat her testimony a number of times—which she did without changing key phrases that Steuer believed were perfected before trial. In his summation, Steuer argued that Alterman and probably other witnesses had memorized their statements and might even have been told what to say by the prosecutors. The defense also stressed that the prosecution had failed to prove that the owners knew the exit doors were locked at the time in question.

Soon after Christmas, 1911, the trial came to an end. Deliberating for less than two hours, the jury voted to acquit.

In the next couple of years, the owners did incur some related expenses. In August 1913, Blanck was arrested and fined $20 for locking the door in his new factory during working hours. In addition, Blanck and Harris lost a civil suit when 23 families of Triangle victims sued them for damages. In March 1911, almost three years after the fire, the plaintiffs won compensation in the amount of $75 per deceased worker. Overall, despite these minor set-backs, the owners made good money on the Triangle Waist Company Fire. Their insurance company paid about $60,000 more than the reported losses, or about $400 per casualty.

Pepìn followed the aftermath of the fire with an increasing sense of disillusionment. Justice, it seemed, had been blind-sided, and Corporate Greed, attended by a slick lawyer, had gone to market and, higgledy, piggledy, done a jig all the way home.

Joseph Balzac and the Lopez sisters: Louise and Ianthe, 1909-1915

> Yet if I should get married and it's... snow
> And she gives birth to a child and I am sleepless, worn
> Up for nights, head bowed against a quiet window, the past behind me,
> Finding myself in the most common of situations a trembling man
> Knowledged with responsibility...
> O what would that be like?
> —- Gregory Corso, *Marriage*

After 1901, Pepìn Balzac's early years in New York are sketchy. Although he started out as a newspaper compositor, at some point, he and Lalo Morales became partners in a printing shop making up menus, calling cards, letterheads and logos. But Lalo died young. Working alone, Pepìn struggled to make a success of the business.

Thin and gangly when he first came to New York, by 1909 Pepìn stood 5'11" and his body had filled out. He took pleasure in looking elegant. Even at work, he appeared smartly trim in a starched white shirt with a high paper collar, green eyeshade, a leather apron and sleeves rolled up and secured by garters.

When at leisure, whether listening to the rabble-rousers on milk boxes in Union Square or admiring the fashionable ladies shopping along 6th Avenue or Broadway, he cut a dapper figure sporting a gold pocket watch attached by a chain to his trouser fob.

Louise Lopez, September, 1909

At the turn of the century, bicycles were all the rage. Pepìn bought a Pope "safety bicycle" with same sized wheels and a chain and sprocket drive. On weekends he often took it on the train in order to explore the Jersey Shore or Long Island.

Copper-skinned Pepìn Balzac must have met Louise Lopez around 1909. A studio photograph of Louise from this period shows a handsome young woman with auburn hair piled into an upsweep, full lips, a dimpled chin and a meditative expression.[13] She had the photograph reproduced on a postcard that she sent to Birdie, c/o Sea Breeze (Hospital?), West Coney Island from the Madison Square Station, September 2, 1909.

Seven months later, the 1910 Census taken on April 29 of that year records Pepìn and Louise as living at 145 W. 20th Street. It lists Pepìn, 28, as a printer and Louise, 21, as a factory examiner. By April, however, Louise was no longer working—she was 8 months pregnant.

Louise had to have been pregnant with Joey when she married Pepìn in late 1909 or early 1910. Born May 17, 1910 at the Sloane Maternity Hospital, New York City, Joseph Henry Balsac was blonde and blue-eyed, and though named for Pepìn and Genaro, he was certainly not Pepìn's son. Notwithstanding the doubtful paternity, Joey's birth certificate lists Joseph Balsac as the father. The document also records that Pepìn and Louise had moved since April. By the time the baby was born, they were living at W. 16th Street. It gives Cuba as Louise's country of origin and indicates that she had a child who died before Joey's birth.[14]

Much about the union of Pepìn and Louise is a mystery. In 1939 after Pepìn's death, my mother found their wedding license in Pepìn's bureau drawer. It lists the bride as Louise Lopez Coleman. [15]

Benton Coleman?

Anne and Joey Balzac, 1928

On June 18, 1907, a month before her sisters emigrated from Kingston to New York, Louise Lopez married a U.S. Marine, Benton (Beni) David Coleman. She was 18. Who was he, and what happened to him? The

Marine has watery blue eyes, a cleft in his chin, huge ears and a sensual lower lip. In Joey's wedding picture taken when he was 18, Joey looks remarkably like this man.

Why did Birdie save the photograph? Had she intended to tell Joey about his father at some later date? When and under what circumstances did Louise and Pepìn marry?

Joey, Jr. was not quite 26 months old when Louise gave birth to a second child, a girl. They named her for Pepìn's beloved *abuelita* for whom his sister, Fidela was also named. Pepìn must have been delighted. Born July 2, 1912, little Della looked like the Balzacs. She was dark with black glossy hair like her father.

With two babies to support, Pepìn decided to give up all thought of running his own printing business. It was simply too risky, with or without a partner. Instead, that same year, he joined the Sidney Ross Pharmaceutical Company in Newark, New Jersey. Hired to print labels for their drugs and to translate instructions for their use into Spanish, French, Italian, Portuguese and German, he was to keep the same job for twenty-seven years. It provided him with an excellent salary all through the Great Depression, many times when his was the only check keeping nine or ten people afloat. But the young couple was to know scant happiness.

After Ianthe finished her nurse's training in 1912 at the Sea Breeze Hospital or perhaps at the brand new Coney Island Hospital, she joined Vincent in Rhode Island. She worked as a nurse there, and over the course of a year became engaged to a man named Theodore from Pawtucket.

And Ianthe was poised to marry Theodore when an urgent summons from Pepìn Balzac brought her hastily back to New York probably in June 1913. Pepìn must have begged his sister-in-law to come—possibly to nurse Louise, most certainly to look after the children.

Louise had developed peritonitis as a result of acute appendicitis. On June 27, 1913 a week before Della was a year old, Louise died. Three days later, she was buried next to her sister, Daisy, at the Evergreens Cemetery. Louise was only 24 years old.

Had Louise suddenly fallen ill? When did Birdie arrive? Was she at her sister's bedside at Bellevue Hospital?

The one certainty is that after Louise's funeral, Birdie babysat while Pepìn took a somber vacation at Wildwood-by-the-Sea, New Jersey using the proceeds from Louise's small life insurance policy.

In early autumn, Birdie broke off her engagement to Theodore in order to continue looking after her sister's motherless children and their forlorn father. No doubt Pepìn was thankful for her help. But by October of 1913, just three and one half months after his wife's burial—Louise was scarcely adjusted in the tomb—Pepìn's feelings for his sister-in-law had passed far beyond gratitude. The mignonne Birdie, whom he may never have formally married, was pregnant with my mother.

Always called Nena ("Baby") at home, Dad named his second daughter Mercedes Balzac (this time the registrar spelled the last name with a "z"). She was born in New York City, July 9, 1914. It was a difficult breech birth; the baby couldn't be turned and was delivered rump first. To Pepìn's great relief, Birdie recovered, but she was left with a prolapsed womb, a condition that would eventually lead to a hysterectomy. With a four-year old, a two-year-old and a new baby, the Balzacs had outgrown their apartment and needed desperately to get out of the city.

[9] Thirteenth Census of the United States: 1910, New York City, Borough of Manhattan, Enumeration District 109, Sheet 14A lists Henry "Fitzie" and Daisy "Lopass" boarding at 13 Charlton Street.

The Certificate and Record of Marriage, # 1598, records the Fitze's address as 16 Charlton Street, gives Daisy's age as 24 (she was 26, born January 11, 1885) and her place of birth as London (other documents name Kingston, Jamaica as her birthplace). The Reverend Herbert Roscoe Bates of the Spring Street Presbyterian Church performed the ceremony. (*The Gleaner* article erroneously lists the church as Methodist). Reverend Bates was the same minister who presided at Daisy's funeral ten weeks later.

In a story entitled, "East Side is Plunged into Grief by Saturday Fire," *The New York World*, Monday, March 27, 1911 published the following account:

> Mrs. Daisy Lopez Fitzie, who is dying at the New York
> Hospital, said she jumped from the ninth story window

and broke her hips, legs, and arms after she had been severely scorched by flames. Two months ago she was married to Henry Fitzie, a lace expert. About three weeks ago Fitzie went to Switzerland, there to establish a business and prepare a home for himself and his wife. Fitzie left his young wife with sufficient funds to support herself but she didn't want to make inroads on, what she told the other girls who worked with her, her "nest egg" so she got a position as a shirtwaist maker.

Of French-Swiss descent, Henry Fitze, 20 had immigrated to the United States in 1908 and lived in New York City for three years prior to his marriage. On September 20, 1920—eight and a half years after Daisy's death—Fitze came back to the States sailing as a passenger on the *S. S. Lafayette*. Now a resident of St. Gall, Switzerland, 32 years old, married and en route to visit relatives in Chicago, with what regrets did he enter New York harbor?

Though I knew as a small child that Daisy had died as the result of a fire, I first learned that it had occurred on Washington Place and Greene Street when I began attending New York University in 1954. Tia Fidela Balzac told me that Daisy had died jumping from a ninth floor window of the Brown Building, now part of the University. So notorious were both my Tias for telling wild stories that at first I didn't believe her.

[10] In *The Triangle Fire* (Philadelphia and New York: J. B. Lippincott, 1962), 106, Leon Stein gives Daisy's address as 11 Charlton Street and spells

her last name "Fitze" as do the Ellis Island Immigration Records of her husband, Henry Fitze. But her tombstone and the Evergreens Cemetery official record of interment use the spelling "Fitzi" and list the year of her birth as 1887. At the time of her death in 1911, Daisy was 26, born in 1885. Using contemporary newspaper accounts, eyewitness reports and transcriptions of the Triangle trial, Stein writes the classic account of the fire and its aftermath. See especially his chapter "Ninth," 51-66.

[11] The then New York Hospital was situated on 15th and 16th Streets between Fifth and Sixth Avenues. Relocated at York Avenue and 69th Street, it later became the New York-Presbyterian Hospital/ Weill Cornell Medical Center. In *Triangle: the Fire that Changed America* (New York: Atlantic Monthly Press, 2003), 274, David Von Drehle claims that Daisy was one of the few girls who had jumped into the firemen's net. Tia Fidela told that same story and believed Daisy might have lived, but too many bodies fell on top of her.

[12] Neither contemporary U.S. newspaper accounts, nor Stein nor Von Drehle mention Daisy's actions during the fire. In early March 2004, almost 93 years after Daisy's death, I found the two cited articles in the archives of *The Gleaner* at the newspaper's office in Kingston, Jamaica. In slightly shortened form, "A Flower for Daisy" won honorable mention in the Feature Article category of the 73rd Annual *Writer's Digest* Writing Competition. The New York State Department of Labor printed the essay and featured it in its memorial exhibit on the 94th Anniversary of the Triangle Shirtwaist Factory Fire in Albany, March 22, 2005. The next month, New York State Senator Serphin R. Maltese invited me to talk about Daisy Lopez during his weekly television program. (New York State

Senate Office of Communications, Senator Maltese, Topic: With Guest Diane Fortuna, SUNY Stony Brook," April 19, 2005).

[13] In 1972, I visited Della in California and gave her Louise's photograph. It is now in the possession of her son, Jimmy Redding. In 2005, Joseph Balzac III, my cousin, opened up the back of an old portrait that had belonged to his father and found the postcard with Louise's note and picture. Joe kindly allowed me to copy the postcard as well as a number of his father's snapshots.

I only learned what happened to Louise in February 2004 when I received the Owner Profile of the Evergreens Cemetery, Lot Nazareth #4430. It gives acute appendicitis as the cause of death. Louise's death certificate corroborates that finding and adds the diagnosis of peritonitis (Certificate of Death, City of New York, Bureau of Records, No. 20018).

[14] Certificate and Record of Birth, No. 26340 of Joseph Balsac, Jr., May 17, 1910. This birth certificate, the 1910 U. S. Federal Census and Louise's death certificate all record her place of birth as Cuba; hence, the speculation concerning a possible Lopez residency there. Louise's wedding certificate to Benton David Coleman, however, gives her birthplace as Kingston, Jamaica.

[15] The wedding of Louise Leonora Lopez (she was 18, born in 1889, but claims to be 19) and Benton David Coleman, 23, took place in Kings County, June 18, 1907 (Certificate and Record of Marriage, # 5798). Louise gives her address as 1157 44th Street, Brooklyn. At the time Coleman, 23, a Marine, was assigned to the *U.S.S. Hancock* serving as a receiving ship at the New York Navy Yard in Brooklyn. The son of James Calvin Coleman

and Anna Lamison, he was born in Salinas City, California. I received this document in May 2008 and finally learned the given name and occupation of Louise's first husband.

Though it certainly does exist, I have not been able to locate the wedding certificate of Joseph Balzac and Louise Lopez Coleman in any of the New York City boroughs. Might Pepìn and Louise have married at the Jersey shore? Might that explain why Pepìn went to Wildwood-by-the-Sea after Louise's interment? No wedding license for Ianthe Lopez and Joseph Balzac was found among his papers in 1939, a fact which led my mother to speculate that they may not have formalized their union.

Part 1, Chapter 4
Floral Park: 1915-1948

anyone lived in a pretty how town
(with up so floating many bells down)
spring summer autumn winter
he sang his didn't he danced his did....

children guessed (but only a few
and down they forgot as up they grew
autumn winter spring summer)
that noone loved him more by more
——ee cummings

Only eighteen miles from New York and on the Long Island Railroad line, Floral Park, once called East Hinsdale, grew up around the late nineteenth century estate of John Lewis Childs. A botanist, seed producer and energetic entrepreneur, Childs established the first mail-order seed business in America producing his catalogues in his own printing plant, The Mayflower Press. Among his many other accomplishments, he published a garden magazine, *The Mayflower*, 1885-1906 (23 vols.) and wrote *A Guide to Lily Culture* (7 eds. 1888). He also managed an extensive farm, "Flowerfield" in St. James, Suffolk County where he developed gladioli, cannas and dahlias. In Pasadena, California, he maintained a seed house for the propagation of geraniums, freesia and amaryllis.

Though primarily a horticulturist, his interests were ornithological as well. In mid-career, Childs edited *The Warbler*, a magazine of birds (Mayflower Press, 1907).

A Republican, Childs was elected to the State Senate in 1894. He still found time in 1908 to become Floral Park's first President (a title later changed to Mayor) and to head the Village Board of Education. It was the age of energy, and like his friend Teddy Roosevelt, John Lewis Childs was one of its paragons.

Childs laid out the town, naming almost all the streets for flowers and shrubs, planting thousands of Dutch elms and Norway maples on every byway, lane and road. In spring as the train approached Floral Park, Long Island Railroad riders admired his extensive and beautiful fields of hybrid tulips. Appropriately, the street that crossed the railroad became Tulip Avenue. Only a stone's throw from the press and railroad station stood his turreted Victorian mansion.[16]

Pepìn may have discovered the town on a weekend outing long before he married. As a young man, he often escaped from the summer heat in the city by taking his bicycle on the Long Island Railroad and getting off to explore whatever place took his fancy. Fascinated with place-names, he never forgot the "floral park" with a sea of tulips floating a white estate house clearly visible from the train.

To the Balzacs, the village of Floral Park must have seemed like a perfect place to raise children. It had thriving shops on Jericho Turnpike, yet its many open fields preserved its rural character. On Sundays, the chimes and bells of four different churches marked the morning hours. On weekdays when Joey was old enough, Pepìn could walk the boy to the elementary school on Elizabeth Street and continue down South Tyson Avenue to the L.I.R.R. for the commute to New York. From there, he could take the Tubes to Newark. (Later, when the subway was extended into Queens County, he could save on fare by taking a bus across from St. Hedwig's Church two blocks from 41 Sycamore to the subway in Jamaica, from there to the city and Newark).

Gathering their courage and savings and making the most important investment of their lives, Pepìn and Birdie bought the two-story, clapboard house at 41 Sycamore Avenue on what eventually became the easternmost street in Floral Park.[17] It was a Dutch colonial, probably built from Sears Roebuck plans, with sloping eaves and all the most modern features.

On March 13, 1915, the Balzacs moved from New York City into their new home. No wonder that they thought of it as a poor man's Sagamore Hill. On the first floor of the house was an open, columned sun porch; a glass-doored entry way with a coat closet; to the left, a parlor with pocket doors that led to a large dining room with a grand bay window. A corridor from the entry contained the stairs to the second floor to the right and straight ahead led to a large kitchen.

Used to a cramped New York City apartment, Birdie marveled at the huge eat-in kitchen. She was delighted with its large white-legged porcelain sink and drain board, floor-to-ceiling built-in cabinets and oversized wood burning stove for cooking and extra heating in the winter.

The house had two pantries—a butler's pantry between the kitchen and the dining room and just beyond the kitchen, a small unheated back porch with a closet outfitted with shelves for canned goods. There was just enough space across from the closet for an icebox.

Off the corridor to the kitchen in the stairwell, a large stained-glass window looked out on a narrow side yard where Birdie could grow kitchen herbs, and the back yard was deep enough for an extensive vegetable garden. At the top of the stairs was a bath with a claw-footed tub. Off a long hall were four bedrooms, the master bedroom with an arched alcove ideal for a nursery. Radiators stood in every room including the bath. With a coal cellar and an unfinished attic, the house fulfilled all their needs. Above all, it was full of light and plenty large enough for Pepìn, Birdie, and the three children.

Within nine years, however, Birdie bore three more babies, and Tia Fidela and her infant boy lived in the house for a time. With seven children, three adults and only one bathroom, 41 Sycamore, originally so palatial, began to burst at the seams.

According to Manuel Gil, Dad's lifelong friend and co-worker at Sidney Ross, in those days Pepìn was a handsome, whimsical, bright fellow. Having named his first son for himself, he proceeded to name the next boys for famous kings in history. All three were born in the front bedroom of the new house: in February 1916, Bill, named for William the Conqueror; in April 1918, Pete, named for Peter the Great; and in September 1924, Freddie, named for Frederick Barbarossa, the foremost of the medieval emperors. Pepìn named his daughters, Della (Fidela) and Mercedes, for the virtues, Faith and Mercy. He skipped Hope.

From Sycamore Avenue to Lake Success[18]

> *A lake is the landscape's most beautiful and expressive feature. It is earth's eye; looking into which the beholder measures the depth of his own nature.*
> —Henry David Thoreau, *Walden*

Eight Dutch colonials stood on Sycamore Avenue, built by the same contractor, each a little different from the other. Like the Balzacs, almost all the families who had bought houses on the street were fugitives from the city, and many of them were immigrants. On Sycamore Avenue and the surrounding streets, their rough offspring—from Irish, Italian, German, French, Greek, Polish, English and Spanish backgrounds—walked to school together, played stickball in the road, hide-and-seek in the neighbors' yards. In their wild games, they accidentally trampled Mrs. Bentayoue's prize lilies, stole apples from the Rapetti's backyard and grapes from Martone's arbor and talked red-haired Kitty Bradley into supervising bonfires for roast mickies. They hung on the *wurztman's* truck when he came to sell blood sausages to the Schuhmachers and Fleischers and harassed the milkman and the Dugan Bakery delivery boy by hitching sleds or bicycles to the backs of their vans. In general, the kids raised so much hell and made so much noise that Mr. Hensey repeatedly threatened to call the cops.

Happily, as far as the children were concerned, Sycamore Avenue was only a mile and a half as the crows fly to Lake Success. Spring-fed, it adjoined a golf course and was extensively posted with "No Swimming," "No Trespassing" signs. Nevertheless, the kids in the neighborhood thought of it as their personal beach in summer and their exclusive skating rink in winter.

Any one of the bigger boys knew the back way through the woods over the small stone bridge to the lake. Just walk up Sycamore to Jericho, they'd say, tack almost immediately to the left on Cherry Lane for the half-mile hike past Kuchera's paint store and the open field beyond Kiewra's rambling old farmhouse. Within five minutes, you'll be at the city line on Hillside Avenue. From there, hang a right for four blocks in New Hyde Park, then head north into the woods cross country on the narrow child-worn path.

On hot summer days as the high grass gave way to the first stands of trees, the temperature dropped noticeably, and the only sounds were occasional bird songs, the chirpings of thousands of invisible crickets and the snapping of twigs as the children made their way like so many Hansels and Gretels through a virgin forest. The woods were full of great, old tulip trees and slimmer, bush-like sassafras, tangled hillocks of pink mountain laurel and dogwood so thick in early spring that their white blossoms looked like snowflakes gently blowing in the wind.

The children had to stay close to the trail or risk a severe case of poison ivy. So virulent was the variety that grew along the North Shore of Long Island that even in winter one had to avoid coming in contact with the bare poison ivy vines. Some of the older kids did take a chance, wearing socks and long pants over their bathing suits. Armed with trowels and newspapers brought from home, they left the path to search for the delicate yellow Lady's slippers that grew beneath the oak trees close to the lake's edge. Their mothers prized these already rare native orchids as specimen plants for their wildflower gardens.

At last, the ground became soft and damp, and parting the brush near the end of the trail, they had their first glimpse of the miracle—Lake Success, crystalline, serene and inviting, glimmering through the trees. It was their Walden Pond, spring, summer, autumn and winter: dense woods, dappled sunshine, and the clear blue water, a great open space beneath the heavens.

On hot afternoons, the lake belonged to the kids—despite the police who circled once an hour—despite the guard at the gatehouse entrance on Lakeville Road. They stripped to their bathing suits and hid their clothes behind the bushes. Crossing the narrow sandy beachfront, they waded up to their waists, then dipped in and out of the pure water dolphin-like, hair plastered back, their young bodies shining.

The water was cool and transparent. Even twenty feet out, they could see the fine pebbles on the bottom. Warned by older brothers and sisters, no one dared swim to the middle. The lake, the locals said, was bottomless, fed by underground springs that created two whirlpools near the center. But the edges all around to a depth of ten feet were safe.

On the hour, the cops would spy the swimmers and scream at them to come out of the water. The kids ignored the warnings, swimming around the lake, carefully skirting the center, disappearing into the woods before the police could catch up with them. As soon as the patrol car had passed, the children backtracked to the place where they had hidden their clothes. Their pants and shirts, their pinafores and socks already smelled of thyme and wild onions.

That was their summer routine. In winter, as soon as it got cold enough, usually just after the turn of the year, the kids threw their ice skates over their shoulders and trekked through the snow from Sycamore north through New Hyde Park. They preferred going the shorter back way, but in winter, the snow rarely melted in the woods. Their narrow path was obliterated until spring. Instead, they climbed through the hole in the fence on Lakeville Road and carefully sneaked past the golf course gatehouse, hid their shoes and gutta-perchas and put on their extra socks and skates.

They came to the lake in winter with as much anticipation as in summer. For an hour or two after school on cold bright afternoons, these homegrown Hans Brinkers glided, raced, practiced spins and jumps—even though their skates weren't silver. Many of the kids had been up since 5 A.M. doing early morning chores or finishing homework before school began.

Although they wouldn't admit it, they started to tire as the afternoon light began to wane, as the wind picked up and grew bitter. Reluctantly, they retrieved their footgear and began the long tramp home with red cheeks and stinging fingers.

On moonlit January nights, especially on the weekends, some of the parents accompanied the kids. At such times, as many as fifty people—children and adults from Manhasset, Great Neck, New Hyde Park and Floral Park—might be on the ice. Skating singly or in pairs, they moved gracefully around the edges of the lake, talking and laughing, trying new figures and arabesques. It was a scene out of a Currier and Ives engraving.

The police patrolled the area year round. Local men themselves, they were concerned about the trespassers' safety. If adults were present, however, the cops didn't even stop—though one night, much to everyone's amusement, one of the younger officers got out of the patrol car—only to put skates on himself.

By 9 P.M., people started to leave. Parents and children reached home flushed from the exercise, nipped by the cold. They looked forward to drinking hot chocolate in the warm kitchens of Sycamore Avenue.

Never, never did they foresee that housing contractors would buy their beloved lake, its pristine shorefront and deep woods. Never, never did they anticipate that their childhood refuge would be fenced, its thickets shorn of dogwood and mountain laurel, its wild thyme and Lady's slippers extinct.[19]

Rena C. Hayden of the John Lewis Childs Elementary School[20]

My mother took me to kindergarten on my first day of school. Rena C. Hayden recognized her. "Why Mercedes Balzac, whatever are you doing here?" My mother responded, "This is my daughter."

"Oh, no," Mrs. Hayden replied ruefully remembering my mother's wild brothers. "I'll not outlive another generation of Balzacs."
—Nena Balzac

When the children from Sycamore Avenue went to the Floral Park School No. 22 (renamed June 1, 1921 for John Lewis Childs), they tried not to speak in the mongrel tongues they used at home. Though they were painfully aware that they lived across the tracks on the last street in town, and inhabited, as it were, the latter end of the world, they tried to be Americans. Their starched and sanitized teachers and staff—the Mistresses Darling, Crabbe, Howe, Lynch, Harrington, Thurston, Whitbred, Purdy, De Witt, Chisamore, Plummer, Eames, Smith, Crotty, Martin, and Marshall—demanded nothing less. As late as the 1940s, aside from Mrs. Rosetti, the kindergarten teacher, Miss Heidtman, who taught first grade, and Miss Levy, who taught seventh, the teachers and staff came from English and Anglo-Irish Protestant backgrounds, spoke with refined accents and held conservative political views. In the 1948 presidential election, they voted for Dewey.

From 1914 to 1947, a remarkable woman, Rena C. Hayden ran the Elementary School, K-8, with impeccable taste and an iron hand. Appointed by John Lewis Childs as a teacher in 1908 and then as principal, she hired and fired the staff for its classrooms as well as its kitchen; personally policed the schoolyards at recess, making miscreants walk single file behind her; disciplined, and on occasion, expelled unruly students; and came knocking loudly on parents' doors in her capacity as sometime truant officer. She stood no more than 5'1"; was stocky, with an enormous chest and delicate, small limbs. No animal rights activist, she wore hats with birds on them, tailored suits with a stole of little foxes draped over her shoulders and sensible leather shoes. Her voice, when she chose to raise it, sounded to her pupils like the wrath of God Himself, and her bulging blue eyes exacted attention. Awestruck teachers referred to her as R.C.H.; awestruck children whispered her name. Both teachers and pupils withered under her terrible gaze.

For thirty-three years, Mrs. Hayden personally oversaw the education of nearly every kid in Floral Park. They conquered English grammar by diagramming sentences, writing by practicing the Palmer method; they learned to read by sounding out their letters, to do sums by working with flash cards at school and at home. Those that would not or could not master these skills were remanded to summer school, and if that did not help, they were unceremoniously left back. She commanded so much respect that few parents ever disagreed with her judgments.

Strong in character and social in purpose, she led the Pledge of Allegiance and the 23rd Psalm at assemblies, headed the John Lewis Childs School contingent to the Mummer's Parade at Thanksgiving and marched in the very first ranks of every Memorial Day celebration. During the early years, many of her charges left school upon completing eighth grade. She had only nine brief years to teach them to think clearly and independently, to polish the many diamonds in the rough she believed them to be, to inspire them with the highest ideals of American culture.

That was her public persona; in private, she acted otherwise, with kindness and discretion. I know one anecdote about her benevolence; there must have been others. In 1927, when Birdie died, Peter Balzac was not quite nine years old. Within a year and a half, in addition to Joey and Della, Nena graduated 8th grade and quit school. So Pete quit too. He hung out at the coal yards, going with the drivers on delivery runs, helping maintain the straw for the stable, now and then getting tips.

He was doing pretty well for himself, when one fine morning, Mrs. Hayden came looking for him. She went first to 41 Sycamore Avenue. Not finding him there but given directions by a mortified Nena, R.C.H. proceeded to the coal yards where she finally caught up with the boy. In her severest voice, she asked, "Peter Balzac, why are you not in school?"

"I've quit school," he replied bravely.

"You can't quit school at age ten," she thundered.

Thinking quickly for some kind of excuse, he stammered, "I haven't got any clothes to wear to school." (Little more than a child herself, Nena, 14, tried to keep Pete's shirts and trousers clean and mended, but king of the anthracite heaps, he inevitably came home, clothes tattered and covered with coal dust).

Mrs. Hayden looked down at him. He did look ragged. His pants were ripped, and his once white sailor shirt had taken a beating. Without hesitation, Mrs. Hayden opened her pocketbook and gave the boy a twenty-dollar bill. "Now, Peter Balzac, you have money to buy clothes for school. I expect you to be there."

Working from morning until dusk and trying desperately to raise his motherless children, Pepìn hadn't realized that Pete had been skipping school. Ever grateful to Mrs. Hayden for her intercession, Pepìn paid back the twenty dollars. Mrs. Hayden never referred to the incident again, nor when she saw the boy in the halls of the John Lewis Childs Elementary School did she ever make mention of his new clothes—knickers and an argyle sweater vest—that he had bought at Ted's Men's Store on Jericho Turnpike.

Pete finished eighth grade. In his eighties, Pete told me that story himself. He revered the memory of Rena C. Hayden of Floral Park.[21]

Mayors and fire chiefs came and went; she remained, through World War I, through the roaring Twenties, through the Great Depression, through World War II. In April 1945, when F. D. R. died, she turned out the entire school on the lawn in front of the original bell-topped school building. Solemnly, she lowered the flag to half-mast. Her eyes filled with tears; many of the teachers openly wept. Some of her pupils realized, perhaps for the first time, that like the fallen President, Mrs. Hayden had provided them with an example of commitment, strength and self-reliance. For an even longer time than he, through dark and difficult years, she had led the way. It was her finest hour.

1947 marked the end of an era in Floral Park. Because of the ministrations of Childs and Hayden, it had had a fair seedtime. First, John Lewis Childs' mansion was torn down. Before the demolition, Mrs. Hayden saw to it that all the classes from the school went on a tour of the enormous white house. She wanted them to take away one last impression of her mentor and friend. Most unforgettable to the schoolgirls was Mrs. Childs' charming, round, burgundy-carpeted sewing room in one of the towers.

At the end of the school year in June, 1947 after thirty-three years at the helm, Mrs. Hayden retired as principal of the John Lewis Childs School. She went home to her house on Jericho Turnpike by the Long Island Railroad trestle. For a few more years she continued to march in holiday parades. And then she passed indelibly into our recollections even as she receded into the town's history.

As surely as John Lewis Childs, Rena C. Hayden was a founder of Floral Park.

[16] Biographical information concerning John Lewis Childs comes from Edith M. Purcell, *Across the Years: the Story of Floral Park* (1958).

[17] As late as 1918 both Sycamore and Lewis Avenue were so new that they were not incorporated into any village. Born in the front bedroom of 41 Sycamore Avenue on April 29, 1918, Peter Balzac's birth certificate lists his

place of birth as "outside Floral Park." By mutual agreement sometime afterwards, Floral Park took Sycamore Avenue as its easternmost street, and New Hyde Park adopted Lewis Avenue as its westernmost. From 1915 to 1993, for 78 years, at least one Balzac lived on Sycamore Avenue.

[18] "From Sycamore Avenue to Lake Success" was published in *The Gateway*, the Floral Park newspaper, under the title "A Floral Park Winter and Summer in the Good Old Days," Vol. LXXVIII No. 20, Wednesday, February 4, 2004, 1, 10-11.

[19] Coming back from New York City in 2003, my son, Davin and I took Lakeville Road to Floral Park. On a whim as we approached Lake Success, we turned into Lake Shore Drive, now the entry into an upscale housing development. Huge, expensive homes fronted the lake and all but obscured that pure body of water.

[20] *The Gateway* published this sketch under the title, "In Memoriam: JLC Principal Rena Hayden," in its Memorial Day issue, Vol. LXXVI No. 35, Wednesday, May 22, 2002, 5, 11.

[21] Nena Balzac's version of Mrs. Hayden's encounter with her little brother was neater and more picturesque:

> *When Pete told the principal that he had no clothes for school, Mrs. Hayden had him march directly behind her. They proceeded up Jericho Turnpike to Ted's Men's Store where she bought him an outfit right there and then.*

In a conversation with Pete in 2002, he assured me that it didn't happen that way.

Part 1, Chapter 5
41 Sycamore Avenue

Then read from the treasured volume
The poem of thy choice,
And lend to the rhyme of the poet
The beauty of thy voice.

And the night shall be filled with music
And the cares, that infest the day,
Shall fold their tents, like the Arabs,
And as silently steal away.
—Henry Wadsworth Longfellow, *The Day is Done*

Gentle, ribald and kind, Pepìn read Cervantes' *Don Quixote* at least once a year in Spanish. Seated in his Morris chair on the front sun porch, smoking his pipe full of cherry-flavored tobacco, he would intermittently howl with laughter. When he couldn't contain himself any longer, he would call Birdie, interrupting her housework, and translate a passage from the book so that she would have to laugh too. Alternately, he roared with delight over Rabelais' *Gargantua and Pantagruel* reading it in the original to keep up his French. "Foolie, foolie", he chortled.

He was almost entirely self-taught. He spoke Spanish, French, Italian and Portuguese fluently. He was a good Latinist and read German with facility. (After his death in 1939, Della found a request for Mr. Balzac to print a drug label in Dutch). He even knew a smattering of Chinese. On more than one occasion, he took the whole family to Chinatown and amazed his wife and wonder-struck children by ordering from the Mandarin menu and speaking to the waiter in his native tongue.

To foster his children's learning, he bought hardbound sets of the *Harvard Classics*, the *Book of Knowledge* (18 vols.) and the *French Classical Romances* placing them in the oak and glass bookcase to the right of the pocket doors in the parlor. With these under their belt, plus the mandatory *Complete Works of Honoré de Balzac*, his children, he convinced himself, would have the equivalent of a college education.

For himself, he purchased a leather bound, complete set of Shakespeare in tiny individual volumes slipping a different two by three inch copy of a play into his pocket every day to read on the train as he went to work. His lifelong love of Shakespeare added to his elegant and accented English. Friends of my mother remembered with fondness how he described the long trip from Floral Park to Newark. "When I alighted from the Tubes, a stone's throw from Manzanilla", he would say—much to their amusement—and then recount some incident of his travel. "Descending from the train" (a direct transliteration from Spanish), he would claim with a tired smile to have "trekked from the shores of Bohemia." His diction was exquisite and often archaic. "Use a word three times," he liked to remind his offspring, "and it's yours for life."

Pepìn's pronunciation was so charming that on summer evenings children on the block came to call for him. "Nena, Nena, can your father come out and tell us a story?" Weary of playing Kick the Can or Ring-o-Levio,[22] they sat on 41's wide brick stoop under Birdie's maples, transfixed as he intoned bits and pieces from the *Arabian Nights' Entertainments*. While they liked his version of "Sinbad the Sailor" and

"Aladdin and the Magic Lamp," they clamored to hear "A-lí Ba-bá and the Forty Thieves." Even after Dad had told that particular tale many times, they asked him to repeat it, delighting as much in his accent as in the incidents of the narrative. The way Mr. Balzac said the hero's name conjured up Persian tapestries and oriental splendor.

An artless storyteller himself, he had his children present entertainments on Sunday afternoons. They had a week to memorize a poem or dramatize a play in which one or more of them appeared. They rehearsed in the dining room behind the closed pocket doors. When ready to present their version of "The Children's Hour," Pepìn acted as *Magister Ludi*, the Master of the Games. As soon as he gave each child a fancy introduction, the sliding doors rolled open and the player held forth before the admiring audience of parents and siblings sitting in the parlor.

Joey's favorite piece, one that he still could recite in his sixties, was a rendition of "Home." When he got to the last lines, "Ye've got t' love each brick and stone from cellar up t' dome: / It takes a heap o' livin' in a house t' make it home," all the children felt that Edgar Guest had written with 41 Sycamore in mind.[23]

A wonderful mimic, Della was fond of reciting an eerie poem complete with sound effects: "Have you ever heard the wind go 'WOOOOOOO'?" Mid-way through the recitation, her eyes opened wide, and her voice lowered to a hoarse whisper. "Oh who do you want, oh lonely wind,/ that you wail the whole night through?" At this point, Della trembled and blanched. "And the wind would say in its meaningful way/ "YOUOOOO."[24]

My mother's repertoire contained two old favorites: H. C. Bunner's "One, Two, Three," a saccharine Victorian tearjerker about "an old, old, old lady and a boy who was half past three/And the way they played together/was beautiful to see." Alternately, she sang Eugene Field's "Little Boy Blue," an equally saccharine piece about a child who dies, but his toys remain true. "Ay, faithful to Little Boy Blue they stand,/ Each in the same old place/ Awaiting the touch of a little hand/ The smile of a little face."[25]

They all knew by heart Edgar Allen Poe's "The Raven," Celia Thatcher's "To a Sandpiper," and Henry Wadsworth Longfellow's "The Village Blacksmith" and "Paul Revere's Ride." The most published poet at the turn of the century was the now all but forgotten Ella Wheeler Wilcox. Her poem, "Solitude," a Balzac standard, became a virtual motto for the entire family: "Laugh and the world laughs with you;/.Weep, and you weep alone./ For the sad old earth must borrow its mirth,/ But has trouble enough of its own."[26]

Sometimes even Birdie would get in on the act singing the Protestant hymns of her childhood, "That Old Rugged Cross," or "In the Garden" or "Shall We Gather at the River?"

However clichéd the versification or lachrymose the sentiment, these Sunday entertainments served a noble purpose: the young Balzacs became highly verbal, if not glib; they were poised on their feet before adults and strangers; and even as children, they loved the rhythms and rhymes of the English language. By the time they were teenagers, they knew reams and reams of poetry, ranging from Shakespearean soliloquies to the lowest and funniest of limericks. On occasion,

"Polonius' Advice to Laertes" or "To Be or Not to Be" gave way to Joey's recitation of "Sweet Betsy's Boil"—all twenty-eight verses—or Bill's mildly salacious rendition of "Two old maids in a feather bed/ One turned over and to the other said,/ How am I doing?" Composed of at least another ten stanzas, he declaimed this ditty—with Pepìn smirking despite himself—while the Balzac aunts were upstairs in the bathroom together taking off their corsets after a big holiday meal.

Surprisingly, Pepìn never taught his children Spanish. Though they all knew *dichos*, the proverbial phrases that so constantly peppered Dad's speech, Bill was the only one who became fluent in his father's native tongue, learning formal Spanish in high school and college.

If Dad frequently used Spanish proverbs such as "Hunger is the best sauce" and "He who laughs last, laughs best," Birdie fell back just as often on English traditional sayings: "Wash as far as possible, then wash possible," "Silence is golden," "Children should be seen, not heard," "Spare the rod, spoil the child." Wash cloth in hand, she'd pursue Joe or Bill or Pete. "Let me wash those ears. There's more dirt in them than in the potato patch." Though her adages somehow always seemed harsher than Dad's, she had a wry sense of humor. Should one of her brood have left a coat or hat lying about, she was sure to say, "A place for everything, and everything in its place, and the piss pot on the piano."

Joey often had his mouth washed out with soap for revising Birdie's admonitions. If she began with "A stitch in time," he would finish the line *sotto voce* with "saves your ass" before she could get out "saves nine." Hustling the children off to bed before 7:30 P.M., Birdie would defend her decision with "Early to bed, early to rise" only to hear precocious Joey snidely whisper, "makes for a big family."

Edmundo La Carruba, Jr.

> 'Death,' said I, 'what do you here
> At this Spring season of the year?'
> 'I mark the flowers ere the prime
> Which I may tell at Autumn-time.
>
> But the Spring-tide pass'd the same;
> Autumn-time no earlier came.
> And the flowers that he had tied
> As I mark'd not always died
> Sooner than their mates; and yet
> Their fall was fuller of regret:
>
> It seem'd so hard and dismal thing,
> Death, to mark them in the Spring.
> —Gerard Manley Hopkins, "Spring and
> Death"

Did I ever tell you the story of little Edmundo, Tia's baby, who died during the Great Influenza Epidemic of 1918-1919?

The shadow of death came early to the house on Sycamore Avenue. Tia Fidela, who came to the States in 1914 and was living in Brooklyn, had fallen in love with a handsome young soldier, Edmundo La Carruba. She and her gallant Field Artillery Officer were engaged to be married when suddenly in the summer of 1917, his unit was called up and shipped out to France. Reluctantly that April, President Wilson had finally declared war.

Within weeks, Tia received notification that Edmundo was among the first American casualties, killed on a nameless field in France. Almost simultaneously, she learned that she was pregnant. She fled to Floral Park. Pepìn and Birdie, soon to have their third child, welcomed her with tenderness and understanding. Sister and sister-in-law gave birth weeks apart, to Edmundo at the beginning and Peter at the end of April 1918.

Despite the fact that the babies were born at 41 Sycamore Avenue and their identity was certain, Tia dutifully checked them both. Gently turning their heads to the side, she pointed out a particularly prominent spur of cartilage on the back of their ears. Everyone has this cartilage she said, but only blood relatives have so marked a protuberance. She dubbed it the "Balzac bone". She claimed that every child since the original Joseph and Josephine of 1812 fame had been born with this anomaly. Triumphantly, she declared both Edmundo and Peter to be Balzacs. Thereafter, every new mother in the family for the next two generations would do the same, reassuring herself that the infant born in the more sterile environment of a modern hospital was indeed hers.

During the course of 1918, especially in the brutally cold winter of 1918-1919, a virulent strain of influenza killed an estimated twenty million people world-wide, five hundred forty eight thousand in the United States alone. With no known vaccine, young and old came down with raging fevers and racking coughs. Some recovered, but babies in particular suffered dehydration and uncontrollable scarring of the lungs.

At 41 Sycamore Avenue in early February 1919, Edmundo and Peter contracted the flu and were critically ill. Tia and Birdie isolated them from the other children and took turns dipping the infants into tepid baths to reduce their fevers. A barking cough shook their tiny chests as they gasped for breath. Fearing that they were dying, Tia threw on her shawl and ran to St. Hedwig's for a priest.

When Father Wilamowski arrived, he baptized both infants, but Tia's baby did not survive the night. Edmundo La Carruba, Jr. lived only ten months. Peter Balzac passed the crisis and thrived.

> *Edmundo was such an alert baby—content and chubby. He had wispy curls and huge brown eyes in this photo taken when he was six months old.*
>
> Tia Fidela's baby, Edmundo

If Tia's grief knew no end, so Birdie's compassion had no limit. Once again, Pepìn, Birdie and the disconsolate Tia made the sad journey to the Evergreens Cemetery. Little Edmundo was buried with Birdie's sisters, Daisy and Louise. After a Roman Catholic priest read the Office for the Dead and lead the recitation of the Lord's Prayer,

Pepìn recited lines he had somewhat freely adapted from François de Malherbe's "*Consolation á Monsieur du Perier:*"

> *Mais il estoit du monde, ou les plus belles choses*
> *Ont le pire destin,*
> *Et rose il a vescu ce que vive les roses,*
> *L'espace d'un matin.*
> (But he was of this world, where the most beautiful
> Share the worst fate.
> Rosebud, he lived as the roses live,
> For the space of one morning).

Despite Pepìn's and Birdie's entreaties for her to stay with them in Floral Park, Fidela moved to an apartment on Pennsylvania Avenue, Brooklyn and took a job as a lace tatter in a glove factory. On one side of the living room archway into the kitchen, she hung a portrait of the dashing Edmundo, Sr. in uniform, complete with jodhpurs, Sam Browne belt and high leather boots; on the other, a large oval-framed study of their son. She had been so busy caring for Edmundo that she had forgotten to pick up a studio photograph taken of him in December. She ended up sending it to Birdie and Pepìn on March 16, 1919, a month after the baby died. On the back of the photo, she wrote:

> *Mis queridos hermanos. Vaya este retrato como recuerdo de tu sobrino y ahijado que ya no existe Edmundo. Murió el 8 de Febrero de 1919.*
> (My dear brother and sister. This portrait comes as a remembrance of Edmundo, your nephew and godson, who no longer exists. He died February 8, 1919).

Grieving and alone, she became increasingly pious. She certainly believed that her afflictions, sent by an offended God, resulted from her sin. She went to early Mass daily, praying for the repose of the souls of her lover and her son. Her constant prayers earned them years and years of remission from Purgatory and perhaps salved the hurt of her once wayward heart. Comforted by her devotion to the Rosary, she went on repenting for the rest of her life.

In 1922, Rosa Balzac came from Puerto Rico to live with her older sister. Within weeks, Rosa found a job with the cookie and baked goods concern, Nabisco, first as an inspector, eventually as a supervisor in the Brooklyn factory. Together, the sisters continued to visit Sycamore Avenue showering Birdie, Pepìn and the children with presents, picking wild flowers on the way.

Birdie's Works and Days

Work, for the night is coming,
Work through the morning hours;
Work while the dew is sparkling,
Work 'mid springing flowers;
Work when the day grows brighter,
Work in the glowing sun;
Work, for the night is coming,
When man's work is done.

Work, for the night is coming,
Work through the sunny noon;
Fill brightest hours with labor,
Rest comes sure and soon.
Give every flying minute,
Something to keep in store;
Work, for the night is coming,
When man works no more.

Work, for the night is coming,
Under the sunset skies;
While their bright tints are glowing,
Work, for daylight flies.
Work till the last beam fadeth,
Fadeth to shine no more;
Work, while the night is darkening,
When man's work is o'er.
—Words: Anna L Coghill, 1854; Music:
"Work Song," by Lowell Mason, 1864

Pepìn was gone from early in the morning until seven o'clock at night. Harried by the responsibility of raising six active youngsters virtually alone, Birdie resorted to whaling them with a cat-o'-nine tails. Pepìn never approved of lickings. "Birdie, Birdie", he would say, "Try not to notice. They're only children."

But Pepìn wasn't home very much, and so the task of disciplining the children fell to her. For her part, she did try to be fair. If one of them tattled, the snitch got the first lashing; the wrongdoer, the next. Joey did get flailed more than the others, though, and it wasn't just because he was the eldest. He seemed always to provoke her, and, in truth, she didn't like him. When my mother was very young, she remembered that Joey would cry, "Don't you hit me! You're not my Mommy"! He was three years old when Louise died, but like the children in ee cumming's poem, as up he grew, down he forgot the other, gentler lady who more and more rarely frequented his dreams.

Birdie didn't mean to be irritable and probably didn't realize how very tired she was or how ill. She wore herself out economizing to clothe them all: turning Pepìn's collars, making the boys' blouses, mending endless rips in their knickers, cutting and hemming hand me downs, darning socks, sewing identical dresses for herself and the girls. As a child, my mother was ashamed of these garments even when they were brand new. There just wasn't enough money to buy readymade blouses and skirts that many of the girls at school wore.

Birdie maintained a large garden in the spring and summer and did extensive canning and preserving in the fall. She propagated and raised a quince bush in the back yard, and like her mother, prided herself on her quince jam. On Mondays, she washed sheets and towels on her knees leaning over a galvanized wash board placed in the claw-footed bathtub upstairs. On Tuesdays, she did the clothing, separating the whites from the colored fabrics, scrubbing them all with homemade lye soap that reddened and coarsened her hands. Wednesdays were devoted to starching, ironing, sewing and mending; Thursdays, if the weather was good, to special tasks like placing the washed and blued lace curtains on the pin-pricking stretcher that she set up in the yard or airing the goose down pillows and virgin wool blankets that she hung out the back upstairs windows. On Fridays, she baked five large round loaves of bread and at least one special dessert, a pie or cobbler, a tapioca or rice pudding for the weekend in case someone came to visit.

She took time out of her busy schedule to teach her girls to cook and sew. "If you don't know how to make rice by the time you are seven, you'll never be a woman". The girls beamed when their rice came out perfectly, each grain separate, firm and flaky. Della took to needlework, but impatient Nena constantly knotted the thread, and finally Birdie gave up trying to teach her embroidery.

Once a year in the fall, Pepìn dragged a huge iron kettle and a four-foot long paddle from the cellar. In the back yard, he improvised a low hearth of loose bricks and made a fire with kindling and small logs. Dressed in her oldest clothes, Birdie decanted the animal fat that she had saved all year into the cauldron, added lye to the mixture, and stirred the caustic yellow brew until it boiled. When it cooled, she cut the soap into bars and stored them in the back porch pantry. Her wash soap, she claimed with pride, would cleanse a chimney sweep's coat.

Germ-conscious from her training as a nurse, she kept the house in immaculate order, scouring the big kitchen floor on her hands and knees, pushing up her prolapsed uterus as she scrubbed. She cooked, baked, shopped, swept, waxed and, draping the sisal parlor rug over the back-yard clothesline, whacked it with a wire rug beater until she was exhausted.

The children, of course, pitched in. (God help the ingrate who shirked his duty). If any of them tarried, she would glare all the while at the malefactor as she read Joy Allison's "Which Loved Her Best?" from the 1917 New Barnes Reader.

> "I love you, mother," said little John;
> Then forgetting his work, his cap went on,
> And he was off to the garden swing,
> Leaving his mother the wood to bring.
>
> "I love you, mother," said rosy Nell;
> "I love you better than tongue can tell."
> Then she teased and pouted full half the day,
> Till her mother rejoiced when she went to play.
>
> "I love you mother," said little Fan;
> "To-day I'll help you all I can;
> How glad I am that school doesn't keep!"
> So she rocked the baby till it fell asleep.
>
> Then stepping softly, she took the broom,
> And swept the floor, and dusted the room.
> Busy and happy all day was she;
> Helpful and happy as a child could be.

"I love you, Mother," again they said,
Three little children going to bed.
How do you think that mother guessed
Which of them really loved her best?

Hearing the poem, the kids groaned. They came to despise anyone named "Fan," but usually a little guilt went a long way, and whatever the job, they learned to give "it a lick and a polish."

Everyone had a chore. The girls dusted and took care of the baby after school. The boys stoked the furnace, took out the garbage, turned over the garden and weeded. On weekends, Pepìn chopped wood for the kitchen stove, put up screens and took down storm windows as the season demanded. As his wife sang "Bringing in the Sheaves," Pepìn artfully pruned the hedges on the property line. "Work for the night is coming when man's work is done," was Birdie's household mantra.

Sometimes on the weekend, Dad's co-worker at Sidney Ross, Manuel Gil, would ride his bicycle all the way from Brooklyn to Floral Park. He admired Pepìn's skill as a printer, his erudition as a translator, and his devotion to his big family. Manuel was a Cuban, a diminutive, gentle man with a hooked nose who could have posed for a Mayan sculpture. He genuinely liked kids and never failed to bring them a bag of candy.

When he came for Sunday dinner, the children were allowed to sit quietly in the parlor, a room that during the week was off-limits to them. For their benefit, their father and Manuel traded funny stories about Puerto Rico and Cuba when they were boys. Then seated at the dining room table, the children's table manners had to be impeccable. Birdie had only to raise an eyebrow, and they immediately knew which fork to use or whether they might ask for a second helping.

Manuel was a bachelor with an enormous appetite who devoured Birdie's Caribbean rice and bread pudding with gusto. Birdie always made him feel welcome, and how could she not? He praised her home cooking so sincerely that she didn't mind how much he ate. She sympathized with him: a recent émigré, he missed home and his family in Havana. Manuel needed a wife, but neither Pepìn nor Birdie knew any petite Spanish girls.

"Where does that little man put all that food?" the kids wondered. When Dad and Manuel went for a postprandial stroll, Joey composed a limerick in their guest's honor:

"There was a young man from Cuba
Whose stomach was big as a tuba.
He ate till he split and then had a fit—
This hungry young man from Cuba."

The kids howled with laughter. Needless to say, Birdie was not amused.

Birdie Lopez Balzac, ca. 1922

On Sundays when she wasn't entertaining, Birdie sometimes walked to the Lutheran Church on Spooner Street off Plainview Avenue. She found comfort in the sermons of its engaging young pastor, Reverend Durr.

Despite her rare church attendance and the Protestant hymns that she so often sang, Birdie wasn't particularly religious. Her father's family had been nominal Methodists paying organized worship no mind. Lopez is a common Sephardic name, but he never acknowledged having Jewish blood. Since that was the case on her father's side, she considered herself an Anglican like her mother and approved of Pepìn's counsel that the children read the Bible, both the Old and New Testaments. She was pretty lax about formalities—some of the children had been baptized, some not. Aside from Bill who attended the Catholic School of the Holy Ghost in New Hyde Park, none of the kids went to Sunday school or made their Holy Communion or Confirmation.

Pepìn was even less orthodox than his wife. Raised as a Catholic with two sisters fanatically devoted to the Church, Pepìn eschewed the whole enterprise of belief. He thought that Jesus was a great prophet; so were Buddha, Confucius and Mohammed. Though he admired the style of St. Augustine's *Confessions*, he found Lucretius' *De Rerum Naturum* more to his taste. Scandalizing his sisters, he claimed to be a perfect pagan and wanted no priest when he died. "High Mass, high money," he teased them, "Low Mass, low money; no Mass, no money."

[22] Both Kick-the-Can and Ring-o-Levio were urban street games that the children on Sycamore Avenue brought with them from the city to Floral Park. The games were variants of Hide-and-Seek. When there were only a few children, they played the former, setting up a tin can in the middle of the street. The child who was "It" had to find those who were hiding and put them in "jail" (usually a chalked out square on the asphalt). If "It"

went too far away from the can, one of the hidden children could dash out into the street and, by kicking the can, automatically free all those who had been placed in jail. When "It" had captured everyone, the first child caught became "It." With greater numbers of children, one played the team game, Ring-o-Levio. One person from Team 1 was jailer. All other members of Team 1 went actively searching for those hiding. Captured children went to jail, but should a child from Team 2 touch the perimeter of the jail without being caught, he freed all his captured teammates. As he did so, he would scream, "Al-ee, Al-ee, Oxen-free!" (The cry may have been a perversion of the German, *alles, alles, aus und früh!*—all, all, out and free!). When Team 1 had rounded up all their opponents, Team 2 became "It."

[23]. *Home*, by Edgar Guest

It takes a heap o' livin' in a house to make it home,
A heap o' sun an' shadder, an' ye sometimes have t' roam
Afore ye really 'preciate the things ye lef' behind,
An' hunger fer 'em somehow, with 'em allus on yer mind.
It don't make any differunce how rich ye get t' be,
How much yer chairs an' tables cost, how great yer luxury;
It ain't home t' ye though it be the palace of a king,
Until somehow yer soul is sort o' wrapped 'round everything.

Home ain't a place that gold can buy or get up in a minute,
Afore it's home there's got t' be a heap of livin' in it;
Within the walls there's got to be some babies born, and then
Right there ye've got t' bring 'em up t' women good, and men;

And gradjerly, as time goes on, ye find ye wouldn't part
With anything they ever used—they've grown into yer heart:
The old high chairs, the playthings, too, the little shoes they wore
Ye hoard; an' if ye could ye'd keep the thumb-marks on the door.

Ye've got t' weep t' make it home, ye've got t' sit an' sigh
An' watch beside a loved one's bed, an' know that Death is nigh;
An' in the stillness o' the night t' see Death's angel come,
An' close the eyes o' her that smiled an' leave her sweet voice
dumb.
Fer these are scenes that grip the heart, an' when yer tears are
dried,
Ye find the home is dearer than it was, an' sanctified;
An' tuggin' at ye always are the pleasant memories
O' her that was an' is no more–ye can't escape from these.

Ye've got t' sing an' dance fer years, ye've got t' romp an' play,
An' learn t' love the things ye have by usin' 'em each day;
Even the roses 'round the porch must blossom year by year
Afore they 'come a part o' ye, suggesting someone dear
Who used t' love 'em long ago, an' trained 'em jes' t'run
The way they do, so's they would get the early mornin' sun.
Ye've got t' love each brick an' stone from cellar up t' dome:
It takes a heap o' livin' in a house to make it home.

[24] Small wonder that Della saw apparitions on occasion! Here is the
text of the poem for which she was noted but couldn't remember
at age 60 (unlike Joey whose memory at 62 was faultless):

The Wind (Author unknown)

Have you ever heard the wind go...
"WOOOOOOO?"
It's a pitiful sound I hear.
It seems to chill you through and through
With a strange and speechless fear.
It's the voice of night that broods outside
When folks are still asleep,

And many and many a time I cried
To the darkness brooding far and wide
Over the land and the deep.
"Oh who do you want, oh lonely wind,
That you wail the whole night through?"

And the wind would say in its meaningful
way...
"YOUOOOO."

My momma told me years ago, when I was a
little tad,
That when the wind went wailing so,
Somebody had been bad.
And then when I was tucked in bed,
Where I had just been sent,
With the blankets pulled around my head,
I'd think of what my mother said.

"And who's been bad today?"
I'd ask of the wind that harshly blew
And the wind would say in its ghostly way...
"YOUOOOO!"

One, Two, Three! by Henry Cuyler Bunner

It was an old, old, old, old lady,
And a boy that was half past three;
And the way that they played together
Was beautiful to see.

She couldn't go running and jumping,
And the boy, no more could he;
For he was a thin little fellow,
With a thin little twisted knee.

They sat in the yellow twilight,
Out under the maple tree;
And the game that they played I'll tell you,
Just as it was told to me.

It was Hide and Go Seek they were playing,
Though you'd never have known it to be—
With an old, old, old, old lady
And a boy with a twisted knee.

The boy would bend his face down

On his one little sound right knee,
And he'd guess where she was hiding,
In guesses One, Two, Three!

"You are in the china closet!"
He would cry, and laugh with glee—
It wasn't the china closet;
But he still had Two and Three.

"You're up in Papa's big bedroom,
In the chest with the queer old key!"
And she said: "You're *warmer* and *warmer*;
But you're not quite right," said she.

"It can't be the little cupboard
Where Mamma's things used to be–
So it must be the clothespress, Gran'ma!"
And he found her with his Three.

Then she covered her face with her fingers,
That were wrinkled and white and wee,
And she guessed where the boy was hiding,
With a One and a Two and a Three.

And they had never stirred from their places,
Right under the maple tree–
This old, old, old, old lady,
And the boy with the lame little knee–
This dear, dear, dear, old lady,
And the boy who was half past three.

Little Boy Blue, by Eugene Field

The little toy dog is covered with dust,
But sturdy and stanch he stands;
And the little toy soldier is red with rust,
And his musket moulds in his hands.
Time was when the little toy dog was new,
And the soldier was passing fair,
And that was the time when our Little Boy
Blue
Kissed them and put them there.

"Now, don't you go till I come," he said,
"And don't you make any noise!"
So toddling off to his trundle-bed
He dreamt of the pretty toys.
And as he was dreaming, an angel song
Awakened our Little Boy Blue,—
Oh, the years are many, the years are long,
But the little toy friends are true!

Ay, faithful to Little Boy Blue they stand,
Each in the same old place,
Awaiting the touch of a little hand,
The smile of a little face.
And they wonder, as waiting these long years
through,
In the dust of that little chair,
What has become of our Little Boy Blue
Since he kissed them and put them there.

26   Solitude," by Ella Wheeler Wilcox

Laugh, and the world laughs with you;
Weep, and you weep alone.
For the sad old earth must borrow its mirth,
And has trouble enough of its own.
Sing, and the hills will answer;
Sigh, it is lost on the air.
The echoes bound to a joyful sound,
But shrink from voicing care.

Rejoice, and men will seek you;
Grieve, and they turn and go.
They want full measure of all your pleasure,
But they do not need your woe.
Be glad, and your friends are many
Be sad, and you lose them all.
There are none to decline your nectared
wine,
But alone you must drink life's gall.

Feast, and your halls are crowded;
Fast, and the world goes by.
Succeed and give, and it helps you live,
But no man can help you die.
There is room in the halls of pleasure
For a long and lordly train,
But one by one we must all file on
Through the narrow aisles of pain.

Part 1, Chapter 6
Birdie and Her Brothers:
Melancholic Uncle Charlie and Uncle Vincent

Aye, in the very temple of Delight

Veiled Melancholy has her sov'reign shrine

Though seen of none save him whose strenuous tongue

Can burst Joy's grape against his palate fine,

His soul shall taste the sadness of her might,

And be among her cloudy trophies hung.

—John Keats, *Ode to Melancholy*

Nonetheless, there were respites from the daily routine. Birdie's handsome younger brother, Charles, whom everyone referred to as Melancholic Uncle Charlie, came from Kingston for a visit at least two or three times when my mother was a child. The children eagerly anticipated his arrival and openly grieved when he had to return home.

Did I ever tell you the story of Melancholic Uncle Charlie? The picture that we have of him seems to commemorate his high school graduation if the rolled booklet in his left hand has any significance. He looks about eighteen, and though his face is smaller than Daisy's, he most resembles her. He has fine features, large dark eyes and a gentle sympathetic expression. As with Eliza's portrait, the family had A. Duperly & Sons take the photograph of Charlie.

Melancholic Uncle Charlie ca.1905

The children simply adored him. Loaded down with gifts for each one of them, he was in such high spirits when he sailed in from Jamaica that every day seemed like an outrageous garden party.

During the couple of weeks that he stayed, Charlie engaged the older children in a whirlwind of activity, a season of joy. He took them on every ride in the carnival set up in an empty field a few blocks away in New Hyde Park. He took them to the ice cream parlor on Jericho Turnpike and bought them as much store-made candy as they could eat. He took them swimming at Lake Success and amused them by swishing his head under water making noises like a walrus. He took the four oldest on the Long Island Railroad to New York for a Yankee game.

When Uncle Charlie visited, even Birdie was gay. Not only did he give her a break from all but the littlest child, he got her laughing. He made her dance the latest two-step in the parlor, and when, flustered, she protested that she had to get dinner on the table, he threw her apron high out of reach onto the dining room chandelier and marched up to the German delicatessen on Jericho Turnpike. He bought enough cold cuts, potato salad, cole slaw, black bread and *charlotte russe* for two families. Despite her rebuke that he was "spending money as if it grew on trees," she was diverted by his visits and touched by his thoughtfulness.

And then Charlie returned to Kingston. Ordinary life on Sycamore Avenue resumed. The older kids wrote him elaborately decorated thank you notes, but they didn't hear from him for a year at a time. The children asked sadly, "Why doesn't Uncle Charlie write? Doesn't he know how much we miss him?" Birdie shook her head slowly: "You know Charlie. He's melancholic."[27]

Brother Vincent

O mind your feet, O mind your feet,
Keep dancing like a wave,
And under every dancer
A dead man in his grave...
A drunkard is a dead man,
And all dead men are drunk.
—William Butler Yeats, *A Drunken Man's Praise of Sobriety*

Just as much as the kids looked forward to seeing Melancholic Charlie, so much did they dread the visits of Uncle Vincent, the youngest of my grandmother's family and the one who most took after his father, Christopher Lopez, Sr., in temperament.

Vincent and Birdie shared a special bond; as a baby, she had half raised him. As a teenager, he lived with her in Providence, Rhode Island until she returned to New York to care for their sister's children in 1913. Soon thereafter, Vincent followed her to New York. He was 20 when Louise died, and he went off on his own developing an immoderate fondness, as he put it with typical braggadocio, for "fast cars, hard liquor and light women."

Anna and Vincent Conway Lopez, 1915

Living in Yorktown and working as an express man, Vincent met an imposing German-American girl named Anna Oetgen. When she firmly rejected his blandishments, he proposed. On May 16, 1915, they were married at the Church of the Holy Spirit on E. 88th Street in Manhattan.

From the moment that Pepìn first caught a glimpse of her, he called her *Anna Culo Grande.* Their wedding photograph shows that however unkind, Pepìn didn't exaggerate. She was at least as tall as Vincent was and broader in the beam. For such a large body, her head seems small.

114

With thin lips and big expressionless eyes, Anna looks resolute and somewhat cold. He is probably only 5'5" or 5'6", and like many little men, he has puffed out his chest and stands up very stiffly to offset his slight stature.

Vincent was the fairest of the Lopez, brown eyed and blonde, but even as a young man, there is something unpleasantly tense about his flaring nostrils and turned down mouth.

The match between Vincent and Anna must have been made on the outskirts of Hell. They quarreled from the get-go. Arrogance had met arrogance; but Vincent, who had all the markings of a classic bully and coward, could not intimidate his wife. *Anna Culo Grande* was not a submissive woman like Vincent's mother. For one thing, she was bigger and stronger than Eliza had been. Vincent found that he was living with a woman who could take him in a fight.

In due time, she gave birth to a boy and named him George for her father with Vincent for a middle name. Though they both doted on the child, their marriage was a disaster. Anna hated Vincent's drinking, and he hated her nagging. The truth of the matter was that when Vincent had had one too many, he "turned the corner" like his father and became vicious and violent.

Eventually, nothing could make Anna stay with a drunk. She packed up her belongings, dressed the boy and left. Although Vincent searched for years on end, he never found a trace *Anna Culo Grande* nor of his son.

Or so he said. Actually, Anna and George were living with her parents in New York City according to the 1920 Federal Census. The 1930 Census has them residing in Sunnyside, Queens, no more than 12 miles away from New Hyde Park where Vincent had rented a house.

Vincent now had an excuse to get plastered on every possible occasion when he wasn't working. He alternately slobbered and sobbed about his lost child, or he swaggered and got belligerent over his bucket of beer. Some years after Birdie and Pepìn bought 41, Vincent brought a fat former whore, Helen May to live with him in New Hyde Park. A blonde with droopy, red-rimmed eyes, she was the polar opposite of Anna. An alcoholic herself, she didn't mind Vincent's heavy drinking. Unlike Vincent, however, Helen May was kind and, torn by her inability to have children, she devoted herself to him, a huge Great Dane, the meanest bulldog that anyone ever saw, an assortment of puppies and anywhere from two to five cats. Their house smelled of human sweat, stale beer, unbathed dogs and dirty litter boxes. Though they lived together for more than thirty years, he never married her. "Once bitten," he used to say, "twice shy."

Birdie was to blame if the children actively hated Uncle Vincent. He visited once every two weeks, and since Pepìn turned a deaf ear to her complaints about the children, she told her brother which kids had lied or stolen a penny from her purse or talked back to her. With great ceremony, he would drag the offenders into the butler's pantry one at a time, take down their pants and spank their bottoms until they glowed. He enjoyed making them howl.

When my mother was eleven and almost a young lady, Vincent made the mistake of whipping her until she literally couldn't sit down. Worse even than the pain of the beating was the humiliation. She was still weeping at 7 p.m. when Pepìn walked home from the train station.

"*Suleiman bitch!*" he screamed at Birdie. "If that sadistic brother of yours ever touches one of my children again, I will put him through the wall."

With that, Pepìn took Birdie's cat o' nine tails, went down into the cellar and heaved it into the furnace. Thereafter Vincent visited less often, almost never when Pepìn was at home. The beatings stopped. The kids, careful not to exult openly, silently blessed their father's holy name.

Mean Uncle Vincent

Aunt Rosa Gets Married

> *Let me not to the marriage of true minds*
> *Admit impediments. Love is not love*
> *Which alters when it alteration finds,*
> *Or bends with the remover to remove:*
> *Oh, no! it is an ever-fixéd mark...*
> —William Shakespeare, *Sonnet 116*

Do you remember Aunt Rosa's lovely wedding picture? She was so pretty seated in front of her tall and serious 'Americano.' By marrying her on July 4, he declared his independence from his wealthy and overbearing father.

Rosa and Arthur
McClintock, 1925

Pepìn's youngest sister, Rosa came to Brooklyn to join Tia Fidela in 1922. Rosa was innocent, even child-like, and neither Pepìn nor Fidela thought she would ever marry.

But Nature, it would seem, abhors vacuums and celibacy in equal measure. Rosa took a job at the Nabisco Biscuit Company and met a young veteran of World War I, Arthur McClintock who worked in the stockroom.

If ever opposites attracted, this was a classic case; though they were both tall—Aunt Rosa stood 5' 11", Arthur was easily 6' 2"—she was as dark as he was fair. She was a devout Catholic; he, a strict Methodist. She was preternaturally shy, partially because she spoke English with a thick accent, partially because she was self-conscious about having "a slow eye." He, on the contrary, was voluble and easily excited. If he spoke for her and acted strangely at times, she didn't mind, so taken was she with this carrot-topped dynamo who had deigned to notice her.

He came from a fine Scots family who could trace their lineage back to eighteenth century upstate New York landowners. According to the McClintocks, Rosa was a nobody, one step up from a wet-back, a penniless factory girl. The Balzac name and social standing in Puerto Rico meant nothing to them. In particular, Arthur's father, William McClintock, a well-known architect, didn't fancy his son courting a semi-literate Spanish girl who spoke English haltingly when she spoke at all. To discourage her, he told Rosa that Arthur was mentally unstable and had spent much of the past seven years in and out of veterans' hospitals. When that didn't faze her—she didn't believe him—he assumed that Rosa was a fortune hunter and cut Arthur off without a cent. The young couple was not to be deterred. In fact, his father's opposition only cemented Arthur's resolve to marry Rosa.

As her only nearby male relative, Rosa thought it important to ask for Pepìn's blessing. The couple, all a-glow, visited Floral Park. At the end of the day, if Pepìn found Arthur somewhat eccentric—he talked wildly about becoming an artist, but he liked his job at Nabisco because it didn't take much concentration—Pepìn also recognized the young man's devotion to his sister.

Fidela reacted to Rosa's love affair with characteristic geniality: "My time is over," she told them both happily, translating a Spanish proverb. "Your time has come." Significantly, Rosa and Arthur were married on July 4, l925 Independence Day.

Amor vincet omni. Love conquers all, it seemed.

Some two years later the couple had a little boy, William *Segundo*, named for his Scots grandfather. Unfortunately at the same time, Arthur's behavior became increasingly erratic. A few years after the birth of his son, he suffered a complete breakdown. Diagnosed as a paranoid schizophrenic, he was confined to a mental asylum until his death in 1941.

Devastated by the incurable illness of her beloved Arthur, Rosa again moved in with her sister, Fidela, this time with a carrot-topped little boy.

Cousin Bill was brilliantly red-haired when he made his Confirmation at

age 12. His hair was still red when he applied to college. A talented artist, who probably took after his paternal grandfather in this regard, Cousin Bill won an art scholarship to McGill University, Montreal. His mother and aunt, Tia Fidela, were thrilled he would study at a Catholic college that would reinforce the religious ardor they had instilled in him.

William Segundo Mc Clintock
(Cousin Bill of the Red-Hair)

The rest of the family was amazed and amused, however, when William *Segundo* came home for the Christmas vacation that year. With pitch-black hair, Cousin Bill looked very Hispanic indeed. From then on, he refused to allow either his mother or his aunt to wash his hair with the "special" shampoo that for the last seventeen years they believed might make him more acceptable to his wealthy, red-haired grandfather.

Let Us Love and Let Us Live

With light heart may she rise,

Gay fancy, cheerful eyes,

Joy lift her spirit, joy attune her voice;

To her may all things live, from pole to pole,

Their life the eddying of her living soul!

- Samuel Taylor Coleridge, *Dejection: an Ode*

Sometimes Birdie did something silly, like hide from Pepìn. Having gone to bed, Della and Nena had not yet fallen asleep in the yellow bedroom near the top of the stairs when Birdie came in on tiptoe, her finger over her lips, gesturing to them not to make a sound. "Daddy and I are playing a game," she whispered as she opened their closet door and snuck inside silently. Sure enough, a few minutes later, suppressing their giggles, they heard Dad coming up the stairs, crooning softly, "Birdie. Birdie. Where are you? I'm looking for you."

So it was that in 1924, Birdie found herself pregnant again. Without Pepìn's knowledge, she borrowed the money for an illegal abortion from Brother Vincent but fainted at the bus stop in front of St. Hedwig's Church. She revived to find a Polish nun holding her. The nun was so concerned that she walked Birdie home.

Baby Frederick was born September 6 at 11:40 p.m. in the front bedroom at 41. The doctor who attended her warned Pepìn that another pregnancy would kill her. The doctor suggested that she take a year or two to regain her strength and then have a hysterectomy.

With Birdie's operation put off and a new baby in the house, life at 41 went on happily. The next summer, Pepìn took the whole family on an outing to the Hamptons. The children loved the train ride on the Long Island Railroad. They adored Hampton Bays where the water was shallow and warm enough to go swimming. Pepìn particularly delighted walking to a sandy area known as Good Ground, named for the tract in the Biblical parable of the mustard seed. Someday, they would buy land in the Hamptons and build a summerhouse. When he retired, Birdie and he would live there year round.

That was his long-range plan. He had one project for the immediate future. In the fall of 1925, he called in a carpenter and had the open porch enclosed, in effect adding an extra, though unheated, room to the house. With windows on three sides, the sun porch became his smoking den, an auxiliary nursery for the baby, a playroom for the older children.

When a sudden rain shower threatened, Birdie would bring the colander full of beans or peas that she was preparing for dinner to their new room and snap or shuck them. Eagerly she watched the storm gather. As the Long Island sky turned yellow and then black, the birds would stop chirping. The wind would come howling through her beloved maples, and huge raindrops, the size of silver dollars would stain the dry ground. "It's pouring the rain down!" she would exclaim with a Jamaican lilt. She adored summer storms.

Joey Marinero

I must go down to the seas again to the vagrant gypsy life,
To the gull's way and the whale's way where the wind's like a whetted
knife;
And all I ask is a merry yarn from a laughing fellow-rover,
And quiet sleep and a sweet dream when the long trick's over.
—John Masefield, *Sea-Fever*

Within a year after Joey graduated from John Lewis Childs, he began working at the Lake Success Golf Club. Tall, blonde and anxious to please, Joey made good money during the day accommodating wealthy putters. At first, Birdie heartily approved of his job. He put in long hours on the links and from the outset had given her at least two dollars a week from his tips. But of late, she had reason to worry about the hours and the company Joey was keeping.

At night, he began running around with a wild bunch of caddies that he had met at the Golf Club. Recently translated from East New York and Corona, these boys were from the rough back streets of Mineola. A number of them were one step away from being criminals. They boasted about having broken into a clothing store in Flatbush some months before and were planning to steal a fancy car, strip it and sell the parts for real money.

The 18-year-old leader of the group was a good looking, wisecracking joker named Donny Hilker. With mischievous blue eyes and tousled wavy brown hair, Donny prided himself on having a way, his way, with the ladies. He was always talking about his latest conquest, and he spared his fascinated crew few details. Girls loved Donny. Joey could see that the very first night Hilker invited him to a party. Hilker seemed dangerous, and that was partly why he was so attractive. He genuinely liked women and acted in turn so attentive, gallant and saucy that few females could resist him.

Men liked Donny, too. He was smart and iconoclastic, forthright, yet appealingly dishonest. His language was salty: he talked about "boosting" radios, "knocking over joints," "parlaying hooch" that had "fallen off the back of a truck." At first, Joey didn't believe Donny's stories about "easy pickings." To Joey Balzac, Hilker was a charismatic blowhard, a womanizer and a prankster, but he hardly qualified as a robber.

Miffed by Joey's scoffing, Hilker determined to take him along on a job—something simple to break him in—like stealing tires. One Friday evening, more out of curiosity than anything else, Joey foolishly consented to go with Hilker to Jamaica in Donny's old jalopy. They parked on a side street, and Donny went around to the back of the car and hauled an athletic bag out of the rumble seat. They began walking down Jamaica Avenue. Near 168th Street just after dark, Donny spotted a late model Ford with practically new tires. "Go hang out on the corner," he told Joey. "If you see a cop coming, whistle 'My Wild Irish Rose.'" Donny then took a tire iron, jack and flashlight from the bag and proceeded to let the air out of the tire.

Joey quickly reached the corner and leaned over as if to tie his shoe. Within two minutes Donny had jacked up the car and had just finished loosening a couple of the lugs when Joey began whistling furiously.

Simultaneously, Joey was also praying, "Please, Lord, please help me. Please, Aunt Daisy and all the saints, please help me. I promise that if I get out of this scrape, I'll never do anything bad again. So help me God."

At the same time, Hilker pretended to be having trouble with the last lug as a cop car made the turn onto Jamaica Avenue and came cruising down the block. The car slowed as it approached him, but before it could come to a full stop, Donny ran out into the road and flagged the cops down.

"Gee, fellas. I got a flat, and I can't unscrew one of the lugs. Could you give me a hand and hold the flashlight for me?" One of the policemen ambled out of the car and took the proffered light. From that point on, Donny never stopped talking.

Transfixed on the corner, Joey was dying a thousand deaths—he knew enough not to run and draw attention to himself, and he couldn't just saunter away and leave his friend literally holding the bag. He strained without success to hear what Donny—crouched over and spinning the tire iron—was saying. Whatever it was, the cop looked amused.

That damned Hilker! Joey stewed. He had a hundred funny stories and more gall than a den of pit vipers! Jesus! Now Donny was prattling on like they were old buddies, the policeman laughing as he held the light steady. Donny finally finished removing the tire. "Thanks a lot, officer." Donny flashed a big smile, and the cop tipped his hat. "Glad to oblige," he said strolling back to the patrol car. The cop never asked Donny for his registration or driver's license.

Ashen-faced, Joey immediately rejoined his friend. As Hilker rolled the stolen tire back to his parked car, he was nonchalant. "You did good, Joey. Next weekend, we'll hoist a Studebaker, and you can be the lookout." Joey was nauseous. If he continued seeing Hilker, he feared they both would end up in jail.

The episode so frightened Joey that two days later he went to a recruiting office and obtained papers for admission to the Navy. Joey was under age–sixteen–and had to have parental consent. That night, he paced back and forth on the cement walk in front of 41 waiting for his father to come home. Finally he spied Pepìn coming down Sycamore Avenue from Charles Street. He hardly let Dad step into the sun porch and light his pipe before he was begging his father to fill out the form. "Please, Dad. If I stay around here, I'm going to get into real trouble. Please."

Reluctantly, Pepìn signed. Birdie made no objection. The first of the Balzac children left home in 1926.

And then there were five.

---

[27] Uncle Charlie's "melancholia" seems to have been a bi-polar disorder caused by a chemical imbalance, and Uncle Vincent's alcoholism may have begun as a way of coping with depression. A severe manic-depressive syndrome afflicted Freddie as an adult, and initially, Bill may also have been affected by it. Two of Louise Lopez Balzac's great grandchildren have the disorder as well as one of Birdie's grandchildren and one of her great-grandchildren. In all cases, those so disposed have been male.

Part 1, Chapter 7
The Death of Birdie

A slumber did my spirit seal;
I had no human fears:
She seemed a thing that could not feel
The touch of earthly years.

No motion has she now, no force;
She neither hears nor sees;
Rolled round in earth's diurnal course,
With rocks, and stones, and trees.
—William Wordsworth, A Slumber Did My
Spirit Seal

Finally, Birdie couldn't postpone the operation any longer. In early February 1927, she kissed the children good-bye and left for Flower Hospital in New York City.

They never saw her again. On emergency leave from the Navy, Joey donated blood to no avail. Early on the morning of February 11, Birdie died on the operating table. The doctors said the operation was a success, but heart failure brought on by exhaustion killed her.

Pepìn was not quite forty-five years old, once again a widower, left this time with five kids: Della, 14; my mother, 12; Bill, 11, the day after his mother's death; Pete, nearly 9; the baby, Freddy, less than 2½.

Those Crazy Aunts:
Tia Fidela and Tia Rosa

Insanity runs in my family. It practically gallops.
—Joseph Kesselring, *Arsenic and Old Lace*

Did I ever tell you what happened at Birdie's funeral?

They lifted Freddy up to kiss his mother in the coffin that had been placed in front of the three parlor windows. That brief glance constituted his only recollection of her. The neighbors came bearing dishes of food, and many of them made the trek out to the Evergreens Cemetery, Brooklyn for the burial. Now all three sisters, Daisy, Louise and Ianthe, and the baby, Edmundo, lay side by side in the grave donated by the City of New York.

Maudie Porth, Birdie's one close friend from the next block, assumed that Joey and Della knew about Louise. "Poor motherless children," she said with genuine sympathy, "and you two have lost a mother for a second time."

They were shocked. Why hadn't Dad told them? What had their mother Louise been like? Since in his sorrow, Dad wouldn't or couldn't talk about his wives, Della cornered the Balzac aunts. Under the veil of their piety—"Ah, Louise. R. I. P. Rest in peace," Aunt Rosa murmured—they were terrible and often misinformed gossips. They had made Pepìn furious with their fanciful explanation of why Pete was born with a double first joint on his thumb. Knowing nothing about polydactylism, they ascribed the abnormality to the fact that while she was pregnant with him, Birdie had drowned a litter of puppies. *Claro que sí*, of course, Baby Pedrito was born with a paw.

Out of earshot of her father, Della coaxed the aunts for information. It didn't take much to get them started. The aunts told Della that her mother's body turned black when she died. Such a young woman! Whatever could Louise have died from?[28]

Della was sixty, in a wheelchair, the victim of multiple sclerosis, when she told me this story.

"Those crazy aunts," she said. "What kind of a thing was that to be telling a little kid? That her mother turned black?"

As Della thought about it, big tears began to roll down her wasted cheeks. "Those crazy aunts!" Then she started to giggle just recalling them. With that she took her good hand and slapped it on her knee. "Ah, hell! Ain't life grand?"

The aunts by any standards were, if not crazy, poised on a banana peel between eccentricity and a superstitious otherworldliness.

Somehow for them, a time warp had set in. When Rosa was in her mid-thirties and Tia Fidela only in her forties, they both looked as if they were sixty. Two huge women, each at least 5'11", they wore their wavy black hair pulled back in tight buns and covered their olive complexions with the yellow-tinged face powder that Hispanic women so often use. It had a sweet and distinctive odor. They used no lipstick or any other makeup.

Their once merely sensual features broadened as they grew older, and their bodies thickened. Lacing themselves into heavy corsets under dark dresses, wool or gabardine in the winter and floral crepe in the summer, they never adopted bras. Clasped with a brooch, the bodices of their dresses cascaded over large sagging breasts. Lisle or black stockings and heavy, thick heeled tie-up shoes completed their almost invariable costume.

They did everything together: attending daily Mass before work, visiting shrines here and abroad to pray now not just for the Edmundos, father and son, and for their sister-in-law, Birdie, but for Arthur as well.

Tias Fidela and Rosa, 1939

"With a tongue, you can go to Rome," they were fond of saying, sending postcards to Pepìn and the family from St. Joseph's Shrine in Montreal, Mass cards from Lourdes and Loreto and scapulars from the grotto of the Virgin of Guadalupe in Mexico City. They were a peripatetic team in search of the earliest or latest miracle or manifestation, Mother Goose and Cuckoo the Bird Woman *á l'española*, leftovers from the 19th century.

All this with a flaming-haired boy in tow.

Despite their odd appearance, credulous piety and ridiculous white lies, they were very dear and generous beyond measure. Invited for Christmas dinner, they arrived hours late—the bus had broken down, the subway was flooded, the L.I.R.R. was operating on a diminished holiday schedule—but who could be annoyed with them? Like the Magi, they came bearing precious gifts: an onyx ring for Pepìn, leather jackets for the boys, delicate sixteen jewel Bulova watches for Della and Nena.

They never missed a family occasion, often coming to Sycamore Avenue when everyone was asleep, leaving presents in the unlocked back porch: from Nabisco, large fondant-covered birthday pound cakes; from Fidela's shop, beautifully crocheted white gloves for the girls' Sunday wear and fur-lined leather gloves for Pepìn and the boys. At least three or four times a year when one of the boys went to the icebox for milk early in the morning, he would find a stack of packages placed just inside the back door. He'd call upstairs, "Dad, your sisters were here." They were like the good elves of the children's story that work all night long and disappear before dawn.

Where they got the money for all these extravagances no one ever knew. They were as silent and evasive about their personal affairs as they were vocal about others' intimate relations. They loved a good gossip—their imagination verged on the mythopoetic—but there wasn't an ounce of malice in them. When they talked about long dead Balzac cousins, uncles and aunts in Puerto Rico, they gave every name the pious suffix, R.I.P. If they fib on occasion about defunct subways, busses and trains, their sins were only venial.

In truth, they liked to sleep late, then bathe in turn using the heavily perfumed *Jabon Maja*, soap imported from Spain, and *Pretty Feet and Hands*, a rough skin remover. Once their toilette was complete, Tia would cook a large breakfast of poached eggs over brown Spanish rice and fried green bananas, toast, juice and boiled coffee. Having washed the dishes, they put out milk for the cat, fed the canary and covered its cage. They then lit candles below the two portraits—one of Baby Edmundo and the other of Edmundo, Sr., jaunty in the uniform of a Field Artillery Officer. Finally, having said a short prayer for father and son, they were ready to sally forth. By that time back in Floral Park, dinner was ready.

Then the aunts' two-hour trip began: the elevated to Penn Station, the L.I.R.R. to Tulip Avenue or, alternately, the subway to Jamaica, then the bus to St. Hedwig's. Often on Easter or Labor Day as they walked from the train or the bus stop in front of the church, they would spot some lovely wild flowers growing in a field and pick them as a bouquet for the holiday table. They were on mañana time, but back at 41 Sycamore, the turkey, pulled from the oven, was getting cold on the counter top.

As the aunts aged, their tardiness increased. Finally, from the 1940s on, to avoid ruined holiday dinners, my father drove to Brooklyn to pick the aunts up in the morning, and Pete took them back to Pennsylvania Avenue at night.

𝔓𝔥𝔬𝔱𝔬𝔰 𝔣𝔯𝔬𝔪 𝔍𝔞𝔪𝔞𝔦𝔠𝔞

This earth of majesty, this seat of Mars,
This other Eden, demi-paradise,
This fortress built by Nature for herself
Against infection and the hand of war,
This happy breed of men, this little world,
This precious stone set in the silver sea...
This blessed plot, this earth, this realm, this
England.
—William Shakespeare, *King Richard II. II, i, 40*

After Mama died, we lost touch with our Jamaica
relatives. All we have to remember them by are five
photographs.

Eliza Mary Purcell Lopez, ca.1898

Christopher Augustus Lopez III studied dentistry in England where he met Eliza Mary Purcell, his future wife. Watts & Co. Photographers, 15 Royal Promenade, Clifton, England is responsible for this engagement portrait of our beautiful aunt in a formal ball gown. When race relations in Jamaica deteriorated in the early 1930s, Eliza Mary may have influenced Christopher and Charles to relocate to England.

133

Signa Elaine, Winnifred and Mingaurette Allison, 1908

Posing for A. Duperly and Sons are the Lopez girls dressed identically in white lace, crocheted stockings and high boots. I guess their ages to be 6, 4, and 5. On the back of the photo is the inscription: 'To dear Auntie Daisy, With love from her three little nieces.'

Winnifred, Signa Elaine, Charlie's Daughter, and Allison Lopez

ca. 1914

This next studio photo shows the girls some five summers later. Posing with them in front of a beach backdrop is their dark haired cousin, Charlie's daughter.

Christopher A. Lopez III and his 1914 Model T Tourer

In the back seat from left to right: Unknown woman, unknown man, (Adeline Campbell Lopez and Christopher Augustus Lopez II?) and Eliza Mary Lopez, (Mrs. C. A. Lopez III). In the front seat: Christopher III behind the wheel, Winnifred next to him, Melancholic Uncle Charlie in the passenger seat and Charlie's daughter, Allison and Signa seated on the back fender and running board.

J.B. Valdés, a fashionable society photographer, came to the Lopez home to snap this picture of the family.

Taken about ten years after the photograph with their new car, the Lopez have had a fourth daughter, Dorothy who has dark eyes like her father. Our three older cousins have become pretty young ladies even as their mother's good looks have faded. Clean-shaven and serious, Christopher's turned down mouth and added girth mark him as 'a man of substance.' Of all the Lopez, he looked most like his father.

Dr. Christopher Lopez III and Family, ca. 1922

41 𝔖𝔶𝔠𝔞𝔪𝔬𝔯𝔢 𝔴𝔦𝔱𝔥𝔬𝔲𝔱 𝔅𝔦𝔯𝔡𝔦𝔢

I meant to find Her when I came—
Death had the same design—
But the Success—was His—it seems
And the Surrender—Mine
I meant to tell Her how I longed
For just this single time—
But Death had told Her so the first—
And she had past, with him—
—Emily Dickinson

The directors of the Sidney Ross Pharmaceutical Company were more than generous to the bereaved Pepìn after Birdie died on February 11, 1927. To help put his affairs in order, his bosses gave him the rest of the month off with pay. When Louise had died, her life insurance had provided a little extra money. This time, however, there wasn't even a small policy to cover the expenses of the funeral. Years earlier, a John Hancock representative had urged Pepìn to make some provision for his second wife, but Birdie had sent the agent away. "I don't want insurance," she had told Pepìn with a laugh. "You're not going to take a vacation at Wildwood-by-the-Sea when I die." Her words were prophetic: Pepìn didn't go to Wildwood or anywhere else. What little savings he had went to the funeral director.

Inevitably, March 1 came, and a drawn and worried Pepìn dutifully went back to work. From the Floral Park railroad station to the Tubes to Astor Place in Newark, he reviewed his instructions to his daughters repeatedly. But would the boys cooperate, and could the girls manage?

Joey, Apprentice Seaman, was somewhere off the Virginia coast on naval maneuvers. Della had graduated the year before from John Lewis Childs and quit school. Nena was still in 7th grade. His daughters were too young to assume Birdie's exhausting responsibilities, but there was no one else. Even more disconcerting to Pepìn than the waves of grief that would spontaneously sweep over him, was the gnawing sense that the family had begun to unravel.

Pepìn comforted himself with the knowledge that Maudie Porth, Birdie's dearest friend, lived just around the corner on Lewis Avenue. In an emergency, his children could always count on her for help. She had already been too kind—overseeing the food and drink for the funeral and greeting people when he was too overwhelmed to do more than say hello and shake hands. Nevertheless, he didn't want to impose on Maudie or on her cantankerous but kind husband, John, any more than necessary.

As the oldest girl, Della ostensibly was to take charge of the house, pay the bills, do the shopping and cook dinner. Nena was to help with the food preparation and to care for little Freddy. On weekdays before school, she dressed and fed him while Della made breakfast. While Nena was at school, Della bathed the baby, fed him lunch and put him down for a nap. By the time he awoke, Nena would be home to watch him in the afternoon. Then Della was to shop and cook; Nena was to do her homework and help Della with preparations for dinner.

On weekends, the two girls shared the household chores. Pete and Bill were to chop and stack kindling for the kitchen stove and wash and dry the supper dishes. In actual fact, the jobs of taking care of the baby as well as running the house devolved more and more on Nena, a situation she resented and that eventually caused a rift between the sisters.

Della and the Electric Company

> The best laid schemes o' mice an' men
> Gang aft a-gley,
> An' lea'e us nought but grief and pain
> For promised joy.
> —Robert Burns, *To a Mouse*

Della and Nena were as different as starlings and cocker spaniels when Birdie died. At 14, Della was fully developed, flighty and popular, such fun that a whole bunch of boys hung out at 41, on the sun porch or on the stoop.

Knowing now that Birdie was not her mother, Della grieved very little. She barely felt related to her younger sister and brothers. As far as Della was concerned, her beloved brother, Joey, was her only sibling.

At 12, Nena was as fair as Della was dark, and her body had just started to bud. She was desolate after her mother's death. She couldn't see how they would keep up with all the things that Birdie used to do. Always a serious and imaginative child, she was prone to vocalizing her worries. From early on, the family had given her the nickname, Nena the Complainer.

Within a few weeks after Birdie's funeral, Della began neglecting her duties and foisting them on her half-sister. Like any kid of fourteen, Della preferred being with her friends to cleaning the house and doing the shopping. With no adult to keep her on track and in check, Della was free to wield absolute power, and it corrupted her absolutely. Case in point: her feud with the Electric Company.

Pepìn had instructed Della to pay both the milkman and the newspaper boy weekly. The Electric Company had an office on Jericho Turnpike where she shopped. Once a month, he told her, she was to stop by and take care of the electric bill.

Not used to budgeting, Della constantly overspent. She managed to deal with weekly accounts, but by the time the electric bill came due, she had run out of money and had to defer paying it until the following month. Once in arrears, she stayed in arrears. Unbeknownst to Pepìn, she accrued substantial late charges. By early May, the Electric Company flagged the Balzac account for tardiness. Knowing Dad would be furious with her, she simply never told him that the bills were now marked "Delinquent." What he didn't know couldn't hurt him.

"What right have they to overcharge honest working people in these hard times? Do you know the company mails out letters with 'Final Notice' stamped in red on the envelope so that even the mailman can see it? Isn't that a violation of some American Constitutional right to privacy? She shook her finger under her friends' noses. The Electric Company ought to be glad that her Dad wasn't a lawyer because he'd sue it for price fixing. "Is this any way for a public utility to act?" She'd be damned if she would pay one extra dime!

With her Spanish up, Della was formidable to behold–her eyes flashed, her nostrils turned white. Her whole sweet young body shook with rage. "Della," her awed friends reminded her, "Don't be mad at us!" They knew enough to beware Della scorned.

To ingratiate himself, one of her beaus, an 18 year-old Jamaica Vocational student, generously volunteered to break into the locked electric meter box. He had been studying circuitry. "By the time I'm finished, Della, every month you just reset the clock that records the kilowatts used. With the money you'll save," Mr. Fix-It calculated, "you'll be able to pay all the current and extra charges."

Della clapped her dainty hands, absolutely gleeful. Dad would never have to know. With her full knowledge and undying gratitude, Della's swain took a hacksaw to the lock, opened the box and reversed the dial hands. Then, he put the severed lock back in its original position. From five feet away, no one would ever suspect anything was wrong. (Between them, Dad fumed later, they didn't have the brain of a *cucaracha. Que tonteria!* (Such stupidity!)

When after two months the Balzacs seemed to be consuming about one tenth the electric that they had formerly used, someone at the company smelled a rat and sent out a technician to check the meter at 41.

The company charged the chagrined Pepìn Balzac with theft of services and tampering, fined him exorbitantly and, as added punishment, turned off the electric at 41 Sycamore Avenue for six months. Dad was furious. For her part in this fiasco, Pepìn forbid Della to go out after dinner for the duration and barred Della's friends from visiting her at home. They would not darken the door of his darkened house until January at least, when the lights came on again.

It wasn't so bad in the summer to live without electric. At first, Della thought that candlelight was "romantic" (though she dared not even whisper such an idea when Dad was around), but as fall came on and the days became shorter and shorter, all of the Balzacs found it tough to read, cook and eat in semi-darkness.

To cause trouble and make Dad angry with Della all over again, Bill took to singing the refrain from W. C. Handy's "St. Louis Woman" whenever she lit the candles. "I hate to see," he would croon, "that evening sun go down." Finishing the blues, he would then launch into the opening stanza of Henley's "Invictus:"

> Black is the night that covers me
> Black as the Pit from pole to pole
> I thank whatever gods there be
> For my unconquerable soul.[29]

If Pepìn looked up at all from squinting at his newspaper in the dim glow, he merely scowled and sucked his teeth in disgust.

By December, darkness visible was making everyone wretchedly unhappy. Holiday time was barely festive. The week before Christmas, the boys cut down a little pine tree in the woods. Without lights, it looked forlorn. When Della suggested that maybe they could put tiny candles on its branches, Pepìn all but exploded. *"Suleiman bitch!"*

he cried. "First, a daughter of mine engages in petty theft and ruins my good name. Now she wants to commit arson and burn down my house! Because of you, this entire family is suffering from the ninth plague, 'the darkness which may be felt!'"

Christmas 1927 was bleak. There were presents under the tree, and the baby was happy enough playing on the floor with a new red truck. The girls did their best to serve a holiday meal, and the aunts came from Brooklyn loaded down with gifts, but somehow no one felt much like eating or talking either. Night came on so early. To Pepìn, the darkness seemed symbolic. On the first Christmas without Birdie, they had no electric. She was the sun. Had she only been here, he thought, the day would have been bright and joyous. And he looked balefully in Della's direction.

Everybody except little Freddie castigated Della, but nothing and no one could tame her wild exuberance. In July 1927, the summer after Birdie died, she had turned fifteen. With snappy black eyes, curly black hair and a shapely figure, she was both exotic and exciting. She had an infectious laugh, a quick wit and high spirits. Tired of the pall that hung over 41 Sycamore Avenue, she declared as she pirouetted around the kitchen that she wanted to embrace life, eat caviar and dance the tango with a rose between her teeth.

> *"Yeah? Try dancing the dishes back into the china closet,"* Nena responded.

Unfortunately, Della seemed older and more mature than she actually was. Getting all gussied up, she easily passed for eighteen. Poor unwitting Pepìn! Easier to stop a *hurricano* than keep Della under wraps for six months! She stayed grounded for all of two weeks, then waited until he went to bed to make her weekend escapes. Since her friends were barred from the house, she met them on the corner. More often than not, they ended up at local speakeasies where they could dance and have a couple of drinks. When she came in at midnight or later, she tiptoed up the stairs, vaulting over the squeaky fourth step from the top. The sleeping denizens of 41 Sycamore went on dreaming their dreams and never stirred.

The night after Christmas 1927, when Pepìn had fallen asleep, Della once again sneaked out to go drinking with Johnny Jones from up the block and his friend, Bill Redding, who owned a car. Some weeks before, Bill had introduced Della to his older brother, Jack, a twenty year old, six-foot-two, rugged electrical lineman. Della and Jack instantly hit it off and had begun to date, but Jack was working that night.

At an Elmont club, Johnny, Bill and Della began jazzing with three college boys who found her funny and flirtatious. At two o'clock when the place closed, they decided to go for a ride. No one was feeling any pain. Della piled into the back seat of Bill Redding's car with the three college boys she hardly knew. They assumed she was fast and began getting fresh with her. What began as mere fooling around and touching escalated into a full-blown attack. As the three tried to pin her down, Della bit and scratched, punched and kicked, fighting furiously. Bill, who was driving, kept turning around and telling the guys to leave her alone. Coming to a curve at high speed, he lost control of the car. All six ended up in the hospital. The Jones boy had a broken arm, Della, a concussion; the others sustained severe cuts and abrasions.

When the police officers learned Della's age, they detained her. They never charged the men—not with attempted rape, not with aggravated assault, not with reckless endangerment, not with contributing to the delinquency of a minor, not with drunk driving. The cops wanted to know just one thing: what was a fifteen year old doing out at three o'clock in the morning with five men? The State stepped in.

Aside from the purchase of his house, Pepìn had never needed legal counsel before. In desperation, he swallowed his shame and went to see an acquaintance, a retired lawyer. Once Children's Court was involved, the attorney explained, there was little anyone could do. It would stand in *loco_parentis* and, acting in what it considered to be Della's best interest, would probably remand her to a juvenile facility. He wisely counseled Pepìn to hire a housekeeper immediately, no matter the cost, or face the possibility of losing his other children. In desperation, Pepìn turned once again to Maudie Porth, who immediately came to his aid. John Porth, however, didn't like his wife to work. He would only permit her to serve as housekeeper until Della's case was settled; then Pepìn would have to find someone else.

Pepìn would worry about a permanent arrangement later; for the moment, he couldn't thank Maudie enough. In early January, she accompanied him to the hearing in Mineola. Despite Maudie's testimony and Pepìn's earnest entreaties, the Court adjudged Della "willful and intractable" and sent her to The House of the Good Shepherd, a Catholic home for wayward girls in New York City, until she was eighteen. Pepìn suffered a tumult of contradictory emotions: he was both aggrieved for Della and grateful that his other children were safe.

As innocent as she was headstrong, Della was no longer at 41 Sycamore Avenue when electric power was restored in mid-January, 1928, and there was no fine that Dad could pay to bring her home and make things right.

And then there were four.

For the next two and a half years, Pepìn went once a month to see Della on visiting days at the bleak brownstone on 116th Street in Manhattan. Jim Redding sometimes went with Pepìn. The Reddings knew that Della was "a good kid" and felt she had been given "a bum rap."

Della and Jim (Jack) Redding, ca. 1932

As for Della, once she got used to the place, "It wasn't so bad," she reassured her worried father. She bonded with an Albanian runaway, Lillian Bartolino, who had also lost her mother. Treated with respect, the nuns were kind, and they were teaching the girls a trade. Under the nuns' tutelage, the two became excellent seamstresses. Della learned tailoring and made herself "a swell black wool coat" with a sateen paisley lining and buttons covered to match.

Forgetting all about dancing with a rose between her teeth, Della became more serious, less impetuous. She looked forward to Jim Redding's visits and kept up a steady and increasingly loving correspondence with him. When she was released in July 1930, he was waiting for her at the door.

[28] Della died in 1992 without learning that her mother had died from appendicitis. See endnote 13.

[29]
> *"Invictus" by William Ernest Henley*
> *Out of the night that covers me,*
> *Black as the Pit from pole to pole,*
> *I thank whatever gods there be*
> *For my unconquerable soul.*
>
> *In the fell clutch of circumstance*
> *I have not winced nor cried aloud.*
> *Under the bludgeonings of chance*
> *My head is bloody, but unbowed.*

Beyond this place of wrath and tears
Looms but the horror of the shade,
And yet the menace of the years
Finds, and shall find me, unafraid.

It matters not how straight the gate,
How charged with punishments the scroll,
I am the master of my fate;
I am the captain of my soul.

Part 1, Chapter 8
"Me Imperturbe"

Knowledge enormous makes a god of me.

Names, deeds, gray legends, dire events, rebellions,

Majesties, sovran voices, agonies,

Creations and destroyings, all at once

Pour into the wide hollows of my brain

And deify me, as if of some blithe wine

Or elixir peerless I had drunk,

And so become immortal.

—John Keats, *Hyperion*

In Floral Park, the burden of running the house fell on Nena's frail shoulders. In February 1927 when her mother died, she was 12, a seventh grader. During that next winter in early 1928 when Della was sent away, Maudie Porth took care of little Freddie at her house until 3 p.m. so that Nena could go to school. Once Nena got home, however, she assumed the full duties of chief cook, bottle washer, laundress and surrogate mother to her three younger brothers.

Whenever Nena had an extra moment, she delved into Pepìn's bookcase. At his suggestion, she began with the *Collected Works of Honoré de Balzac* initially reading *Père Goriot*, weeping at the trials of the old man as he beggars himself to help his selfish daughters. She consumed *Eugenie Grandet*, shuddering when with his dying breath the avaricious Grandet desecrates the Last Rites blasphemously grasping at the golden cross used to bless him. She sighed at *La Peau de Chagrin*, stirred by the grotesque fantasy on the vanity of human wishes. Poor Pauline, poor Raphael de Valentin! Balzac was magnificent! No wonder Dad was so proud of the family name!

One afternoon while Freddie was napping, Nena came upon a green cloth-covered copy of Whitman's *Leaves of Grass and Other Poems* in Dad's bookcase. She loved the silky feel of the small volume with its embossed ivy decoration and was thrilled by the lines from "Song of Myself."

> I am the poet of the woman the same as the man
> And I say it is as great to be a woman as to be a man,
> And I say there is nothing greater than the mother of men.
>
> 426-8 (1855)

Whitman's poem was so passionate and all-inclusive; Nena had never read anything like it. She committed whole sections to memory: the wondrous simplicity of "A child said 'What is the grass?'" and the transfiguring beauty of "I ascend from the moon, I ascend from the night."

With what was to become a life-long practice, she began applying the diction from her reading (later, from movies as well as from books) to daily life at 41 Sycamore Avenue. Brothers no more, she'd say to Bill or Pete, *Look here, 'camerados', we need some milk for supper. Which one of you is going to the A&P?* She couldn't go to the store herself because she had *quintillions* of things to do. If anyone made fun of her newly acquired vocabulary, she'd look down her nose haughtily, toss her recently bobbed hair and quote what she (and possibly the poet) thought was Spanish: *Me Imperturbe.* For two or three months, she ate, slept and spoke Whitman.

Her intoxication with Walt came to a screeching, if temporary, stop when Nena made the unfortunate mistake of taking *Leaves of Grass* to school. During a lunch period, Rena C. Hayden came upon the girl in the cafeteria immersed in reading "Crossing Brooklyn Ferry." Horrified, Mrs. Hayden confiscated "the filthy book" and packed it into a decontaminated manila envelope along with a stinging antiseptic note to Pepìn.

 "Whitman," R.C.H. asserted, "was not suitable reading matter for a child." Crushed, Nena went home sure that she was in for a scolding, but when her father opened the sealed letter, he laughed merrily.

"O Diós mio! I'm so glad it was only Whitman! What would Mrs. Hayden have said if she had found you with Balzac's *Droll Stories*? Foolie, foolie," he uttered with glee. "Just imagine that scene!"

He didn't believe in censorship, he told his grateful daughter, and although he had nothing but respect for Mrs. Hayden as a principal, he didn't think she came up to the bar as a literary critic. Then genuinely interested, Pepìn asked Nena if she had a favorite Whitman poem. When she replied, "Out of the Cradle Endlessly Rocking," he heartily approved. He thought it one of Walt's best, too.

As far as Pepìn was concerned, Nena could read anything in his library, but since discretion was the better part of valor, perhaps it would be better if in the future she kept his books at home. With her father's encouragement, Nena read as much as time allowed, first going through his bookcase, later using his card at the Floral Park Public Library. (Not until she was fourteen would she be able to check out adult selections in her own name).

Nena managed somehow to complete 8th grade, but in June 1928, the situation at 41 forced her to quit school. In order to care for little Freddie, she put aside all thought of attending high school.

Heart-broken, she bought the group photo of her graduating class, but she wasn't in it; nor did she attend the graduation ceremony. Maudie Porth was out of town, and she couldn't get anyone she trusted to stay with the baby. She treasured the photo and the State Education Department's certificate dated June 18-22, 1928 declaring she had "satisfactorily completed the requirements" for graduation.

To mark the occasion, Pepìn gave Nena her mother's gold ring with a small diamond in a gypsy setting. When she had completed grammar school, Birdie herself had received it from Eliza, her mother. Along with the Balzac and Lopez portraits, the graduation photograph, school certificate and ring became Nena Balzac's most valued keepsakes.[30]

𝔎𝔦𝔱𝔱𝔶 𝔅𝔯𝔞𝔡𝔩𝔢𝔶 𝔞𝔫𝔡 𝔱𝔥𝔢 𝔅𝔩𝔲𝔢 𝔅𝔬𝔶

She played it fast, she played it light and loose
Her several parts could keep a pure repose,
Or one hip quiver with a mobile nose
(She moved in circles, and those circles moved).
—Theodore Roethke, *I Knew a Woman*

Once summer came, Nena and the baby were often alone. In her isolation, she sometimes turned to Kitty Bradley, a wild, brash Irish-born neighbor living across the street who had a soft spot for all the kids on the block. Good hearted, but without much taste, Kitty tried to comfort the girl, inviting Nena and the baby in for tea, showing her how to use makeup, dyeing and bobbing Nena's hair to lift her spirits.

Brother Bradley, the Blue Boy

When Rena C. Hayden came looking for Pete, she first came to 41 Sycamore Avenue. Nena, 14, a strawberry blonde thanks to Kitty Bradley, answered the door. Mrs. Hayden took one look at her and queried: "Why, Mercedes Balzac, whatever have you done to your hair?" The girl shriveled

155

beneath Mrs. Hayden's stare. Nena let her hair go back to its natural color, a light reddish brown.

To lift her own spirits, Kitty drank and caroused, bringing men home in broad daylight while her husband was working. According to the rumor mill or, as Pepìn put it, *les emissions de la radio des putes* (the radio waves of the whores), any number of teenage boys, including Joey Balzac, were beholden to her. She was notorious in the neighborhood, a laughing scarlet lady with dyed titian hair and a faint Galway brogue. An independent, fast-talking hip-swinger, she just didn't give a fig for what anyone thought.

Nena loved her, understanding instinctively that Kitty couldn't get past her grief—the loss of her six-year old boy—born with a malformed aorta who had died the year before Birdie. Kitty always called him Brother Bradley, but everyone on the block knew him as the Blue Boy. Because the slightest exertion or excitement caused him to lose his breath and become cyanotic, Kitty became expert in giving him mouth-to-mouth resuscitation. She breathed for him; she would have died for him. The doctors told her that the child wouldn't live to see his fourth birthday, but Kitty turned herself inside out to amuse Brother and make him comfortable; she carried him in arms and indulged him in every whim. What did the doctors know? Every ounce the boy gained, every mouthful he ate, every breath that he took was Kitty's personal triumph.

Then two months past her boy's sixth birthday, Kitty swore that she had heard a strange moaning sound during the night. She didn't know until later that it was the cry of the banshee, the woman of the fairies, presaging death. In the morning, Kitty was cradling Brother Bradley on her lap telling him a story when he just stopped breathing. Nothing could bring him back.

He was a beautiful boy with such a sympathetic face. Looking at his photo, I always associated him with the child in Eugene Field's poem:

'And as he was dreaming an angel song
Awakened our Little Boy Blue.'

Bill and Pete

Behold a race of young ones...
A race of real children; not too wise,
Too learned, or too good; but wanton, fresh
Mad at their sports like withered leaves in winds
—William Wordsworth, *The Prelude*, V, 407ff.

Nena had her hands full trying to manage the house, keep Bill and Pete from running wild and take care of Freddie, too. *Mirabili dictu*, she had no trouble getting Bill to go to school. In 1924, Rena C. Hayden had expelled him from the John Lewis Childs' third grade for repeatedly disrupting the class. Sitting in the back of the room, he would turn his eyes up so far that only the whites showed. Then acting like the living dead, he would stand up and lurch toward his terrified classmates. Legend has it that he was so agile and athletic that once when his exasperated teacher made him stand in a corner as a punishment for some peccadillo, he climbed out the second floor window, shimmied down the drainpipe and ran home.[31]

He was full of high spirits at school as well as at home where he often talked six-year-old Pete into aiding and abetting him. Somewhere Bill had found a pair of handcuffs, a prompt for them to play cops and robbers one rainy day in their bedroom. Bill was the bad guy, Pete, the policeman. Having fun, Pete handcuffed Bill to the bed, but without the key, Bill really was locked up.

Birdie thought they were being too quiet and got doubly suspicious when she caught Pete going down into the cellar. Fortunately she intercepted him at that point and saved her furniture. Pete was on his way to find a saw to cut through the bedpost. "You are going to cut through what?" she cried.

Going upstairs to their bedroom, she tried to free Bill, but the wrists of the Prisoner of Zenda remained firmly cuffed. Angrily taking money out of the sugar bowl, Birdie sent Pete to the hardware store for a hacksaw and a file. After spending an irate quarter of an hour to free Bill, she took Pete by the upper arm and asked him what he was thinking when he locked his brother up. Already in tears, Pete sobbed that Bill had told him to do it.

"And if Bill had told you to jump off the Brooklyn Bridge, I suppose you would you have done that too? What will you get into next, you bloody kids?"

The boys knew she was really angry—she hated swearing.

Birdie whacked them both for that antic. They had made her spend extra time and money—but nothing dampened Bill. He was having great fun, and neither Rena C. Hayden nor Birdie could get him to stop.

When Bill was expelled from John Lewis Childs, the only alternative nearby was the Catholic school attached to the Church of the Holy Ghost in New Hyde Park. Birdie hesitated because of "idolatry and popery," Pepìn because of religiosity itself. There was no other choice. Fortunately, it turned out to be a good one.

During Bill's school interview that both his parents had to attend, Mother Superior asked Bill why he had been such a bad boy. She was amazed when the eight-year old answered with a translation of a Martial epigram that Pepìn had taught him some time before.

> I do not like her, Dr. Fell,
> But why it is I cannot tell.
> It's not her mental prowess that I fear
> But rather that I deem her queer.

For the first time Pepìn realized that Bill had something close to an eidetic memory. The nun saw that the boy was exceedingly bright and that an inexperienced and unimaginative instructor had failed to present challenging classroom work.

Se aburrió como una ostra. He was bored like an oyster, Pepìn thought to himself.

Mother Superior saw to it that Bill was kept busy. His teacher, Sister Mary Agatha, made Bill the class monitor. When he finished memorizing the Catechism and made his Holy Communion and Confirmation, Father Anselm selected him to be an altar boy. By fifth grade, Brother Michael chose him and two other bright kids to learn Latin after school every day. And he blossomed until Birdie died.

He was eleven that cruel February 1927, tall for his age, slim, powerful and lithe as a panther. He was dark like Della with Hispanic features and his father's wavy black hair. And he was angry; angry that his mother had vanished; angry that, despite Nena's best efforts, near chaos reigned at 41.

The nuns kept him in check at school, but at home he could be vicious. Not only would he do nothing to help around the house, but he would lose his temper and throw things at Nena if she didn't do exactly as he demanded.

Fortunately, he wasn't home that often; sometimes he didn't even show up for dinner. A young couple, Edna and Jack Fenty, were renting the house at 30 Lewis Avenue, diagonally behind the Balzacs. Just as Nena had turned to Kitty Bradley, so Bill found comfort and support at the Fenty house. Jack, 25, was a slim man with a dapper little mustache. He was a cashier in an ice cream plant and had hopes of becoming assistant manager.

In 1927, Edna was 22, a pretty, soft-spoken young woman with a new baby, Jimmy, born in July. She came from an educated family; one of her brothers was a teacher, and her genteel sister, Grace taught piano.

Unlike their rough and ready immigrant neighbors, the Fentys were cultivated and civil with middle class values and culture.

Though Pete was two years younger than Bill, he didn't treat Nena much better than his brother. He wouldn't help with the baby; he wouldn't run errands. If Nena dared to berate him, he would hide the iron so that she couldn't get Pepìn's shirts ready for work. A house devil and a tormenting tease, Pete then scampered away.

Even before Birdie died, Pete would come home from school, change into his old clothes and be off to his favorite haunt—the coal yards. With tight black curls and the smile of a gremlin, he was the darling of the delivery wagons, the pet not only of the drivers and customers, but also of the owner.

One afternoon his mother caught Pete dunking a donut into a glass of milk. "And where, pray tell, have you picked up that disgusting mannerism?" she asked him. He was just doing what all the drivers did with their "coffee and," but Birdie considered the habit neither couth nor masculine. From then on, if Pete dunked, he did so away from 41.

In the summer of 1927, the year that Pete lost his mother, unbeknownst to the yardmen, he made extra money as a spotter. Paid by the number of deliveries they made, the drivers never suspected that the 9-year-old who came along for the ride was keeping accurate accounts of their stops.

While they unloaded bales of hay or a ½ ton of coal, Pete made a straight line on a small pad, every fifth line crossing the former four as his employer had taught him. With Pete's tally marks in hand, his boss could challenge any employee's count.

This undercover work appealed to Pete's love of intrigue, but there was one thing that he didn't understand. Why, week after week, did some customers buy so much hay? They didn't even have animals.

Then one day in the stable after he had fed apples to the gentle dray delivery horse, he tripped on a bale and discovered that it held two dozen tall-necked bottles full of a tawny liquid.

He waited until he got home to tell Della. She giggled, then explained that the coal yard owner was making hay while the sun of Prohibition was still shining—but warned her little brother not to tell anyone else—including Nena, Bill and Dad. Nena had always been a prig, afraid of her own shadow, and since Bill got religion going to Catholic school, he would condemn Pete's actions as immoral. If Dad suspected that Pete was helping to deliver bootleg whiskey, he wouldn't allow his son to return to the coal yards, and if anyone there learned that Pete knew about the contents of the bales, he probably would be fired. Look, listen and say nothing, his sister counseled him. Pete wisely took her advice and kept his job.

The owner of the coal yards sincerely liked Pete, admired the boy's pluck and wanted to adopt him. In 1928, he actually came to 41 to broach the idea. His wife and he were childless; he was a wealthy man and could give the boy every advantage. Grateful that such a kind man had taken an interest in his son, Pepìn politely but firmly rebuffed him.

To add to all of Nena's other worries, Uncle Vincent began coming by on a regular basis, and he wasn't drunk. On one of his visits the year after his sister died, Vincent invited Pete to his house to see a new puppy. When the boy dropped by the New Hyde Park house one June day after school, Helen took him out on the back porch. There in a cardboard box, a small auburn fluff ball was sleeping, hind legs splayed out. The puppy had the pointed snout of a Shepherd, the red coloring of a chow, and because of a pure white mark on its forehead, Vincent had already named him Star.

Pete loved animals. When his mother was alive, she had refused to have house pets around, no matter the number of garter snakes, cats, dogs, turtles, frogs and fish that Pete dragged home. (They were unclean, Birdie told him, and besides, didn't she have enough of a menagerie with six kids?)

He was still there playing with the pup when his uncle came home from work. While Helen made dinner, Vincent watched thoughtfully as Pete, giggling and roughhousing, rolled on the floor with Star. "My sister was wrong about that," Vincent thought. "Every boy should have a dog to grow up with."

A neighbor had given the puppy to Vincent, and she still had the runt of the litter. Though Pete had turned ten at the end of April, Vincent brought the runt to 41 the next day and presented it to Pete as a belated birthday present.

Vincent could be generous, even thoughtful, when he wasn't drinking.

But Nena wasn't overjoyed with the prospect of having a dog around.

> *He doesn't come in the house, and you walk him and feed him,* she told Pete.

Eventually, they compromised: Pete agreed to make a dog house in the back yard for the summer and fall; by the time the weather got cold, the puppy would be house-broken and could sleep in the cellar.

Initially overjoyed with his gift, Pete turned apprehensively to Uncle Vincent. "But what if Dad won't let me keep him?" Vincent smiled. "Don't worry. I'll talk to him. Just promise to train the puppy and take good care of it." That night, to his surprise, Pete didn't have to convince his father of the benefits of having a dog. Pepìn was immediately taken with the roly-poly little thing. Smaller and squatter than Star, Dad remarked that with its thick reddish ruff, it looked like a tiny brown bear cub. Pete's 4th grade class had just gone on a field trip to Oyster Bay. "That's what I'll name him," Pete exclaimed with glee: "Theodore Roosevelt Balzac." And so it came to pass that in the spring of 1928, Teddy Balzac became the mascot and protector of 41 Sycamore Avenue.

Que años aquellos! What years those were! Pepìn sighed. In May 1927, a little over three months after Birdie died, he and millions of others exulted at the news that Charles A. Lindbergh, flying from Roosevelt Field only a few miles east of Floral Park, had landed safely in Paris. When he returned to the United States, the shy young airman was a national hero. In Washington, President Coolidge presented Lindbergh with the Distinguished Flying Cross, and in New York City, Mayor Jimmy

Walker gave him a huge ticker tape parade and the New York Medal of Valor. Everyone was talking about "The Lone Eagle." The elation caused by Lindbergh's solo flight temporarily allayed Pepìn's grief.

In late August, however, when Sacco and Vanzetti lost their final appeal and Gov. Fuller of Massachusetts did nothing to stop their execution, Pepìn's despair returned full force. A professed pacifist and opponent of capital punishment, he found himself almost sympathetic to the riots and bombings that occurred as protests against the injustice of their deaths.

𝔏𝔦𝔱𝔱𝔩𝔢 𝔉𝔯𝔢𝔡𝔡𝔦𝔢, 𝔓𝔞𝔤𝔞𝔫 𝔑𝔬 𝔐𝔬𝔯𝔢

Suffer the little children to come unto me,
and forbid them not: for such is the kingdom of
God.
—Mark. 10. 14.

Thank God for Freddie, an affectionate and delicate little blond boy. When he was three, he would sit on his sister's lap and ask, "Nena. Nena. Can I kiss your lipstick?" They adored one another.

Nena was the only one who could bathe him. Like most little kids, he was afraid to put his head under the tub faucet to rinse his hair. To make sure that he wouldn't get soap in his eyes or sputter and half drown, Nena took extra pains with him. She handed him a triply folded washcloth to hold tightly against his eyes. Then with just her index finger under his chin, she could get him to thrust his head back. Telling him to be a soldier, she poured entire pots full of water over his scalp and rinsed his hair two or three times almost never wetting the washcloth.

In the summer, sometimes Maudie and John Porth, who owned one of the few cars in the neighborhood, would invite Nena and Freddie to Bar Beach on the North Shore of Long Island. The water in the Sound was generally warmer than at the ocean, but the pebbles on the shore and in the shallows were sharp and hurt Freddie's feet.

On very hot days, Nena preferred to pack a small lunch, perch Freddie on a towel in her bicycle basket and ride the three miles up to Lake

Success, skirting the guardhouse at the Lakeville Road entrance. The shoreline was sandy and pebble-free; the water, cool and bracing. They would go for a dip, Freddie holding on to her shoulders, then come back to the clearing where they had deposited their things. After lunch, they would rest for a while and ride home refreshed with plenty of time to make dinner.

In the winter, she bathed Freddie in the kitchen in her mother's large washtub. Drying him briskly, she dressed him in pajamas that she had warmed on the radiator. How he loved hot pajamas! Then she carried him upstairs to his bed in the unheated back bedroom, wrapped the covers around his feet, and said,

Now you are as snug as a bug in a rug.

Her attentions were necessary. Like Brother Bradley, Freddie had been born with a congenital heart defect, an incomplete closure of the mitral valve. Fortunately, the condition was not life threatening, and as long as he didn't overexert himself, he didn't show any ill effects. If, however, he ran around and jumped too much or became overwrought, he could have a weak spell. The color would drain from his face and tiny beads of sweat would appear on his upper lip and forehead. At that, Nena would hold him on her lap and chafe his arms and legs. In a few minutes, his cheeks would become pink again.

Of course, the aunts were worried about him. Their youngest nephew seemed frail, but his heart condition was only a part of their concern. What troubled them most was that Pepìn and Birdie had not thought to baptize the boy. Finally, on one of their visits to 41 Sycamore

Avenue, his sisters brought up the subject with Pepìn. As far as he was concerned, Freddie's mortal or immortal soul seemed to be functioning just fine without the benefit of aspersion. Nevertheless, he understood instinctively that Edmundo's baptism *in articulo mortis* weighed heavily on Fidela's conscience. Because he cared about his sisters' peace of mind, he consented to Freddie's baptism—on condition that they make all the necessary arrangements.

I do not know who served as Freddie's sponsors; aside from Fidela and Rosa, I don't think that Pepìn knew many church-going Catholics. Fidela was an obvious choice; perhaps Popeye Martone also consented. He was the grandfather of the Italian-American clan who lived three doors away, and his daughters, Anne, Rose, Louise and Elvera were Nena's best friends. Vincent and Helen May had once been Protestants at the beginning of time, but they could not be Freddie's godparents. Father Wilamowski of the Polish Church would never have allowed anyone but good Catholics to stand up for a child of the faith. As it was, the priest was horrified to learn that Freddie was not a babe in arms, but a boy of three and a half.

In the spring of 1928, the appointed baptismal Saturday finally came. Both Aunt Rosa and Tia Fidela certainly attended the ceremony. Father Wilamowski baptized three tiny babies and then turned to Freddie. The boy had never been in a church before. Awed into absolute silence, he didn't mind when the priest's hand rather heavily pressed on his head, nor did the child react when anointed with oil on his shoulders and chest. But when Father Wilamowski sprinkled the boy with holy water three times, Freddie went into an outraged pet and called the priest "a bummer."

Freddie was not usually a fresh-mouthed kid, but his indignation at being spattered with water had an irksome and recent history. As they washed the dishes, Bill and Pete would sometimes have a water fight at the sink. To get a rise out of Freddie, they would splash him, too. They were bummers when they did that to him. Wasn't the man in black a splasher just like his brothers?

Despite Tia Fidela's embarrassed apology, Father Wilamowski was incensed. The child had no respect. Tia was mortified; she had saved Freddie from the anguish of Limbo, but she vowed never again to try to redeem any of the Balzacs.

As for Freddie, he was *salvado*, a pagan no more, but he returned home in utter disgrace. To regain his confidence, he climbed on Nena's welcoming lap. In a muted voice, he murmured, "Nena, Nena, can I kiss your lipstick?"

Cookin' Creole, Cookin' Good

> Sugar cane, syrup (cane), saffron, dill and 'roux',
> Etouffée, café au lait, flan and bisque and stew—
> Sabayon and courtbouillon, corn bread, jambalayas,
> Enchiladas and tostadas, pepper jelly and papayas—
> Crème glacé, sweet parfait, batter breads and mustard,
> Chocolate mousse, duck and goose, caramel cup custard!
> —*Talk About Good!* Foreword, Le Livre de la Cuisine de Lafayette
> (Lafayette, Louisiana: The Junior League of Lafayette, 1961)

By the summer of 1928, Nena had become a considerable cook. At first, she had struggled to get the meat, potatoes and vegetables on the table all at the same time. Once, outraging her brothers, she burned the roast and over salted the string beans, but Pepìn reassured her and ate everything on his plate.

Little by little, she became adept at making Spanish rice the way her father liked it with a large dollop of lard, finely chopped onions and green pepper, flavored with tomato sauce and stuffed olives. Her brothers fought over the *pigau*, the extra crispy layer of rice that had to be scraped off the bottom of the pot. Her *pernil*, a pork shoulder roast, studded with tiny pieces of garlic and sprinkled with tarragon, was succulent, and her fried sausage and thyme stuffing for chicken, turkey or duck was as good as her mother's had been.

She read the *Fanny Farmer* and *Good Housekeeping* cookbooks, got recipes for pot roast and beef stew from Maudie Porth and Kitty Bradley. Popeye Martone taught her to make a creditable Neapolitan spaghetti sauce. Her brothers liked it so much that they would dunk the *puntitas*, (the pointed ends of a good loaf of French or Italian bread) in a cup of the sauce and skip the pasta altogether. For dessert, her standards became a light Cottage Pudding, a type of pound cake, made from a recipe in *Good Housekeeping*, and a black and white icebox cake layered with chocolate snap cookies and whipped cream. Holiday meals featured her *pièce de résistance*, a caramelized pineapple *flan*.

Perhaps when Della came home, Nena began to muse, she might be able to enroll in a cooking school. *Per aspera, ad astra*, through difficulties to the stars, she said to herself quoting Pepìn.

Welcomed by Pete, Uncle Vincent continued to come by usually when Pepìn wasn't home. Ostensibly he came to give Pete pointers about training Teddy, but Pete didn't need any help. At less than a year old, Teddy was an amazing dog who on command rolled over, gave his paw for a handshake, recognized the difference between "out" and "eat," and would "talk" at great length in what seemed like sentences. (On hearing him, Pepìn commented that in his house, even the dog was verbally gifted). Teddy seemed to know when Pepìn would be getting off the bus and nightly would be loping up Depan Avenue just as Pepìn began the short walk home from the bus stop in front of the Polish Church. Allowed to roam at will, everyone in town knew Teddy, the Balzac's gentle red Shepherd.

During these visits, Vincent paid particular attention to Nena and Freddie, and she was disconcerted by his consideration. He was actually pleasant and sometimes even helpful, carrying the heavy laundry basket for Nena out to the line in the back yard, playing with the baby while she hung the wash, slipping a dollar into her apron pocket as he left. "No, no, Nena. You take it. It's for you. Buy yourself something, and think kindly of your uncle." He whispered confidentially that she had been her mother's favorite and his as well. Nena was leery. She didn't know what to make of Vincent's civilities. He wasn't drinking. Had her uncle really reformed?

The answer to that question came in late summer of 1928. All dressed up in their Sunday clothes, Helen May and Vincent came to see Pepìn one weekend afternoon. They found him on the front porch reading Emerson and smoking his pipe with Teddy peacefully dozing at his feet.

It didn't take them long to get around to the purpose for their visit. Now that Maudie Porth was no longer looking after the boy, they wanted little Freddie, almost 4, to come live with them. Helen May was home all day, and Vincent had a steady job delivering meat for Joe's Butcher Shop on Jericho Turnpike. The child would want for nothing, and since they lived only a few blocks away, Nena could bring Freddie to 41 for the day on Saturdays, or alternately Pepìn could visit the little fellow at their house at any time.

Helen May cried. Vincent begged. Pepìn categorically said "No." As a family, they were managing just fine, but he thanked Helen and Vincent for thinking of them. And that ended that, at least for the time being.

𝕳𝖆𝖇𝖑𝖆 𝕮𝖔𝖒𝖔 𝖚𝖓 𝕮𝖗𝖎𝖘𝖙𝖎𝖆𝖓𝖔

> *Language is a perpetual Orphic song*
> *Which rules with Daedal harmony a throng*
> *Of thoughts and forms, which else senseless*
> *and shapeless were*
> —Percy Bysse Shelley, *Prometheus Unbound, IV,*
> *415 ff.*

The big news in early 1929 was the St. Valentine's Massacre. Pepìn read the newspaper avidly and decried the lawless and terrible times. Prohibition had created the era of the gangster. News stories about the infamous Al Capone appeared daily. Though there was a public outcry, especially in Chicago, young people all over the country secretly admired the illicit power of the mobsters; boys wanted "to get in on the action," and girls aspired to be "gun molls."

A new vocabulary had come into vogue. "Bootleg hooch," "the real Mc Coy," "jazz and razzamatazz" and other such expressions had permanently entered the language, and one Spanish-American linguist increasingly shook his head in despair. The elegant English language, the legacy of Shakespeare, the tongue that he had struggled so hard to master, had become hopelessly corrupt in the space of just a few years.

If any one of the Balzac offspring dared to use these new words in his presence, he would sputter in outrage, *"Habla como un cristiano,"* speak like a Christian–as if his children had become latter day Moors once again besieging the gates of the civilized world.

Chaos

> *For what wears out the life of mortal men?*
> *'Tis that from change to change their being rolls;*
> *'Tis that repeated shocks, again, again,*
> *Exhaust the energy of strongest souls.*
> —Matthew Arnold, *The Gypsy Scholar*

The Balzacs staggered along through 1928, through the spring of 1929, but more trouble was just around the corner. One weekend morning, Nena had put up water for the boiled Spanish coffee that her father liked. She was preparing fried eggs for Pete when Bill came downstairs and asked her to make some for him, too.

Pepìn was at the table in his slacks and undershirt reading as he waited for the water for his coffee to boil. Nena served Pete and started to make Bill's breakfast, but as she tapped the eggs on the edge of the pan, the yolks broke. Bill said he wouldn't eat them. She insisted he should. He said she had deliberately ruined the eggs. She called him an inconsiderate brat. One word led to another. Flying into an uncontrollable rage, Bill threw the kettle with near boiling water at her. She was quick enough to turn around, but the water splashed on her back, burning her badly.

Pepìn jumped up to help her. He sent Pete racing up the stairs to the bathroom to get salve and bandages. Her initial screams subsided into sobs. Pepìn cut her blouse open down the back and groaned when he saw the already blistered flesh.

*"Nena, lo siento, lo siento–*I'm so sorry."

When he had dressed and bandaged his daughter's wounds as gently he could, he whirled on Bill. In one of the rare times that he ever chastised one of his children, he lost his temper completely and gave Bill a swift kick in the pants that sent the 13-year-old flying into the vestibule.

Bill already regretted what he had done. He hadn't meant to hurt his sister. He begged her to forgive him—but no apology would serve. Nena was through. Her back healed, but she was left with permanent dark scars across her shoulders. Determined to get away from Floral

Park, she answered a newspaper ad for domestic help. Before the end of the summer, she accepted a job as a cook's assistant in Albany. Nothing Pepìn could say to his fifteen-year old daughter could induce her to remain at home.

And then there were three.

Nena, 15, in Albany

Once Nena left, Maudie again took care of Freddie, but John, now retired, wanted her to be free to travel. With this turn of events, Vincent and Helen renewed their request to look after the boy.

They were relentless. Finally, just after the Freddie's fifth birthday, Pepìn gave in. In late September 1929, Freddie Balzac went to live with his maternal Uncle Vincent and Helen May.

And then there were two, Bill, 13 and Pete, 11.

Sometimes when Pepìn went into Manhattan to see Della, he would take the boys with him. On the train, he would tell them to call him "Chickie," his nickname at work, instead of "Dad." If they met a pretty girl—he rolled his eyes—she didn't have to know that he had such big sons, at least at the beginning. After visiting Della, they would go to *El Fundador*, his favorite restaurant on 48th Street near 6th Avenue, for *paella*. He was popular with the Hispanic waitresses and prosperous Puerto Rican patrons. The boys could see that women admired him, but somehow "Chickie" never struck up more than a casual conversation with any of them.

When they got back home, Bill would be off to tell the Fentys about his day. Though Bill still slept at 41, he was at the Fentys' so constantly that to all extents and purposes, he might as well have been living there. They never saw him in a fit of anger; on the contrary, their gentility spurred him to be thoughtful and mannerly.

In September 1929, Bill began his final year at the Holy Ghost School. Clearly, he was the outstanding student in his 8th grade class. Both Jack and Edna encouraged him to do his best, going over his homework, helping him review for the Regents, New York statewide exams. Their hearts went out to this brilliant, motherless boy. He responded–loving

Jack like an older brother–worshipping Edna like the mother he had lost.

Eventually, the Fentys bought a house on Beechhurst Avenue, one block west of Sycamore, and Edna gave birth to a second boy, Bobby. The Fentys' affection for Bill, nevertheless, remained constant. All through high school, Bill served as a built-in baby sitter doting on the two little boys as he had doted on little Freddie.

And then there was one.

On weekdays as soon as Pete came from school, he went to the coal yards, but on weekends, he devoted himself to a new business venture. In an empty lot on the corner of Sycamore and Jericho Turnpike, 11-year-old Pete designed and built a nine-hole miniature golf course. He collected admission to his putting green, charged the kids in the neighborhood for the use of his clubs (inherited from Joey) and for their own stray golf balls that he collected after they finished the last hole. Business was booming until one day two men showed up and informed him they would be bulldozing his course to make a new commercial building on that spot.

Pete was undone. He had worked so hard on his miniature course. He couldn't wait until he was big enough to work as a caddy at the Lake Success Golf Club, the job that Joey had held before he joined the Navy.

Pete was as enterprising as Bill was studious, but neither thought much about being companions to "the old man," their irreverent name for their father. Many a night when Pepìn got home at 7 p.m., the house was dark. Bill left a note that he was invited to dinner at the Fenty's, and when Pete showed up, he'd have already grabbed a sandwich with the men on the delivery trucks. And so their father would eat alone, drink a beer and go to bed, tired and lonely for his wife and daughters.

Pepìn saw his family dissolving around him. At forty-seven, he felt old and helpless. He had needed Birdie when she was alive but never more than he needed her now, two and a half years after her death. What could he do? He had to travel to Newark every day. After October 1929, there was no chance that he could get another job closer to home.

His problems, moreover, paled in comparison to the economic news. Every day, it seemed, one read of another wealthy, cultured man who had thrown himself out of the window of some high building. The collapse of the stock market was wreaking havoc with the state, with the nation, with the world.

[30] Both the graduation photograph and the certificate were found with the Balzac and Lopez studio photos after Nena's death in 1960. Continuing the tradition, she gave me the gold ring that had originally belonged to my great grandmother, Eliza Kempf Lopez, when I graduated from the John Lewis Childs School in 1950. I gave it to my oldest son, Demi in 1974 when he finished 8th grade, but in San Gimignano, Italy where we lived the next year, his finger grew so large that the ring had to be cut off. When we returned home, I had the ring repaired and still wear it.

[31] My cousin, Bill Balzac told me this story when we were in China together, January 2003. His father, Fred Balzac, Sr. had told it to him.

Part 1, Chapter 9
The House Made Home

Even the roses 'round the porch must blossom year by year
Afore they 'come a part o' ye, suggesting someone dear
Who used t' love 'em long ago, an' trained 'em jes' t' run
The way they do, so's they would get the early mornin' sun;
Ye've got t' love each brick an' stone from cellar up t' dome:
It takes a heap o' livin' in a house to make it home.
—Edgar Guest, Home

The years after my mother died were painful for all of us, but even bad times don't last forever. We may not have had two chickens in every pot as Herbert Hoover had promised, but as a compositor and translator, Dad was both highly skilled and highly valued. His job at Sidney Ross was secure.

In the early years of the Depression, Dad brought home the commanding salary of $50 a week. Unlike some of our less able neighbors, he saw to it that none of us ever feared losing 41 Sycamore Avenue. Other people had houses that they loved, especially if they had grown up in them as children. But no one I've ever met identified with their home in the manner and with the degree of intensity that we did. I cannot say why such a modest structure so powerfully affected us all. It was as if 41 were the manifest symbol of our parents' unexpressed love for us and each another, the seal of our identities, both source and center of our existence.

Can a story explain what is essentially inchoate?

When he had finished enclosing the front porch in 1925, a cautious workman installed a large three-pronged Yale lock on the wooden entrance door. Typically, that night Birdie went to lock it; and just as typically, Pepìn ever so gently stopped her:

'No, 'mira,' let the door to this house always remain open.' His eyes twinkled. 'Birdie, what if a god should come knocking, like in the myths, or the angel of the Lord?'

'Pepìn,' she answered dryly, 'With our luck, if anyone knocks, it will be a vagrant or one of your hungry friends.' But out of mute admiration for him, she didn't bar the door.

Over the years, the shiny brass lock gradually tarnished; never used, it slowly rusted in place. Over the years, the house developed creaks, groans and loose floorboards. One of the boys, probably Pete, had carefully sawn a foot square hole in the pine floor of the bedroom that he and Bill shared. Hiding his treasures in the space between the joists of the sub-floor, he then replaced the boards. I waxed the upstairs floors twice a year, but by the time I discovered the cache, no one would 'fess up' to being the carpenter.

The original wallpaper faded, and our neighbor, Mr. Schuhmacher, a professional decorator, replaced it several times. The kitchen needed and got new linoleum and, when

Pete was old enough, numerous coats of paint. The sisal rugs in the parlor and dining room wore out.

As the years passed, the original cast iron kitchen stove gave way to a green and cream enameled model on legs with a modern gas range and oven. Dad bought me a Spanish Colonial dining room set with a dark oak finish and had a second-hand upright player piano installed in the living room. And Della recovered Mama's mahogany settee and chairs with a Chintz floral print.

Six wild children growing up pell-mell had scarred the house; the births and deaths witnessed within its walls had hallowed it. As it aged, so we aged. Every mark, chip and dent carried the imprint of our collective lives. We would have gone <u>sans culottes</u> and sold apples on street corners rather than let anything happen to 41.

Joey and 37 Flavors

What is love? 'Tis not hereafter;
Present mirth hath present laughter;
What's to come is still unsure:
In delay there lies no plenty;
Then come kiss me, sweet and twenty
Youth's a stuff will not endure.
—William Shakespeare, *Twelfth Night II. iii.40 ff.*

Joey wrote home infrequently, but when he did, it was obvious that he had made a wise choice in going into the Navy. He liked being a sailor; he needed the discipline and order; and he loved the sea. Besides, he wrote to amuse us, blue was his favorite color–it matched his eyes–and having a girl in every port of call wasn't half-bad either. He was playing the field: there were so many girls, and they were all unique! 'Vive la difference!' He wasn't going to settle down, he joked, until like Howard Johnson's ice cream, he had tasted all 37 flavors. He even liked his work. The Navy was training him as a radio technician, a duty that gave him extra privileges.

His letters became utterly serious, of course, whenever he mentioned Della. Initially, he had been worried sick about her, but on further reflection, he wrote—trying to soothe Dad—perhaps a structured environment might be just what she needed.

Over the next two years, he sent us postcards from Panama, Chile and the Caribbean regaling us with his adventures on the bounding main. And then on shore leave in New York when he was eighteen, he met a girl named Anne Caro from a Czech family in Yonkers. She had entered a dance competition there and won first prize doing the Charleston. Joey was in the audience that night; when the competition was over, he congratulated her and asked her to dance. Joey and Anne fell madly in love.

Won't You Come Home, Nena Balzac, Won't You Come Home?

Summer and his pleasures wait on thee,

And, thou away, the very birds are mute;

Or, if they sing, 'Tis with so dull a cheer

That leaves look pale, dreading the winter's

near.

—William Shakespeare, *Sonnet 97*

In Albany, I was working as a cook's assistant for a wealthy surgeon, Irving Halperin, M.D. and his family. They were kind to me, and I learned about balanced meals and nutrition from the doctor and from Mrs. Sauer, their inventive and informed German cook. The Halperins had three children, Marshall, 13, Linda, 11 and Robbie, 7. Mrs. Sauer put me in charge of the children's lunches, menus made up once a week by Dr. Halperin himself.

The two older children were very spoiled. They fought with one another and were persnickety to Mrs. Sauer, but Robbie was sweet. I soon became attached to him, and he promised to marry me when he grew up. He was a finicky eater, so for lunch I made him ground sirloin patties wrapped in bacon; dotted open grilled cheese sandwiches with ketchup to make a smiling face; put the cone on top of a scoop of ice cream on a dish and decorated it to look like a clown. Though he was almost two years older than my little brother, Robbie was my Freddie all over again.

But after ten months, I was homesick, homesick for Floral Park and its tree-lined streets, homesick for 41 Sycamore Avenue, homesick for Dad whose letters, initially light and amusing, gradually betrayed how much he missed and needed me. Sometime in early May 1930, Dad sent me a particularly poignant note, and I became worried. He sounded so weary and disheartened. He had been selfish and thoughtless, he wrote. He realized now that raising little Freddie should never have been my exclusive responsibility–I needed time and space to grow up myself. He accused himself of failure: as a scholar, as a husband, as a father and as a man.

My Dad was no failure. Gentle, generous and humble, he had the respect of intelligent people and the affection of children. He had been a kind and faithful husband, and Mama had cared for him deeply without ever telling him so. And no father had ever been more selfless or patient. Nor had he been thoughtless—he had just desperately tried to keep us all together. I couldn't bear to have him blame himself for circumstances cruelly at odds with his best judgment.

His letter so disturbed me that when I replied, I asked if he wanted me to come home. He answered by return mail that he longed to see my face. The House of the Good Shepherd would release Della in July, he continued, and she had changed. Between the two of us, now that we were older, we would be able to manage. Helen May was devoted to Freddie, and he was well cared for.

In a postscript, Bill pleaded with me to return. He had made a <u>novena</u> and worn out the knees of his pants praying God to help me forgive him. And he promised that Pete and he would help around the house. Pete added a post-post-script that was all Pete (I couldn't help laughing): "Please come back, Nena. We haven't had a decent meal since you left."

I read the letter over and over again. That night I couldn't get to sleep thinking about Dad and my brothers. In the morning I asked to see Dr. Halperin before he went to the hospital. I gave him a month's notice.

At the beginning of June 1930, I left Albany for good and came back to Floral Park. Like a suddenly awakened dreamer needing to be reassured by familiar surroundings, I felt compelled mentally to record everything about 41: Mama's gnarled maples in front of the house; Teddy Balzac standing guard in the side yard, wagging his tail when he saw me; Dad's pipe stand and humidor on the front porch; the ruby Gothic tumblers and pitcher set in the beveled glass and oak China closet; the huge red and white kitchen with a dropped-leaf table under the window; the rounded finial on the newel post at the bottom of the stairs, the yellow-flowered bedroom at the top. I unpacked. I was home.

The very next thing I wanted to do was to walk the six blocks to Uncle Vincent's house in New Hyde Park to see Freddie. The whole time I was in Albany, I had felt guilty. Would he feel that I had abandoned him?

Dad tried to put my mind at ease. Helen May devoted all her time to him; she had taught him his numbers by playing cards with him. She had taught him to read by sounding out cookie recipes; then they made the cookies. He wanted for nothing; together Helen and Vincent had bought the boy enough toys and books and clothes for four children. Vincent, Dad said, was a new man. He hadn't had a drop of liquor for months before he picked Freddie up in September, and he vowed that he would be sober for the rest of his life.

Dad made me promise that I wouldn't talk the boy into coming home for good—it would break Helen May's heart, and it wouldn't be right to disrupt his life again. Though Freddie had missed me as much as I had him, Freddie loved her, too.

I walked up the tree-lined lane to 4th Street in New Hyde Park. Helen May and Freddie were seated on the sun porch playing checkers. Freddie had his back to me and didn't see me come up the front stairs. As soon as Helen recognized me, she let out a gasp and began to sob, sure that I had come to take Freddie away. He turned around just as I called to him.

I didn't dare enter though Helen tearfully told me to come in. A huge mottled Great Dane, a white bulldog and Star were growling and rushing the screen door. She got up and forced them back into the house.

Overjoyed, Freddie ran to the steps and threw himself instantly into my arms. Then he remembered that Helen was in tears.

Momentarily, he didn't know whether to go to her or to cling to me. For both their sakes, I quickly reassured her that I was only there to visit. I finally got her to stop weeping and to wipe her eyes.

Delightedly, Freddie began to tell me all his news, taking me upstairs and showing me his room and his toys. All the time, he was holding my hand as if he'd never let go. He was as slim and pale as ever, but he had grown so tall.

Freddie wasn't angry with me for having left, and he was happy living with Helen and Vincent. We would see each other on weekends, and he would continue to live with them.

Comes Love

Come live with me and be my love,
And we shall all the pleasures prove
—Christopher Marlowe, *The Passionate Shepherd to his Love*

Della's birthday was July 2. Though she wouldn't be home until then, Dad had already bought her a beautiful new Singer sewing machine, the only thing she wanted. Heavy duty with a cast iron head, it came housed in a mahogany cabinet with a matching bench. Closed, it functioned as a handsome desk. Dad had it delivered and placed in the small back bedroom that was to be Della's. The boys had also moved her bed and bureau there from the yellow bedroom, and I went out and bought new white lace curtains for the three windows. With pale pink wallpaper, dark furniture and lace doilies, the room took on a decidedly feminine air. Surveying our handiwork, we all were sure that Della would be pleased.

Pete had taken over the back room after Freddie went to live with Vincent. With Della coming home, however, Pete moved his things out and was bunking once again with Bill in the large green bedroom next to Dad's. At first, Pete was a little annoyed at being displaced, and Bill wasn't thrilled either to share space with his raucous younger brother, but the boys soon accepted the new arrangement. When Bill was home, he rarely studied in his room anyway. He preferred working at the dining room table under the crystal chandelier where he could spread out his books and papers and close the pocket doors for quiet. And aside from sleeping in it, Pete never stayed in his bedroom. He was always out doing something.

They both loved Della and wanted to make her happy to be home. They wanted me to be happy, too. For the first time, I officially had a room to myself, the yellow bedroom at the top of the stairs that I had always shared with my sister. With the return of both his daughters, Dad's notion that young ladies should have rooms of their own tacitly demonstrated that things were going to be different.

It seemed to be a season of gift giving. My sixteenth birthday on July 9 came one week after Della's. Dad bought me a Spaulding English racer and a white ankle length summer dress with a purple organdy cape. It was so light and sheer that wearing it, I felt as if I were floating. Vinnie Rapetti from down the block said I looked like a South American Blue Morpho butterfly. He took my picture posing with my new bike that day, and later, when he shipped out to Buenos Aires on a tramp steamer, he sent me an enlargement of the photo mounted in a butterfly-filled ebony frame.

When Della was released from the House of the Good Shepherd, Jim Redding met her in the city and drove her to Floral Park in his beat up old Packard. The years away had matured her. She was quieter and more considerate. Now, when gangs of boys congregated on the stoop or in the sun porch on fine summer nights, they were my friends. Della dated no one but Jim, and both were serious enough to talk about getting engaged. She and I also got along better because we established and maintained a genuine division of labor: she shopped, I cooked; I did the wash, she, the ironing and mending; she cleaned the bedrooms and bath; I took care of downstairs.

Surprisingly, Joey–the swabbie who didn't want to get serious with any one girl–was the first of us to go to the altar. In September 1928 before his three-year hitch in the Navy was over, he and Anne married. He was 18 years old. He liked to say that he had tasted vanilla and strawberry, but that she combined the remaining thirty-five Howard Johnson flavors.

When he came home for good, they first took rooms on Caroline Avenue in Yonkers. But like all of us, Joey loved Floral

Park. Shortly after his discharge from the Navy, he brought his bride back to the village, renting an apartment on Tyson Avenue, a block from the railroad station. Though jobs were not easy to come by, he found work with the W.P.A. building the new Floral Park Town Hall. His boss liked his easygoing manner, approved of his naval record and even found his recent marriage commendable. Eventually Joey worked as a grounds-keeper at Belmont Racetrack and wrote occasional poetry.

He joined the Rescue Company of the Floral Park Fire Department in 1933 and for many years served as its Secretary. From 1935 on, he kept extensive notebooks, full of inspirational poems published in various newspapers and clippings of all stories concerning Rescue. Until the onset of the war, his chapbooks preserve a week to week history of the village Fire Department.

However content he was to trade in his bell-bottoms and sailor's cap, we all thought that Joey had missed his calling. He should have been in vaudeville. Anne and he often came to 41 visiting on weekends. Uninvited, they managed to show up just at dinnertime (Anne hated to cook). But Nena didn't care; Dad said that in Albany she had learned to cook for an army. There was always enough food. Besides, like little Tommy Tucker who sang for his supper, Joey told jokes and recited hilarious risqué poems all through the meal. He was so entertaining—alternately telling and pantomiming droll stories—that he made everyone roar.

After Sunday dinner, Joey would bring his victrola and records into the living room and roll up the rug. Anne and he would dance the Cakewalk, the Black Bottom and the Broom Dance. They were elegant, our own Fred Astaire and Ginger Rogers. They taught us all the new steps; then Joey would play hit tunes of Bessie Smith, Sophie Tucker, Al Jolson and Ted ("Is Everybody Happy?") Lewis. And he introduced us to stride piano and Fats Waller, the Blues and good New Orleans jazz.

1933

> From harmony, from heavenly harmony
> This universal frame began:
> From harmony to harmony
> Through all the compass of the notes it ran,
> The diapason closing full in man.
> —John Dryden, A Song for St. Cecilia's Day

In 1933, when Sidney Ross Pharmaceuticals was feeling the effects of diminished sales, Dad's bosses asked him to take a voluntary cut in salary. He had worked for them faithfully for twenty-one years, and they didn't want to lay him off. Dad's reaction to this looming crisis was characteristic: on the weekend, he called for a family conference including Joey and nine-year-old Freddie. Dad announced that he was going to accept the 33⅓% cut in salary. "What can we do to reduce expenses?" he asked.

That was all he had to say–he had mobilized his family. Mama had always kept chickens when we were kids, so Della and I bought some baby Rhode Island Reds. Pete was becoming a decent carpenter; he had already built an oversized doghouse for Teddy in the backyard. With Joey's help one Sunday morning, he made a serviceable coop and roost from a bunch of old boards lying around the cellar, some leftover shingles and chicken wire. We raised a rooster and twenty hens and never wanted for fresh eggs.

When our hens produced more than we could use, we gave the extras to Pete to sell. At 15, he was quite the entrepreneur. The 'egg money' was our slush fund–we used it for special treats or for going to an occasional movie.

Bill volunteered his lunch money; instead of eating at the high school cafeteria, he took a sandwich and fruit from home. On Saturday mornings, he cultivated and Freddie weeded the tomato and corn patch.

As part of our concerted effort, Dad had decided to cancel his subscription to the New York Times, but we wouldn't hear of it. He had taught us well. We were the majority—we vetoed that sacrifice. Aside from his cherry-flavored tobacco, the paper was his only luxury. Besides, we reminded him, our newspaper boy was a Martone–they had scads of kids to feed.

Tightening our belts, we ate meat or fish three times a week at most and used up every scrap of leftovers. In Albany, I had learned to make vegetable soups with stock from saved bones and drippings. I served ratatouille like Mama used to make, fish cakes and apple fritters, baked macaroni, cheese and vegetable crepes, frittatas of every description and rice pilaf or jambalaya. With bread made from scratch and eggs from our chickens and with corn, pole beans and tomatoes from our garden, we never felt deprived.

When Della was 'under wraps' as she humorously put it, she had learned invisible weaving. Evenings when Jim wasn't around, she rewove worn spots on coats and jackets, darned socks, patched pants, and turned the collars of dress shirts. Our clothes were not new, but they were always clean and in good repair. Della recycled buttons and zippers, and when garments were too frayed to wear, she cut the fabric into strips and braided yards and yards of them. Then she sewed the braids together by hand for what seemed like endless hours to create multi-colored rag rugs for the living room and dining room. She was absolutely ingenious with a needle and thread.

In March 1933, we huddled around the radio console in the living room to hear Franklin Delano Roosevelt's Inaugural Address. One phrase from the new President's speech became justly famous: 'the only thing we have to fear is fear itself.' Because of our father, we had never feared, but the passage that Dad had us note came later in F.D.R.'s text: 'Happiness lies not in the mere possession of money; it lies in the joy of achievement, in the thrill of creative effort.'

Even with Dad's weekly check reduced to $33, we had turned crisis into victory. Because we had acted as a family, 1933, a bleak time for many others, was turning out to be a good year for the Balzacs of Floral Park.

Edna Fenty

That pleasant cheek, hair smooth and brown.
Clear brows, and wistful eyes—yet gay:
You stand, in your alpaca gown,
And ghost my heart away.

I was a child then; nine years old—
And you a woman. Well, stoop close,
To heed a passion never told
Under how faded a rose!
—Walter de la Mare, Lucy

We were so happy in our happiness, but for Bill's friends, the Fentys, life couldn't have been more painful. Early in October 1932, state police appeared one night at Beechhurst Avenue and arrested Jack. He had been playing the ponies at Belmont Park, had lost money and tried to cover his debts with some liberal 'borrowing' from the cashier's till at the ice cream company where he worked. Charged with embezzlement, he was sentenced to five years in prison.

Even before Jack was sent away, Edna took a job as a checkout girl at Bohack's supermarket on Plainfield Avenue. With her mother caring for the baby and five-year-old Jimmy, on weekends she cleaned houses in Garden City. Every extra penny she made, she gave to the company to make restitution.

When Jack went to jail, Bill lost his best friend, and to make matters worse, he worried helplessly about Edna. She would sometimes come home from work so exhausted that she couldn't speak and wouldn't eat. She'd just go up to bed and fall asleep in her clothes. He did everything that a boy of seventeen could think of to please her. As soon as he got home from school, he weeded and hoed her garden, ran errands and shopped for her mother. The very chores that Della and I had to beg him to do, he did voluntarily for Edna.

She was young and lovely and noble. Neighbors on both streets felt sorry for her. They knew about troubles. Tiny Mrs. Jones, up the block on Sycamore, had two alcoholic sons, Jimmy and Johnny, who constantly got drunk, fought each other in the house and broke up all her furniture.

Mary Fallon, a sad frail spinster with a domineering mother, lived on the corner of Sycamore and Charles. Shy and retiring, she was in and out of Creedmore Hospital for the Insane.

Across the street from the Balzacs, Kitty Bradley was still in mourning having lost Brother, her only child. The Martone's blonde, blue-eyed four-year-old, Jeanie, playing in a nearby driveway, had been crushed and killed, run over by their neighbor's car. Behind the wheel, Mr. Peterson couldn't see Jeanie as he backed out–she was so small. Ruth Martone was never the same after her little girl's death.

Mr. Peterson never recovered from the accident either and gradually slipped away into senility. He'd wander all over town late at night and forget his way home, and poor Mrs. Peterson would be out, a long coat over her nightgown, looking for him. The very people who had armfuls of grief themselves went out of their way to be kind, from time to time sending Edna and her family some vegetables from their gardens, a freshly baked pie, a loaf of homemade bread.

Little by little, Edna paid off Jack's debt—all of it. Her husband was released almost half a year early because of her efforts and his contrition. In April 1937, Jack Fenty returned from prison, a saddened little man who drank heavily. He had lost more than four years of his life and all of Edna's respect.

𝕍𝕚𝕥𝕒 𝔹𝕠𝕟𝕒 𝔼𝕤𝕥

My mind to me a kingdom is;
Such perfect joy therein I find
That it excels all other bliss
My wealth is health and perfect ease;
My conscience clear my chief defense;
I neither seek by bribes to please,
Nor by deceit to breed offense.
Thus do I live; thus will I die!
In Praise of a Contented Mind
—Anonymous Elizabethan lyric

On the sun porch, Dad puffed contentedly on his pipe and made great clouds of cherry-flavored smoke. It was all ebb and flow: one cycle took away, and the next renewed. For now at least, he mused, the tide was coming in. Emerson, Pepìn recollected, had said: "This time, like all times, is a very good one, if we but know what to do with it." *Quizá sí, quizá no.* Perhaps yes, perhaps no.

Pepìn, Anne,
Freddie, and Jo Jo, 1934

Vita bona est, he thought as he tapped out the ashes from his favorite Meerschaum pipe. Life is good. His children were near. Joey lived within

197

walking distance and was the father of a tow-headed boy, Joseph Balzac III. His daughters were engaging, responsible and marriageable young women. Bill, 17, continued to do brilliantly at Sewanhaka High School winning both the English and Latin prizes. Pete, 15, had finished grammar school and was such a go-getter that he often had two jobs, and living with Uncle Vincent but visiting often at 41, slim, sandy-haired Freddie, "a dillar, a dollar, a fourth grade scholar," was as thoughtful as he was gentle.

In two years, Pepìn could rip up the mortgage; the house would belong exclusively to him and his six children as Birdie and he had planned. In four years, after 25 years at Sidney Ross, he would be eligible for a small company pension when he retired and, if Roosevelt got his way with Congress, monthly Social Security checks as well.

Though money was tight now, his salary still fed four kids, himself, a big dog and anyone whom his generous daughters asked to stay to dinner.[32] What more could a man want?

[32] When Della's friend from the House of the Good Shepherd, Lillian Bartolino eloped with Larry Dentico, they were so broke that they didn't have sheets. They came to Floral Park for dinner, and as a wedding present, Nena gave them linens intended for her father's bed—much to his consternation.

Please don't be upset, Dad. We have two sets of sheets for every bed, and they have nothing.

Part 1, Chapter 10
September 21, 1938

Hence, viper thoughts, that coil around my mind,
Reality's dark dream!
I turn from you, and listen to the wind,
Which long has raved unnoticed.
—Samuel Taylor Coleridge, *Dejection: An Ode*

It had been raining on and off for nearly two weeks. Since daybreak, stiff winds accompanied the downpour. Pepìn was on vacation. He had been planning to go to Hampton Bays on the train with his bicycle to explore the area around Good Ground where he had bought property. Some years before, an East End real estate agent had come to the door, and for the price of one dollar a week for two years, Pepìn was able to purchase five lots, each 20' by 100', a parcel large enough for a modest summerhouse. Regretfully, he remembered that distant radiant blue summer with Birdie at Canoe Place and their plans for retirement.

Pepìn had just finished reading *My Country and My People* (1935), a study of modern China. Placed at the very end of the book, the ancient poem "The Spirit of Early Autumn" by Hsin Ch'ichi had caught his eye. Lin Yutang's translation summarized Pepìn's mood almost completely.

In my young days,
I had tasted only gladness,
But loved to mount to the top floor,
But loved to mount to the top floor,
To write a song pretending sadness

> *And now I've tasted*
> *Sorrow's flavors, bitter and sour,*
> *And can't find a word,*
> *And can't find a word,*
> *But merely say, "What a golden autumn hour!"*

At eighteen in Puerto Rico, he had written poems full of pathos. And he had known nothing about life. Ah well, Pepìn sighed, youth tends to over-dramatize. It promised to be a beautiful fall, his favorite time of year, even if the weather today was miserable. Perhaps he still might get to the Hamptons if it cleared up over the weekend.

By 10:00 a.m. Pepìn was on the sun porch reading *The New York Times* (September 21, 1938) with Teddy at his side. The lead story, "Czechoslovakia Decides to Give Up," alarmed him. All one heard about for the past three years, it seemed to him, were predatory politics and territorial invasions. In the West, hard on the Italian conquest of Abyssinia in 1935, the Nazis had taken over the Rhineland, and not content with that expropriation, this March, they had occupied Austria.

And since 1936, civil war had raged in Spain. For the first time in modern history, an armed force—the Nationalists—had deliberately bombed a civilian population. Pepìn still shuddered to think of the photographs that came out of the Basque town of Guernica on April 27, 1937, two days before Pete's nineteenth birthday. Was this the wave of the future? Blanket bombings used to terrify non-combatants?

But nothing compared with the inhumanity of the Japanese in China. In 1937, they had taken Peking, and soon afterwards subjected the Chinese to unspeakable brutalities. At the movies, Pepìn had seen the Pathé News coverage of what reporters were calling the "Rape of Nanking." Little children put to the sword! Women violated and murdered! Thousands of decapitated corpses thrown into the river! *Diós mio*, it was horrifying! Perhaps, Pepìn hoped, the current meeting of European ministers in Munich might stop the war in Spain and put an end to some of these terrible demands for *lebensraum*, living room. Thank God, this time the Americans were staying out of it!

𝔚hat a 𝔏ittle 𝔐oonlight 𝔠an 𝔇o

> I sing of books, of blossoms, birds, and bowers,
> Of April, May, of June, and July flowers.
> I sing of Maypoles, hock carts, wassails, wakes,
> Of bridegrooms, brides, and of their bridal cakes.
> I write of youth, of love, and have access
> By these to sing of cleanly wantonness.
> —Robert Herrick, *The Argument of His Book*

At least at home these past few years, life had developed a certain romance. The procreant urge, Pepìn noted tongue in cheek, was everywhere. Joe and Ann were parents of a tow-headed boy, Jo Jo, who was the spitting image of his father. And Della and Jim finally decided to marry, but when they went to see Father Wilamowski at St. Hedwig's, he refused to officiate because Jim wasn't a Catholic. So license in hand, they called on Rev. Durr, the Lutheran minister whom Birdie had liked so much. He married them on the spot.

Then in 1936, Nena surprised everyone by marrying Mauro, a quiet Italian fellow who had taken to hanging around the house. Moe, as he was often called, had a car and was the brother-in-law of one of Pete's buddies who had needed a ride to Floral Park one night. They came to 41, and Moe met Nena.

Pete never thought that serious Moe, who didn't talk much and didn't dance, would take a fancy to Nena, the social butterfly. Or vice-versa. Nor in Pete's wildest imaginings did he think that Moe would squeeze out Johnny O'Neil, Nena's steady boyfriend for five years.

At first, Pepìn was leery of Mauro because he owned a car. Cars? Whorehouses on wheels, Pepìn called them. He preferred Della and Nena to entertain their beaux at home—none of this "rumble seat, let's-go-for-a-ride" stuff, but Mauro was earnest and clearly in love with his daughter.

Pepìn quickly came to like Mauro; he was modest and sober–unlike Della's Jim and some of Nena's other boyfriends. Pepìn had been amused when Jim Redding had attempted to be sociable, inviting Mauro to Belmont Racetrack. They'd spend a couple of bucks, Jim said, have a few beers and a couple of laughs.

Mauro declined. "Sorry, Jim. Racing's not for me—that's the other side of the family." He was a steady fellow, Pepìn reflected, just what his fickle daughter needed. But why, with such a beautiful name, why did he allow himself to be called "Moe?"

Until Mauro appeared on the scene, Pepìn worried about Nena. She was such a coquette. Sometimes five fellows would be in the parlor taking turns dancing with her.

It was outrageous, Pepìn told his daughter when she came into the kitchen to make a drink for her friends. Nena just laughed,

> *Daddy, you're so old-fashioned! Nowadays, everyone plays the field.*

And then she'd serve all five young men lemonade, while they smiled at her but glared at one another! Such a thing would never have happened in the islands, Pepìn had thought sucking his teeth in disapproval. No girl would have gotten away with such behavior. One of her sweethearts would have stabbed her.

Despite Pepìn's doubts about modern dating, both his daughters had married hard-working fellows and blessed him with grandchildren. Della's curly haired, green-eyed boy was named for his father, and two months after Della gave birth, Nena had me. She named me Diane, the title of a popular ballad of the day, but acknowledging my initials, everyone called me Dee Dee.

Then, soon after Nena brought me home from the hospital on December 16, Pete experienced his first real romance. That evening, Moe's sister, Mary, came from the city to see her new niece. As Mary was about to leave, Pete came in from work. He took one look at her and said, "Give me five minutes to shower and change, and I'll drive you."

It was a cold night, and the roads were icy. As they came across the Brooklyn Bridge, Pete's car went into a spin. Mary was terrified, sure they were going to end up in the river, but Pete managed to regain control of the car. Looking up after the skid, he saw Mary's white face and jokingly reassured her. "You didn't have to be afraid." He smirked. "If we had gone off the bridge, I would have held your hand."

My father was Catholic and insisted on having me baptized. Four months later, his whole family came to the Christening with Elvera Martone acting as godmother and Pete as godfather. At the gathering Mary met Pete for a second time. She thought he was cute. Soon they were seeing each other seriously.

For the past six months, Pete had saved all his extra money in order to buy Mary a diamond ring. They planned to get engaged on her birthday in July and marry December 16, 1939, exactly three years from the day they met.

Only Bill remained unattached. In 1936, he had won a full tuition scholarship to St. John's University in Queens starting out as a Pre-Law student. Now in his junior year, he had switched to English intending to go to graduate school and teach on the college level. He was a shoo-in for Phi Beta Kappa, Phi Kappa Phi and Summa cum Laude. The clever and pretty daughter of the iceman, Dottie D'Angelo, had set her cap for him, but Bill's only interest seemed to be his studies.

In 1936 with both his sisters married and living at 41, Bill had moved into the Fentys' house as a boarder helping Edna financially and giving him a more congenial place to study. Finally released from prison in April 1937, Jack had taken a job as a bookkeeper in Hempstead. Edna no longer worked, and the young Fenty boys, now 11 and 6, were both in school until 3 p.m. With a three-day college schedule, Bill had two full weekdays to study without interruption plus most of the weekend. 41 Sycamore—where people were always dropping by—just couldn't compare with the peace and quiet that Beechhurst Avenue afforded.

Pepìn was proud of his son, but they had argued loudly ending in Spanish, and afterwards Bill avoided seeing him. Pepìn thought Bill should come home and give the Fentys a chance to put their lives back together again, but Bill didn't see it that way.

Stormy Weather

> There came a wind like a bugle;
> It quivered through the grass,
> And a green chill upon the heat
> So ominous did pass
> We barred the windows and the doors...
> And fences fled away,
> And rivers where the houses ran
> The living looked that day.
> —Emily Dickinson

Just as Pepìn began considering once again Pete's upcoming nuptials—brother and sister marrying sister and brother—he heard his grandchildren's laughter. Released from the confinement of our highchairs in the kitchen, Jimmy and I, both almost two years old, came running out on the porch. While Della ironed and Nena cleaned up the breakfast dishes, Pepìn volunteered to watch us.

Making believe that he hadn't heard us, Pepìn pretended to read until we banged on his newspaper. Peeking over the top, he said with feigned surprise, "Oh, you found me again!" How we laughed! We played the same game with him every morning that he was home, my mother said, and never tired of it. Grateful to forget the morbid news, he put the paper aside. Giggling, we both climbed onto his lap—but only for a moment.

Jimmy almost immediately spied the toy box and got down to take out a set of blocks. I wriggled off my grandfather's knee and followed Jimmy. He was prattling on, actively playing with the blocks on the floor. "See, Poppi. See my house."

According to my mother, I never took my eyes off my cousin. I would hand him a block every now and then, but I didn't speak. "Nena has to pay more attention to this child," Pepìn thought. He went into the kitchen looking for something to drink. "You must talk to her more, Nena," he told his daughter, but Nena didn't seem to share his concern.

> *Dad, she understands everything. When she's ready, she'll talk.*

He returned to the sun porch to take up his paper again, but he was so absorbed thinking about his granddaughter that he never saw Pete, soaking wet, come rushing around the corner of East Hitchcock Avenue. Suddenly, the front door burst open.

"Dad, I just heard the Coast Guard advisory down at the Firehouse." Like Joey, he had joined the Floral Park Fire Department as a volunteer and often stopped in there. "This isn't just a storm; we're in for a real hurricane. They've been tracking it from Norfolk, Virginia. They're saying it's going to make landfall somewhere on the south shore with winds around 120 miles per hour. Help me tape the porch windows. If we open them top and bottom, the wind may just pass through. If we're lucky, we won't lose them."

Pete moved swiftly into the kitchen to get some masking tape and mobilize his sisters. "Forget the ironing, Dell. Go upstairs, and clean out the tub. Then fill it with cold water." He patted the pockets of his work jacket and pulled out a bunch of kosher candles. It was September 21, 1938, and the stores had stocked them for the Jewish holidays.

"Here, Nena. These are all the A.& P. had. We're going to need them. I'll try to borrow a couple of kerosene lamps from the firehouse for tonight." He turned to go back to the porch. "Bring the babies into the dining room away from the windows, and see if you can find a flashlight and candle holders. I'll put Teddy downstairs. The porch won't be any place for him this morning."

Before noon, Pete and Pepìn had secured all the windows upstairs and down, great swatches of tape crossing each pane. Then Pete brought the ladder and a piece of plywood up from the cellar, and somehow, despite the angry gusts, he managed to get outside and board up the stained glass window over the stairwell. His mother had loved that window, and he wasn't going to take a chance on something happening to it.

Pepìn sat at the kitchen table and quickly downed two glasses of Nena's "Sinless Sangria," a refreshing grape juice drink containing slices of oranges and lemons but no wine. He had gotten very thirsty from the exertion of taping the windows, but as Nena started to ask about the storm, he was already on his way upstairs.

> *Gee, Dad,* she called after him, *I can't even have a conversation with you before you're running off to the bathroom.*

While Nena waited for him to return, she found two working flashlights and some long tapers in the kitchen cabinets' junk drawer. She took the pink Cambridge Glass candlesticks that had belonged to her mother from the oak china closet in the dining room and placed them on the kitchen table. Then she went back for the pair of silver candelabra that stood on the buffet. Used only on holidays until now, they flanked the fretted silver bowl his bosses at Sidney Ross had given Pepìn in 1937 to celebrate his 25th anniversary with the company.

When her father came upstairs, Della had just finished drawing enough fresh water in the tub for two or three days. With that chore done, she returned to the kitchen. Her sister had already begun to cook.

I'm going to start some Spanish rice and chicken, Della. The men will want food—whenever they get home.

Coming up from the cellar where he had replaced the ladder and tools, Pete asked Nena to make him a couple of sandwiches. "Anything you've got."

He was excited. "They're saying the storm is 500 miles wide, and it's moving very fast, around 70 miles per hour. If it's as bad here as it's been coming up the coast, I may not get back until late."

Pete was working for the town. If trees or branches blew down, he would be on one of the work crews clearing the streets. As an afterthought, he remembered his brothers-in-law who had left the house around 6 a.m. He told his sisters not to worry, but they shouldn't expect Jim, an electrical lineman, or Moe, a machinist, tonight. "If the electric goes out, Della, Jim may be working all night, and I sure hope, Nena, that Moe has enough sense to stay in Jersey at the shop and not try to make it home."

Daddy I'm Coming Back to You

For he comes, the human child,
To the waters and the wild
With a faery, hand in hand,
From a world more full of weeping
than he can understand.
—William Butler Yeats, *The Stolen Child*

No sooner had Pete left 41 to return to work, than Freddie, a freshman at Sewanhaka High School, came in, dumping his slicker on the porch and taking his shoes out of his boots. At 11 a.m., the Superintendent of Schools had dismissed all classes in the district. Freddie and his best friend, Babe Schuhmacher had started to walk from Sewanhaka under wildly blowing trees in the driving rain when Mr. Schuhmacher appeared like an angel in a pickup truck and brought both boys home.

Freddie was wet through and through. Nena made him go get a towel. She roughly dried his hair, then heated up the leftover breakfast coffee. Drink this, and get into some dry clothes. Don't go getting a chill now, she said gently. She handed him a steaming cup, he recalled, just as she had the night he came home from Vincent's.

Two and a half years before, he had fled his Uncle Vincent's house running the six blocks from New Hyde Park to Sycamore Avenue. It was a rainy March night in 1936 before Nena and Moe got married. Freddy was terribly upset, praying all the way to 41 that Dad and Nena would let him stay. Everyone was around the kitchen table: Dad, Jim and Della, Pete, Nena and Moe. They were shocked to see Freddie in such a state. Pete jumped up. "Jesus, Freddie! What the hell is going on?" The boy's face was white and all contorted, and he could barely catch his breath.

Between convulsive sobs, he finally blurted out what he had been afraid to say for a couple of years: when Vincent was sober, he was mean; when he was drunk, he was meaner. Under the guise of solicitude, Vincent punished him for having a heart condition. At home, he wouldn't let Freddy have roller skates or a bike; after school, he wouldn't let Freddie play with the kids on the block. They were too rough, his uncle contended, and Freddie had to be careful for his heart. Though Dr. Buckley had recommended light exercise for the boy at school, Vincent saw to it that his nephew didn't take Physical Education. Instead, Freddie had to sit in the bleachers feeling like a useless lump until the coach, Mr. Glenn came to the boy's rescue and appointed him record keeper for the baseball and basketball games.

When Vincent was drunk, it was even worse. He'd often come home at 2 a.m., wake the boy out of a sound sleep and make him walk the dogs. If Vincent had turned vicious, he'd take a switch from the hedges and beat the sleepy child across his bare legs. "I'll teach you to neglect my dogs! Let's see you dance, you lazy thing!"

Many times Helen May got between them to protect Freddie, and then Vincent would go off on her. She had nothing but bruises and an occasional black eye to show for her kindnesses. Then the next day when Vincent sobered up, he'd be penitent begging Freddie and Helen for forgiveness. And they had forgiven him–too many times.

When Freddie first came to live with his uncle, Vincent had been on the wagon, but for the past three years, his uncle had begun drinking again and his bouts with the bottle had gotten progressively worse. He had blackout spells and couldn't remember where he had been. Stumble drunk, he fell down a flight of stairs and swore that someone had beaten him up. He had terrible nightmares and would wake up screaming about Verdun or the Somme–but he had never been to war.

If he were suffering from a hangover when he came home from work, Vincent would look for something that the boy said or did to find fault. Following Helen's lead, the boy believed that Vincent couldn't help himself—he was someone else when he was drinking or unhappily sobering up. So Freddie had overlooked Vincent's bullying, the taunting, even the lashings.

That morning Freddie must have slept through the alarm, and hurrying to get to school, he forgot to put out the garbage, one of his recently assigned chores. Helen had been upstairs washing clothes in the tub all morning and hadn't even realized that it was collection day. To spare Freddie a confrontation with his uncle, she would have put the garbage out herself.

Vincent came home at lunchtime, saw the neglected cans still standing on the side of the house and went into a fit. He was so beside himself with rage that he couldn't eat the leftover rice and beans that Helen had set out for him. Instead, he fumed and railed, then vaulted up the stairs. Helen could hear him opening drawers in Freddie's room. Late for work, he sped back downstairs with a box under his arm and jumped into his old black Model T.

He had been angry with Freddie for over a week ever since the boy, according to Vincent, had deliberately let Star get hit by the Clinton laundry truck. As Freddie was walking the dog on a leash, Star had spied another dog across the street and slipped his collar. Before Freddie could catch the barking, growling animal, Star ran into the street right in front of the truck. The driver had swerved, but the bumper clipped Star's back leg and narrowly missed running him over.

It had cost Vincent $10 for the vet's bill, $10 that he expected Freddie to pay back by doing extra chores, one of which was putting out the garbage. Freddie was also to bathe the Great Dane, the bulldog and Star once a month with the garden hose, a responsibility the boy hated. He was a finicky little bastard, Vincent snarled, afraid of getting a little wet.

Freddie got home from school at 3 p.m. Helen was worried. "I didn't see the garbage cans until it was too late. I would have put them out, but he noticed them before he got into the house," she said nervously. "Whatever you do, make yourself scarce after supper tonight, and maybe he'll forget about it."

Downcast, Freddie went to his room to do his homework, but everything was in disarray. The drawers of his bureau had been rifled, clothes tossed on the bed. Worst of all, Freddie's prize possession, his collection of baseball cards was missing. Ever since second grade, he had saved every penny of his birthday money to buy new ones as they came out, avidly selling and trading pictures of the athletes at school.

Trying to hold back his tears, the boy waited anxiously for his uncle to come home. Vincent finally arrived well after 8 P.M. Since quitting time, he had been drinking at the Sawmill Tavern on Mc Kee Street with Popeye Martone. When he got home, he was none too sober.

"Uncle, I'm sorry about the garbage. I…" Freddie began, but Vincent cut him off triumphantly. "I took those baseball cards that you're always mooning over and threw them down the sewer. I told you, I told you what would happen if you didn't earn your keep around here." He had threatened before that he would make the boy's life a misery if Freddie "didn't straighten up."

"You only have yourself to blame. Let this be a lesson to you. You'll never see those cards again," Vincent sneered.

The loss of his prize collection was too much for Freddie to bear. "And you'll never see me again either," Freddie screamed. Before Vincent could get out of his chair, the boy ran out the front door slamming it behind him. Fearful that his uncle would pursue in his car, Freddie cut across neighbors' backyards looking frantically behind him until he got to Lewis Avenue and Maudy Porth's house. Soaking wet in the heavy rain, he jumped her fence to get to Sycamore and finally to 41.

"Please, please don't let him take me back! Please let me stay! Please don't make me go back!" By that time, Freddie was nearly hysterical.

Pepìn immediately put his arms around the boy. "Freddie, you'll never go back there, I promise. *Bastardo!* That sadistic bastard! I should have known he hadn't changed."

But all this time, why didn't you tell us, Freddie?

He had been too afraid even to tell Nena. Vincent had told Freddie that Dad didn't want him, that Freddie's birth had killed Mama. And that's why Dad had given him away. "No, Freddie, no!" Nena and Della had both exclaimed. "That's a damned lie," Pete added.

"*No es verdad.* That's not true, Freddie," Pepìn cried, cradling the boy in his arms. "I've always wanted you to be here with us, but Della was in New York, and Nena was in Albany, and Maudie couldn't continue looking after you. And I knew Helen loved you desperately." Pepìn was almost weeping himself, soothing the slim boy and stroking Freddie's tousled wet hair. "That's not true at all. You mustn't believe anything that Vincent says. He's always had a mean streak. Your mother died of heart failure from the shock of an operation. Your birth had nothing to do with it."

Nena joined in,

> *And you could have come home at any time. We thought you were happy with them.*

She had dried his hair with a towel and given him a cup of coffee to warm him up that night, too.

He was eleven and a half when he returned to 41, small for his age, a sixth grader. For the first time in his life, he had a friend, Alvin

Freddie, 14, with 1 year olds Jimmy and Dee, Winter 1938

(Babe) Schuhmacher, a sweet gangly boy his own age, who lived diagonally across from 41.

After school, they played stickball in the street or cards on the sun porch. Nena let Freddie ride her English racer, and Babe and he cycled all over town. Either Babe was in the dining room doing homework with Freddie, or Freddie was at the Schuhmachers' listening to broadcasts of Yankee baseball games with Babe.

An excellent student, Freddie had graduated from John Lewis Childs near the top of his class in June. He and Babe had just entered their freshman year at Sewanhaka High School a few weeks before. They were going to audition for the Sewanhaka chorus and try out for the debate team. They were inseparable.

Gone with the Wind

> *There rolls the deep where grew the tree.*
> *O earth, what changes hast thou seen!*
> —Alfred, Lord Tennyson, *In Memoriam A. H. H.*

True to form, less than an hour after he got home, Babe ran across the street to 41 during a momentary lull of the wind and rain. He found Freddie and Pepìn playing gin rummy in the parlor. "From my house I could see the giant oak in the lot bending and waving in the wind. I think it may come down."

The empty lot between Sommers' house and 41 was where the kids on the block made bonfires of autumn leaves, erected snow forts and built clubhouses. The tree was a fixture in their play: they climbed it and swung from its low-lying branches imitating Tarzan of the Apes, strung ropes and an old tire from it for a swing, collected acorns at its foot to use as missiles for their slingshots. It was huge, venerable and seemingly indestructible.

Abandoning their card game, Pepìn and Freddie led Babe on tiptoe through the dining room. Undisturbed by the gigantic storm, both babies had fallen asleep there in a playpen. When Pepìn and the boys came into the kitchen, Nena and Della were having coffee.

From the kitchen window, they all watched as the hundred-year-old tree twisted, groaned and sighed with each successive gust. At times the rain was so heavy on the windowpane that the tree was completely obscured, but as the water ran off the glass, they could see the oak bending, then leaning closer and closer to the ground and slowly rebounding. Its breaking branches screeched louder than the howling wind. It cracked, it creaked, it moaned, a living thing suffering a prolonged agony.

Around 3 p.m., the winds intensified, bombarding the house until it shook convulsively. The oak whipped about wildly but survived the onslaught. Then the rain virtually stopped, and a strange yellow calm settled over the street. For over a half-hour, Sycamore Avenue remained in the 50-mile-wide eye of the storm.

Suddenly, without warning, the sky turned black. The storm began again, more violently this time as bands of wind at the far side of the eye wall blew with horrific force from the opposite direction. They blasted the careening oak. Yanked back and forth, back and forth, the four-foot wide trunk leaned almost horizontally one final time. As its roots tore, a great mound of earth rose up. It seemed as if a giant hand were pushing the tree from below. With an enormous crash that shook the neighboring houses, the oak fell over, a mountain of splintered branches. Its huge exposed root ball created a crater over sixteen feet wide. The boys were awestruck. "If it hadn't been raining for almost two weeks," Pepìn remarked sadly, "the roots might have held."

By 8 p.m. the sky had cleared. Floral Park had lost many trees, and branches were down everywhere. At 41, the electric went out until the next morning. One of the upstairs windows in the back bedroom had cracked when a limb hit it, but held in place by the tape, the glass hadn't shattered. Some shingles had blown off the roof—nothing that Pete couldn't fix in an hour.

The Balzacs survived the Great Hurricane of 1938 virtually unscathed, but it devastated the Eastern Shore of Long Island and the New England coast. The Category 3 hurricane made landfall at Bellport, Long Island at 3 p.m. during a high tide that was already causing waves higher than usual because of the autumnal equinox. Battering the low-lying coastal towns nearby, it produced a storm surge 17' above normal sea level. Whole towns were submerged under water, houses along Dune Road in the Hamptons were swept out to sea, and a new channel, the Shinnecock Inlet, ripped through and bisected the South Fork, just east of Hampton Bays. More than 100 people died, some buried under collapsing buildings or struck by flying and falling debris, some drowned in the storm surges and subsequent floods. Others simply disappeared.

In New England, the destruction was even worse. Gloucester, Massachusetts reported peak wave heights of 50'. At Providence, Rhode Island, wind gusts of 186 miles per hour lashed the coast. Warned too late, 600 people lost their lives. When the storm ended, the Northeast had 8,900 ruined homes, and 63,000 persons were homeless. The amount of wreckage from buildings alone was staggering. Compounding that damage, the hurricane had uprooted an estimated 2 billion trees.[33]

[33] Scott A. Mandias, http://www2.sunysuffolk.edu/mandias/38hurricane/ Mandias cites Everett Allen, *A Wind to Shake The World: The Story of the 1938 Hurricane* (Little Brown: Boston, Massachusetts) 1-91 and Arthur A. Frances, "Remembering the Great New England Hurricane of 1938", *The Salem Evening News*, September 21, 1998, among many other sources.

𝔎𝔬𝔪𝔪, 𝔖ü𝔰𝔰𝔢𝔯 𝔗𝔬𝔱
("Come, Sweet Death," Mozart oratorio)

though dull were all we taste as bright,
bitter all utterly things sweet,
maggoty minus and dumb death
all we inherit, all bequeath

and nothing quite so least as truth
i say though hate were why men breathe—
because my father lived his soul
love is the whole and more than all
—ee cummings, *my father moved through dooms of love*

Winter came on early that year. The frigid skies did nothing to offset Pepìn's equally gloomy mood. Reading the daily news reports made him more and more apprehensive. By mid-December 1938, it was clear that the Munich Pact of late September had been an illusion.

Neville Chamberlain's "peace in our time" was an empty promise. Despite the concession of the Sudetenland to Germany, Hitler now fixed on Czechoslovakia delivering increasingly violent denunciations of that small and abandoned country.

The Munich Conference, Pepìn feared, had been the eye of a worldwide political storm. The Great Cyclone had wheeled about, and now with augmented force, it threatened to destroy millions of people and deracinate entire nations.

Pepìn read *The New York Times* avidly, but his eyes were bothering him. He promised himself that after the holidays he would get a new prescription for eyeglasses. He was also preternaturally chilled; his hands and feet seemed particularly affected by the wintry weather, and he was running to the bathroom all the time. He must have gotten a cold in his bladder.

In late January 1939, Pepìn came home one night from Newark feeling poorly. At work, he had had a blinding headache. By late afternoon, he was seeing double and could barely set up type. He slept on the subway and was shaking as he walked home from the Polish church in a freezing drizzle. At 41, Nena quickly made him some tea, but he couldn't eat his dinner.

In the morning, though his headache was gone, he was still brutally tired and desperately thirsty. Uncharacteristically, it didn't take much coaxing from Nena for him to stay home. The weather was colder and wetter than yesterday, he told himself. He needed the day off.

Nena wanted to make him breakfast, but he wasn't hungry, just thirsty. He wanted a glass or two of orange juice; then he'd go back to bed.

Pepìn Balzac, 1938

When he didn't respond to her call to come down for lunch, Nena went upstairs.

> *Dad,* she called outside his bedroom door.

He didn't answer. She opened the door tentatively. He was lying in bed, his face towards the wall. She took his hand, but it was clammy to the touch. His breathing was shallow, but she couldn't wake him.

> *Oh, no, Dad.*

She ran downstairs.

> *Della,* she cried. *Something's wrong with Dad. I'll run to Martone's and call Pete.*

Pat Martone, three doors up the block, was a cesspool contractor who had an office in his house and one of the only telephones on the street. His wife, Ruth, was in the kitchen when Nena knocked frantically on the back door.

> *Ruth, it's Dad. Can I use your phone? I've got to get in touch with Pete.*

When she couldn't reach her brother at work, she called the firehouse. Bobby Hermann, a volunteer fireman like Pete, was manning the phone. "Don't worry, Nena. We'll send over Rescue and get Dr. Buckley. And I'll find Pete."

The ambulance came and took the unconscious Pepìn to Mineola Hospital. He was in a coma. Dr. Buckley suspected undiagnosed diabetes. From what Nena told him, Pepìn seemed to have had symptoms for some time.

They took turns around the clock: Nena and Freddy stayed during the day, Della and Pete, all evening. Joey came between shifts at work relieving whoever was there. Going to classes by day, Bill spent the night at the hospital, sleeping on an upholstered chair next to his father's bed.

Pepìn came out of the coma on the morning of the fifth day. He could barely whisper; his lips were cracked, and he motioned that his mouth was dry. Hoarsely, he asked for a pineapple ice cream soda. Dutifully, Freddy went down to the coffee shop and brought his father's favorite treat back for him. As Nena held the straw for Pepìn, he took two sips but was too weak to drink more. By nightfall, he lapsed into a coma for a second time. He died two days later on a bleak Monday, February 6, 1939.

In accordance with Pepìn's wishes, there was no Mass for the Dead. At Della's request, Reverend Durr said a few words at the house. Pepìn was laid out in front of the living room windows where Birdie's coffin had stood twelve years earlier. A somber Joey and a swollen-faced Della greeted the neighbors from Sycamore Avenue and Pepìn's friends from Sidney Ross who had come all the way from Newark. Ashen from shock, Manuel Gil requested to be an honorary pallbearer. Throughout the funeral, Nena stayed in her room upstairs unable to speak without breaking into sobs. As a measure of their respect for Joe and Pete, the

Floral Park Fire Department sent a delegation in parade dress to the wake. Pale and solitary, Freddy was mute.

Bill wrote the obituary for the Floral Park newspaper and gave the now lost eulogy. He said something like this:

> Our father was a Creole, proud of his French name and Spanish and French origins, who came alone to New York as a youth. He was proverbially tall, dark and handsome with wavy black hair and a pronounced and prophetic widow's peak. Co-workers who knew him then said, "He had April in his face." He loved to tell jokes. Often he was so amused by the story he was recounting that he laughed harder than anyone else did. He was a printer, translator and linguist eventually fluent in six languages. If *la vida es sueño*, if life is a dream, his life was an American dream, self-taught and self-realized.

> Our father married two sisters in turn, and by them had six children whom he raised with consummate gentleness. No Puritan, he was fond of saying that if God had made anything better than sex, he had kept it for himself. No mere sensualist, he never took up with another woman after the death of Birdie Lopez. If ever a man was patient in the face

of adversity, it was he; if ever a man exemplified kindness and generosity of spirit, it was he.

Dad loved life and did not fear death. He was fond of quoting from Fitzgerald's version of the *Rubáiyát of Omar Khayyám:*

> O threats of Hell and Hopes of Paradise!
> One thing at least is certain—This Life flies;
> One thing is certain, and all the rest is Lies—
> The Flower that once has blown forever dies.

'Dying can't be all that bad,' Dad often said. 'So many people have done it.' A sleep and a forgetting were the natural ends of all things, a part of the alternating rhythm of the universe. The individual tired and grew old, but the species went on, ever renewed by infancy. He saw his immortality in the faces of his children and grandchildren. And that was enough.

Our father was religious without being a communicant of any church. His religion proclaimed the unfathomable beauty of creation as its temple and the dignity of man as its creed. The True, the Good and the Beautiful were his Trinity. He taught his children that to live in accord with these principles was the *Summum Bonum,* the highest virtue.

He lived simply and, for the most part, contentedly. We, who were brought up by him, will not forget his talents and beliefs nor allow our children's children to forget. His name was Joseph Balzac, and his middle name was Love.

Part 2: The Book of Nena

Mercedes (Nena) Balzac 1947

Part 2, Chapter 1
Kind Spirits: 1939-1960

Now, until the break of day,
Through this house each fairy stray
And each several chamber bless,
Through this palace, with sweet peace.
—William Shakespeare, A Midsummer Night's
Dream

Kind spirit, if you are present in the room, kindly rock the table once for yes, twice for no and three times for I don't know.

Mama, is that you?

After reciting stories or poems or looking at old family pictures, Nena Balzac washed and dressed while I lay in her bed waiting for her return. Perhaps once a week after coming back from the bathroom in an immaculately starched wrapper, my mother carefully removed the antimacassar, alarm clock and small radio from the three-legged table that served as a console to the right of the bed. Then pulling up a straight-backed chair, she laid her hands lightly on the tabletop and called upon her mother's spirit.

I hid under the covers. My grandmother, I knew, had been dead for many years. If the table didn't respond or tapped twice, Nena would intone in a semi-mystical voice,

Dad, is that you?

I shrunk down deeper under the covers. Grandpa died when I was two years old. The idea that he was present but invisible—however benign—somehow didn't comfort me. The table rocked once; Pepìn was in the room. I slipped further down the bed.

Then my mother would ask Dad (or Aunt Louise or Aunt Daisy or whomever else she could conjure) questions about the future. Sometimes the spirit was obliging, patiently answering repeated inquiries, but eventually it would rock the table so hard that Nena would say,

> *The spirit is getting annoyed. It will be better to put the table away for today.*

Armed nonetheless with certain knowledge, mother and daughter could begin the day. Table rocking had a further benefit: at four years old, I acknowledged the unseen familial host—more personal than mere guardian angels—who kept watch at 41 Sycamore Avenue.

The ceremony of rocking the table had begun many years before when a talented and imaginative spiritualist who held sway in South Jamaica taught Nena, Della and a friend, Harriet Richeimer, how to contact the other world. "All old houses are inhabited by spirits of the dead," Mrs. Hurt said.

Della shuddered involuntarily. A number of times she thought that she had seen a man in the butler's pantry hovering near the old printing press that Dad had kept when he gave up his business in the city. Curiously the man was putting on leather gloves carefully tapping between each finger to insure a tight fit. As a child, had Della overheard Dad describing one of his dead partner's most characteristic gestures?

In any case, since Della was certain that 41 was haunted, she, more than Nena or Harriet, was open to Mrs. Hurt's eerie suggestion: "Go into the cellar at midnight with a small table and a chair," the spiritualist advised the young women. "Using only candlelight, call upon the spirits to move the table using this formulary: 'Once for yes, twice for no, three times for I don't know.'" They had all complied, but only Nena seemed to have the necessary psychic powers.

Over the years, Nena was so impressed by Mrs. Hurt's clairvoyance that almost against his will, she dragged her brilliant brother, Bill, to meet the fortune-teller. Bill was not superstitious, but even he had to admit that Mrs. Hurt was impressive. In a trance, Mrs. Hurt saw the Indian chief who served as Bill's guardian angel. Looking at her brother's dark and brooding face, Nena believed the vision, but despite her earnest inquiry, her brother would not repeat any other detail of his reading.

Nena may not have been a professional like Mrs. Hurt, but she definitely was psychic. Everybody said so. If your nose itched, she predicted that before long you would get into a fight. If a shade rolled up suddenly during the day, she foresaw that visitors were coming. If someone dropped a spoon, a woman could be expected. If a knife fell to the floor by accident, surely a man would be knocking later that evening. Nena's prophesies almost invariably came true—though a skeptic might point out that many guests frequented 41 Sycamore Avenue, and some of them were argumentative.

Wasn't it Nena's intuition that had saved Freddie from drowning? One morning when he was about sixteen, she had knocked repeatedly on the locked bathroom door. Freddie was the only one at home; he must have been taking a bath.

When Nena couldn't get him to answer, frantically she called Pete at the Firehouse ten blocks away. Moments later he burst into the house brandishing a long double-headed axe. He hurtled up the stairs two at a time and, with one furious stroke, broke through the panel nearest the lock. Nena and Pete pushed past the shattered door and lifted their unconscious younger brother, Freddie, out of the tub. His body was so white that it might have been made of wax. He looked like the statue of Jesus that I had seen in the church with his head to one side slumped in the arms of his apostles.

They carried him to the bed in the back bedroom and chafed his face and chest just as Nena had done since he was an infant. Slowly, Freddie came out of the weak spell. From then on, Nena made him promise not to take such hot baths. "And for Christ's sake, Freddie," Pete growled, "whatever you do, don't fill the tub up so high."

Nena was an inveterate storyteller. Often after regaling me with some funny song or long-forgotten anecdote, she would sigh,

If only these walls had tongues, the tales they would tell!

Especially on rainy days, I often sat on the stairs beneath the square stained-glass window. Unable to go outdoors, I amused myself by tinting my hands and arms with the reflected crimson, blue and yellow light. Sometimes when I tired of the game of the many-splendored glass, I whispered in my softest voice to the wallpaper on the staircase wall. It had large burgundy cabbage roses flowering profusely on a cream ground. Remembering my mother's words, I begged them over and again to tell me their stories. I cupped my ear to the roses, but ever faithful and staunch, not once did the wine-dark blossoms reveal the wondrous scenes they had witnessed.

Between spirits that rocked tables, intuition that was life saving, and walls that withheld secrets, the invisible world of 41 Sycamore Avenue was shot through with magic and mystery.

As I grew older, the palpable world presented its own marvels: Nena Balzac was a movie buff who took me to see films two or three times a week. In addition, every Saturday I was permitted to go to the Floral Theatre for the kid's matinee—two feature films separated by cartoons, a newsreel, coming attractions and, on occasion, a serial. Saturday afternoons were quiet in Floral Park. Almost all the children were at the movies from 1 until 4:30 P.M. During the forties, the second feature was often a horror film. Some parents did not permit their offspring to see these Poe-Stevenson-Stoker-inspired studies in terror, but Nena Balzac, daughter of Pepìn, never censured the Saturday offerings.

Only once when I was eight did I have a nightmare. That afternoon the Floral Theatre was proud to present the now classic film, *Isle of the Dead* (1945) in which a young woman falls into a catatonic trance. The family doctor erroneously pronounces her deceased. Prepared for funeral rites in a long white gown, the lady awakens immured in a coffin inside a damp mausoleum. Claustrophobic and now totally insane, she exerts demonic strength and breaks out of the nailed-down bier. In her billowing white shroud, she comes sweeping across a desolate island on a windy, dark night to take revenge on those who had prematurely interred her.

My mother had just put up new white lace curtains in my room. August winds caused them to rustle and blow not unlike the lady's flowing burial clothes. When uncharacteristically I woke up screaming, Nena rushed to my bedside. Trembling and sobbing, I tried to describe the nightmare.

"The curtains, Mommy, the curtains! I thought she was coming back from the dead to get me."

My mother rocked me in her arms:

> *Dee Dee, Dee Dee, don't be afraid. Nothing can harm you at 41. Don't you know there are only kind spirits in this house?*

𝔅ill 𝔕evisited

> *Of studye took he most cure and heede.*
> *Nought oo° word spak he more than was neede*   °one
> *And that was said in forme and reverence,*
> *And short and quik, and ful of heigh sentence:*
> *Souning° in moral vertu was his speeche,*   °resounding
> *And gladly wolde he lerne, and gladly teche.*
> —Geoffrey Chaucer, *Canterbury Tales*

In 1935, Bill graduated from Sewanhaka High School at the head of his class. Initially, he was frustrated in his desire to attend college. Applying to a number of New York area universities, he had been named an alternate for a full scholarship at St. John's University in Queens. The principal of Sewanhaka was almost as disappointed as Bill. He wrote a masterful letter to St. John's for Bill and was assured that if the young man reapplied the next year, he would almost certainly receive financial help.

Wisely, Bill stayed on at Sewanhaka for a post-graduate year. If he continued to achieve high grades in Latin, Spanish, Calculus and Physics—courses that he would have taken in his first year of college in any case—the University would look favorably on his application for financial aid. Scholarships were hard to come by in the middle of the Depression; nevertheless, St John's granted a full tuition, four-year scholarship to an ecstatic William Daniel Balzac in September 1936. Dad, the principal, Edna Fenty and the whole family were overjoyed for him.

The only wrinkle in an otherwise brilliant college career came when a Professor of Anthropology told Bill privately that he was a throwback to a primitive man. Always sensitive about his unusual skin color and exotic features, Bill went into a psychological tailspin.

In the fall of 1937, Bill was invited to a Halloween costume party. Still smarting from his teacher's obtuse comment, he went to the affair dressed as Sax Rohmer's Fu Manchu, the villain of a series of 1920s and 1930s films starring Harry Agar Lyons, Warner Oland and Boris Karloff successively in the title role. Bill bought a long black coat, bowler and walking stick at a second-hand store, grew a goatee and, aside from the "cat-green" eyes, resembled the evil doctor to a tee. When asked to identify himself at the party, Bill quoted the squib: "I am the man called Fu Manchu/ I am a greater menace than you/ I kill just to have something to do."

Even darker than the limerick, Rohmer's description of his character stressed his scoundrel's prodigious intellectuality:

> Imagine a person, tall, lean and feline, high-shouldered, with a brow like Shakespeare and a face like Satan, a close-shaven skull, and long, magnetic eyes of the true cat-green. Invest him with all the cruel cunning of an entire Eastern race, accumulated in one giant intellect, with all the resources of science past and present. Imagine that awful being, and you have a mental picture of Dr. Fu-Manchu, the yellow peril incarnate in one man.
>
> —Sax Rohmer, *The Insidious Dr. Fu Manchu*

Nor did Bill put the costume away after the party. He wore the whole outfit for months and posed rather grandly for photographs of himself in full regalia. Impersonating "that awful being" didn't bode well for the way that Bill was thinking about himself. Did he really see Dr. Fu Manchu, "with a brow like Shakespeare and a face like Satan," as an alter ego? What diabolically evil act had he committed?

In 1937, Bill was boarding with Edna Fenty, and after a while, his outlandish garb no longer amused her. To her credit, she insisted that he shave and resume ordinary dress.

Things seemed to right themselves when Bill took a course in Ancient Philosophy and became an admirer of the Stoics, especially Epictetus and Marcus Aurelius. Epictetus appealed to Bill's Catholic background. There is nothing aside from the will that is good or bad, the 1st century A. D. Greek taught; true education consists in the proper use of the will. In so far as man is reasonable, he partakes of the nature of the godhead, and when he exerts reason or will correctly, his own self-interest acts on behalf of the larger social group.

Bill was also moved by Marcus Aurelius' *Meditations:* the goal to be aimed at, the Roman general believed, is tranquility achieved through wisdom, justice, fortitude and moderation in all things. He who obeys reason, "the divinity within a man," will attain tranquility of mind. At least during his later years at St. John's and especially after the death of his father, Bill seemed to everyone who knew him to embody these principles.

In 1939 when Dad died, though my mother was the oldest child, Bill became the head of the family. In pre-law classes, he had learned enough to serve as executor of his father's estate. He prepared all the paperwork for Probate Court and divided Dad's assets so equitably that not one of his five ofttimes fractious brothers and sisters had cause to complain. In so doing, Bill saved the family expensive legal fees.

Ingenuously, Della asked Nena if Bill really was a genius. So sure was Nena about her brother's exceptional abilities that she didn't bother to answer. In truth, all his siblings were in awe of Bill's knowledge and judgment.

Out of the proceeds of Dad's modest life insurance policy, Bill paid for the funeral, and with the remaining monies, saw to it that each one of his brothers and sisters received about $1500 in hand. He put fourteen-year-old Freddie's portion into an escrow account; by the time the boy was eighteen, it would have accrued almost enough to pay for his college education, if Freddie so chose.

In accordance with Dad's final will and testament, the house (free of a mortgage since 1935) and the lots in Hampton Bays were deeded to all six children. Bill convinced them not to sell the properties which would continue to increase in value. Most importantly, as long as any of them needed a roof over their heads, 41 Sycamore Avenue would be there. He especially wanted to ensure that Freddie would always have a home. Clearly, the house would never be sold while Bill was alive.

Over the years, at various times Della, Nena, Pete and their families as well as Freddie and Bill lived there. Joe was the only heir who never came back to Sycamore Avenue, and though he would have benefited from the sale of the real estate, he raised no objection. As far as his brothers and sisters were concerned, the power and integrity of Bill's person gave his decrees the weight of law.

The next year, 1940, Bill was named valedictorian of his class and graduated *Summa cum Laude* from St. John's University. He had majored in History and taken a minor in Classics. He was elected to *Phi Kappa Phi*, the honorary English society, and to *Phi Beta Kappa*. Originally he had intended to go on to law school but became disenchanted, as he put it, "with learning to steal from widows and orphans." With his share of his father's estate, in September 1940, Bill enrolled in Columbia

University's Graduate Program for the Master's Degree in English. He envisioned going on for the Ph. D. with college teaching as an eventual goal.

He would have made a great teacher. He loved to explain things and could be enormously patient doing so—especially with children. The Fenty boys and I were his most ardent pupils.

One morning in the spring of 1941 when I was four, Bill and I were in the back yard feeding Pete's homing pigeons. They surrounded us cooing and pecking at the grain we were broadcasting.

As we came back from their coop, Bill found a baby robin with a broken wing on the ground. It had fallen out of its nest in a cherry tree near the house. The poor thing was terrified. As Bill held it in his hand, I could see its chest thumping with fear. He sent me for some adhesive tape and improvised a splint with a piece of an ice cream popsicle stick. Then he carefully placed the fledgling under an old abandoned car seat that Pete had left by the stoop. Backed up between the stairs and the cellar wall, the car seat protected the bird from the weather and from cats. Warning me not to handle the bird, Bill explained that it could die of fright.

It was my daily job to bring the bird little pieces of shredded lettuce and cooked rice and to dig up worms if I could find them. I was also to give it fresh water in a small shallow dish. Within a week, the bird had become quite tame though Bill did not allow me to touch it. Together he and I checked the bird's progress for about ten days. By then, when we moved the seat, it was hopping and flailing its bandaged wing, so he carefully removed the splint. I was to continue to feed it and set out water daily until we were sure that the wing had healed.

Then one morning when I went out to give the robin some bread crumbs, it was no longer there. Bill said it had flown away. I was crushed to have lost my pet.

"But Dee Dee, that's why we splinted the wing in the first place," he reminded me. In an instant my feeling changed from disappointment to awe, and I looked upon my uncle in a new light. He had saved the bird, and it was a wondrous thing.

"There was a time," Freddy mused later, "when my brother Bill could do no wrong."

1941

> *How sleep the brave who sink to rest*
> *By all their country's wishes blest!*
> *There Honor comes, a pilgrim gray,*
> *To bless the turf that wraps their clay,*
> *And Freedom shall awhile repair,*
> *To dwell a weeping hermit there!*
> —William Collins, *Ode Written*
> *in the Beginning of the Year 1746*

Nena was sure that her daughter had been born under a romantic star. Throughout the fall, the newspapers had been full of stories about Edward VIII, King of England, and his American companion, Mrs. Wallis (Wally) Simpson. Would the Royal Family, the Prime Minister, the Archbishop of Canterbury and Parliament allow the King to marry a commoner and a divorcée to boot? Or would he finally give her up? At last, in December 1936, a few days after my birth, Edward VIII renounced his throne for the woman he loved. It was an act of extraordinary devotion, Nena commented sighing, and most of the civilized world agreed.

Five years later, however, even Nena Balzac had to concede that early December had lost all its romantic connotations.

The night before my fifth birthday, my mother tucked me in under the covers in the unheated yellow bedroom at the top of the stairs.

> *Tomorrow is your birthday,* she said as she kissed me good night.

The next morning, a bright clear Sunday, I woke up happily. "Tomorrow is today," I said to myself. Having bathed me and washed my hair, my mother brought me downstairs in my new white slip. She sat me on the enamel drain board of the kitchen sink to comb my hair. Finally getting out the last of the knots and tangles, she deftly turned the fine auburn strands around her finger and stuck a bobby pin in each sausage curl. With my hands straight up, she slid my dress over my head making sure not to disturb the curls. The taffeta party dress, with tiny green and black checks, had a large square white collar trimmed in lace. She carefully tied a bow in the wide black velvet sash. The unaccustomed silky stiffness of the material "swooshed" when I walked. It was very fancy.

> *Now go sit on the front porch in the sun, and dry up. Don't get your new clothes dirty, and don't play with Teddy. You'll get dog hair all over you, my mother warned. I'll clean up the breakfast things and get dressed, and off we'll go to Aunt Jenny's.*

Unlike her brother Pete, Mommy didn't really like dogs. They tracked in dirt and were always licking themselves, Nena said, making a face. She did allow faithful Teddy Balzac to sleep in the cellar in bad weather, however, and when my grandfather was alive, he insisted that Teddy be allowed on the front porch where he would curl up next to Pepìn's chair. The dog had been devoted to him, and as I grew, I liked to think, Teddy had transferred that devotion to me.

When I was an infant my mother would place me in my carriage on the front walk and tell Teddy to stay. Not even Herbie, the mailman, who knew and liked the dog, could approach the house. He'd have to call to my mother from the street. "Nena, Nena, Teddy won't let me get to the mailbox. Can you come take your letters?"

The morning that I started kindergarten, Teddy accompanied my mother and me to the John Lewis Childs School. Every morning thereafter he would walk with me watching with his head cocked as I entered the huge red brick building. In the afternoon, the dog would come loping up Elizabeth Street to meet me as I was coming home just as he had met Pepìn on his way from work.

After my grandfather died, Teddy missed him terribly. The dog cried so to be allowed on the porch that my mother relented.

That's where he was this morning lying in a patch of sunlight. He was 13, and though he had no white hairs on his muzzle, his joints ached in damp weather. When I climbed into Grandpa's Morris chair, the huge red Chow-Shepherd got up expecting me to pet him. But he lay down again with a soft groan when I ignored him. "I can't pet you today, Teddy. Mommy says I'll get dirty."

The hardest part about birthdays was to sit still so you didn't muss anything up. The second hardest part was waiting. All my big presents would be at Aunt Jenny's and Uncle George's house in Bellerose, a mile away. Aunt Jenny was my father's oldest sister, the first born of seven children. Then after my dad, came Aunts Lee, Mary (now married to Pete Balzac), Claire, Palma and Uncle Frankie. Out of respect for my father, Aunt Jenny had made me a cake and invited their entire Italian family and assorted consorts and friends for coffee.

Soon after Jenny and George had moved into their new brick-fronted cape in 1939, my uncle had finished the basement. It had two large adjoining rooms with a full kitchen and a huge table. In the living room area stood a wicker couch, end tables and two easy chairs. All the big family gatherings were held there. Aunt Jenny could seat ten adults comfortably after having served the kids—her three daughters, her friend's girl, a neighbor's child and me—on a first shift.

My mother appreciated Jenny's thoughtfulness regarding my birthday but had difficulty understanding her in-laws.

(*These Italians,* she'd say to me when my father and his sister, Mary were out of hearing range, *I don't get it. They finally buy a pretty house, and then they live in the cellar and never use their living room or dining room at all)!*

My childhood, I realized later, was lived on the brink of an ethnic Continental Divide.

As I was anticipating the day to come on the front porch at 41, Uncle Pete and Aunt Mary came downstairs with their one-year-old baby, Lenore. "Happy Birthday, Dee," they called onto the porch. Then Uncle Freddie, 17, came out to greet me. "Happy birthday, gremlin," he said with a little grin. They all slept late on Sunday mornings.

I adored my Balzac relatives. In the evening Uncle Bill was coming over from the Fenty's for my second party. Tia Fidela and Aunt Rosa would bring a big cake from the Nabisco Company. And Mommy had invited Uncle Joe, Aunt Anne and my 11 year-old cousin, Jo Jo, to stop by. Uncle Joe would play his records, and everyone would sing, dance, tell jokes and recite poetry. All the Balzacs would congregate—except Aunt Della, Uncle Jim and little Jimmy who had moved to South Jersey and were talking about leaving the East Coast permanently for California.

Even after my parents sent me to bed tonight, I planned to sneak back down with bare feet and sit on the stairs as I always did, scrunched up against the banister so that I wouldn't be discovered. The third step from the top of the staircase was just above the kitchen door. My perch in the dark was like the loge of the Floral Theatre after the lights went down. From there, as if I were at the movies or at a play, I could listen to all the gay chatter coming from the kitchen and the parlor.

My daydreams finally came to an end when Mommy called. She took the bobby pins out of my curls, gave them a swipe with the brush and announced to my father that we were ready to go to Bellerose. He had spent much of the morning washing and polishing his old black Dodge, then had come in to change into his Sunday clothes. As we drove to Bellerose all dressed up, even the car seemed in birthday mode.

It was mayhem at my Aunt Jenny's. Everybody was there—my grandfather, Papa, his seven grown children with husbands, wives, boyfriends, friends and kids. The adults outdid each other shouting to be heard, sometimes engaging in two conversations at once. Children were running around the kitchen playing tag and having a wild time even as Aunt Jenny made coffee and Aunt Lee set the table.

> (*Such noise! It gives me a headache,* Nena always complained after her in-laws' gatherings).

My father's family was big on kissing. When we came in, I had to greet everyone and kiss them starting with my Italian grandfather. I winced as Papa invariably pinched my cheeks saying they were like ripe apples. By the time he had finished mauling me, my cheeks looked like *arancie de sangue,* blood oranges. Then in the middle of the party as I opened up my presents, I had to thank each of my benefactors and kiss them in turn again. At last, when the party was over and my mother and father decided to go home, I would be obliged to say goodbye and kiss everyone once more. Sometimes it took ten minutes to leave.

(*Too many germs*, Nena whispered curling her lip in disdain).

Kisses showed respect, numerous Italian-American relatives informed me. *La famiglia* was big on respect, too. (In contrast, the Balzacs were not as demonstrative as my father's family. They knew I was happy to see them, and I didn't have to prove it).

My Aunt Jenny was always thoughtful and gentle with me, as if to offset my grandfather's brusqueness. She and Uncle George had festooned the cellar with criss-crossing strands of twisted pink and white crepe paper and had taped different colored balloons at every junction. Even the metal support posts, like feminized barbershop poles, were covered with pink and white crepe paper spirals.

Once the party began and the kids settled down, Aunt Jenny had me sit at the head of the table in front of a white sheet cake beautifully decorated with butter cream roses and buds on green stems. In flowing pink letters, she had inscribed on it "Happy 5th Birthday, Dee". To the side of my chair stood a pile of presents wrapped prettily, each crowned with a big fabric bow to be saved and worn in my hair during the next year. As my aunt placed six candles on the cake (five for my years and one to grow on) and lit them, my uncles, aunts, cousins and guests gathered noisily around the table and sang "Happy Birthday." I knelt on the chair to reach the cake, made a silent wish that I would receive a doll carriage for Christmas and, inhaling as deeply as possible, blew out all the candles at once. They clapped and whistled.

Then Aunt Jen inverted a wide-mouthed glass over the center of the cake and pulled out a perfectly round portion. "That's your piece for tomorrow. Don't forget to take it home with you." She gave me a big knife, guiding my hand to cut the first piece. That slice went to Papa to show respect. She dished out cake and a slice of vanilla, chocolate and strawberry ice cream cut from a half gallon "Neapolitan brick." (At my Aunt Jenny's, even the ice cream was Italian). Then she poured big glasses of cream soda for each of the children.

The soda, especially, was a great treat served only on holidays and at gala celebrations. Authorities on both sides of the family had told us that it was bad for our teeth, but cream soda was so delicious that we saved it for last, savoring every drop and not caring if our whole mouth rotted. After we finished, the adults would sit down, and I would open my presents.

While Aunt Jenny and Aunt Claire were clearing and resetting the table, Uncle George decided to put on the radio for some music. But as he quickly tuned in to station after station, he found only news programs. The networks didn't seem to be broadcasting any music at all. That was very strange. What was going on? He finally stopped turning the dial and listened.

Like a shock wave, his deep voice pierced the family's clamor. "My God, be quiet!" he boomed.

George turned up the volume of the radio. Solemnly a newscaster announced that the Japanese had attacked Pearl Harbor and sunk most of the American fleet. A pall came over the room. Seated at the table, my normally voluble relatives were speechless. The national disaster had struck them mute. George tuned into other stations for more details. Every network was reporting the news that a "sneak" attack had left more than two thousand dead and many injured in Hawaii.

My youngest aunt, Palma, sat at the table with her handsome fiancé Mike. They were to be married in August of 1942.

"This means war," Mike said. I had never seen anyone look so woebegone. Stricken, he took her hand. "Palma, Palma, we'll all go."

"War," "soldiers," "barrage balloons," "fighting" had all been in the newspaper. Though I was in kindergarten, since September my mother had me practice writing by copying the headlines of articles in the *New York Daily News*. As she pared carrots or potatoes at the sink for supper, she kept me occupied at the kitchen table and from time to time would look over at my lined writing tablet.

> *No, Dee Dee. That's a 'b', not a 'd'. Look at the letter again.*

She read the block-letter banners to me, and then I would copy the smaller words.

> *That's right. Keep the letters two spaces high and start on the line.*

I knew most of the sounds and could read some three and four letter words, "war" and "guns" among them. "War" was when soldiers fought with guns. That was war. But what did that mean?

I looked around the room. Seated on the wicker couch and easy chairs, even the children were still, and at the table, my aunts and uncles had barely touched their cake. They were drinking their coffee in silence.

Then my father coughed and cleared his throat. He looked worried. He said we had better be getting home. Then everyone decided to go. One by one, they kissed Papa solemnly and held each other close as they said good bye. My mother helped me gather up my unopened presents. I was bewildered; my party, hardly begun, was over. And there would be no celebration with the Balzacs in the evening. My mother tried to explain, but I just couldn't understand it.

I only knew that on my fifth birthday, December 7, 1941, something terrible had happened. The world, such as we had experienced it and as we thoughtlessly expected it to continue, had suddenly changed forever.

Part 2, Chapter 2
The War Years in Floral Park

These fought in any case,
and some believing,
pro domo, in any case

Some quick to arm,
some for adventure,
some from fear of weakness,
some from fear of censure,
some for love of slaughter, in imagination,
learning later
some in fear, learning love of slaughter
—Ezra Pound, Hugh Selwyn Mauberly

The next day, December 8 at 12:30 p.m., a grim President Franklin Delano Roosevelt addressed a joint session of Congress to request a formal declaration of war against the Japanese Empire. The President called December 7, 1941 "a date which will live in infamy." In addition to Hawaii, Roosevelt went on to list concurrent Japanese attacks on Malaya, Hong Kong, Guam, the Philippines, Wake and Midway Islands—"a surprise offensive extending throughout the Pacific Area."

On Tuesday morning, December 9, two days after the Japanese attack on Pearl Harbor, Bill Balzac and Babe Schuhmacher took the bus to the Jamaica Recruiting Station and volunteered for the Marine Corps.

At 25, Bill was enrolled in his second year of English graduate studies at

Columbia Teachers College. In a surge of patriotic fervor, he decided to drop out of school to enlist. He was in perfect physical shape: he stood 5'9½" and weighed 144 lbs. of pure muscle. Walking on the balls of his feet and taking long, swift strides, he always reminded Nena of a young panther. With copper-colored skin, glossy black hair and heavily lidded eyes, strangers couldn't decide whether he was Oriental or mulatto or Amerindian, but in fact he was quintessentially Puerto Rican, an ethnic type rarely encountered or recognized in 1941.

Bill before the War

The Marines accepted Bill immediately but rejected Babe because he had buckteeth. "I thought I was supposed to shoot our enemies," Babe quipped, "not bite them."

Like a lot of other boys who enlisted, Babe wanted to get away from a bad situation at home. He didn't get along with his father.

At Nena's invitation and to Freddie's delight, Babe had lived at 41 for the whole summer. He was 18. He hadn't considered going into the military before December 7, but overnight, he became gung-ho. Unable to join the Marines, he enlisted in the Army. My mother worried about him:

Just because your first name is the same as Sergeant York's (she had seen the movie), you don't have to go into the service. At least wait until they call you up.

On December 11, three days after President Roosevelt's address, in concert with Japan, Germany and Italy declared war on the United States.

Alvin (Babe) Schuhmacher, 16

They were the Axis.

(For a long time, I had trouble reading that word confusing it with "axes").

Once Italy entered the fray, the Italian side of the family became uneasy: Papa, Aunt Jenny, my father and Palma were not citizens. Jenny was 7 and my father an infant in arms when my grandmother sailed from Italy to join Papa in New York. Nine years later, during an extended family visit to Toritto, a small town near Bari, Palma was born. Citizenship was not an issue before the war. Jenny, my father and Palma had all attended school here and considered themselves Americans. Before the war, the U. S. government had referred to them as "resident aliens," but after December 11, they were branded "enemy aliens."

Eventually, just as Palma's Mike had foreseen, all the young men went to war. The Marines sent Bill to Parris Island, South Carolina for boot camp. The Navy drafted Joey and Pete Balzac, Aunt Claire's Jimmy, and Uncle Frankie De Turo. Aunt Lee's Lou and Babe Schuhmacher served in the Army. Somewhat later than the others, my father entered the Sea Bees, a Construction Battalion of the Navy, and received his citizenship papers as he was sworn in. The exceptions were Uncle George, 40, who was too old, Palma's Mike, who received a hardship deferment as the sole support of an aged mother and a passel of younger sisters and brothers and Freddie Balzac, 17, whose heart condition made him 4-F, unfit for duty.

By mid-1942, the population of Floral Park seemed to consist exclusively of old men, women of all ages and children. A year into the war, even the young women were gone until evening, needed for Defense work. They took jobs in the many Long Island airplane and war materiel plants, often leaving home before 7 a.m. dressed in bibbed denim overalls, not returning until 5:30 or 6 p.m. By day, the village seemed almost deserted. Only the elderly, mothers with babies and latchkey children peopled it.

And the War meant:

> *Let it flame or fade, and the war roll down like a wind,*
> *We have proved we have hearts in a cause, we are noble still*
> *It is better to fight for the good than to rail at the ill;*
> *I have felt with my native land, I am one with my kind.*
> —Alfred, Lord Tennyson, *Maud*

- Ya gotta wake up in the dark, but nightfall doesn't arrive until 10 p.m. in the summer because Daylight Saving Time has advanced two hours instead of one

- Ya gotta collect tin cans of any size or condition and foil from cigarette and gum packs for war materiel
- Ya gotta drain all cooking grease for use in explosives and take it to the butcher shop
- Ya gotta put out lights and pull down blackout shades when the air raid sirens begin their deafening wail
- Ya gotta obey the Civil Defense patrol in their white C. D. hard hats should they knock on the door
- Ya gotta "Join the Navy and Free the World", "Build and Fight" in the Sea Bees and answer the Army's "Call to Duty For Home and Country"
- Ya gotta pay attention to the bus and subway placards because "Uncle Sam Needs You" and "We Can Do It", but "Loose Lips Might Sink Ships" since "The Enemy May Be Listening"
- Ya gotta understand that "Silence Means Security" and there's "No Room for Rumors"
- Ya gotta bring 25 cents a week to school for War Bonds stamps because "United We Stand"
- Ya gotta expect mail from soldiers to have heavily inked-out passages marked "Censored"
- Ya gotta learn a whole new vocabulary—Allies, Axis, censorship, C.D., *ersatz*, latchkey, *Messerschmitts*, materiel, profiteering, rationing, Rosie the Riveter, *semper fi*, Zeros—and a formerly unknown geography—Anzio, the Ardennes, Burma, Chungking, Coventry, Dresden, Dunkirk, Monte Casino, Nanking, Okinawa, Tobruk, Truk
- Ya gotta plant a Victory garden—"Grow Your Own, Can Your Own"—even if you've got a black thumb and have never boiled water

- Ya gotta use ration stamps for soap, sugar, butter, meat, gasoline, cigarettes, shoes
- Ya gotta eat Spam and Velveta, make hash from canned corned beef and *ersatz* coffee from chicory, drink Ovaltine instead of Hershey's cocoa, and when there's no butter, color margarine with a pouch-full of yellow dye
- Ya gotta chop and grind cuts of beef at home because some dishonest butchers lace hamburger with cereal and even with horsemeat
- Ya gotta do without chocolate, silk stockings, new tires for the car, rubber-soled shoes
- Ya gotta take care of the chickens and clean out the coop because eggs can be exchanged for butter and sugar
- Ya gotta barter cigarette and gasoline ration stamps for soap and meat stamps
- Ya gotta save lids of ice cream cups and memorize the outlines printed on them of airplanes and ships, both Allied and Axis
- Ya gotta know that beaches, surrounded by barbed wire, close at night so soldiers can watch for enemy submarines cruising in Long Island waters
- Ya gotta love the Andrew Sisters and the Jitterbug and our boys in uniform and pompadours and pin-up girls
- Ya gotta dread seeing the Western Union car on your block and pray that the driver isn't delivering a telegram from the War Department
- Ya gotta be respectful to Gold Star Mothers who've lost a son
- Ya gotta grieve as more and more blue silk rectangles with Gold Stars hang in porch windows or on the front doors of Floral Park homes

- Ya gotta mourn Carole Lombard and Glenn Miller and John Lewis Childs II and Vinnie Raphael from Charles Street and Eugene Gladd killed over Rangoon and gentle Babe Schuhmacher shot dead in the Battle of the Bulge, both from Sycamore Avenue

The Mineola Fair

There are in our existence spots of time
Which with distinct pre-eminence retain
A vivifying Virtue, whence
        our minds
Are nourish'd and invisibly repair'd...
Such moments worthy of all gratitude,
Are scattered everywhere, taking their date
From our first childhood: in our childhood even
Perhaps are most conspicuous.
—William Wordsworth, *The Prelude*, Book XII

With its 200-day, frost-free growing season and proximity to New York City, Long Island once was a huge and lucrative truck farming area. In the spring, families organized forays to strawberry and blueberry "U-Pick 'em" farms, to peach and apple orchards to collect windfalls. On the way, one saw field after field planted with corn, tomatoes and spinach. By late summer throughout Nassau and Western Suffolk, these crops yielded to acres of cauliflower, broccoli, cabbage, squash and pumpkins. On the East End, odiferous chicken, duck and turkey farms competed with potato fields—some planted within steps of the sand dunes fronting the Atlantic Ocean.

Though much of this produce was trucked into the city or sold to large grocery chains like the A&P or Bohack's, for the very freshest vegetables and fruit, locals frequented one or more of the numerous seasonal farm stands. Since 1865, the County Fair in Mineola had celebrated this agricultural embarrassment of riches and was considered so important that schools in Nassau declared a half-day recess to allow students to attend.

My mother and I had gone to the Fair every year for as long as I could remember, but in September 1944, Nena was a lead man at Sperry's in Lake Success. Before working in Defense, she had had little job experience, but having worked six months at Bohack's without a raise, Nena decided to put in an application at Sperry's for a job as a riveter. To her surprise, she scored 92 on their placement test, and they hired her on the spot. My mother's only concern was about me. She wouldn't be home until 5:30 p.m. Could I manage for 2 hours after school? Of course I could—just give me the key. I could care for myself until she got home, finish my homework, have a snack, do whatever shopping was needed and even start supper on occasion.

At Sperry's, despite being terrified at first, Nena quickly adapted to wearing overalls, reading blueprints and riveting airplane bodies. Her foreman, Roy, a likable older man, appreciated her competence and geniality. She was no flibbertigibbet, he told her. Within a few months, he put her name in for promotion to "lead man" in charge of a crew of four girls. My mother loved her work, her crew and her foreman and, since getting the job, had never been late or absent.

Nena was curiously silent when I excitedly told her that on the coming Friday I would have a half-day holiday from school.

> *Dee, I've been dreading the end of September. I'm sorry to tell you this, but you can't go the Mineola Fair this year. I can't get off from work to take you. Please try to understand.*

I did understand, but there was no reason why I couldn't go to the Fair without Nena. I was almost 8 and big for my age. And I knew how to get there. I'd just walk to the city line on Hillside Avenue, pay my fare and ask for a transfer. Then in East Williston, I'd take a second bus to Mineola. I knew how. Hadn't I been taking buses to Bellerose and Queens for two years and to Aunt Jenny's since the war began?

And if I was big enough to shop for food and sundries and stay by myself in the afternoon, then I could surely go to Mineola and have a good time. I knew how to be careful about money—had I ever lost a dime when sent to the store?

Besides, Miss Martin, my art teacher, had selected two of my paintings for the John Lewis Childs School exhibit. I wanted to see them. And it wasn't right—every other kid in the county would be going to the Fair.

For the next seven days, I wheedled and cajoled, argued and reasoned, pleaded and begged until my mother reluctantly agreed that I could go. The wildly anticipated morning of the Fair proved to be sunny and cool with a blue cloudless sky, a typical late September day on Long Island. Much against her better judgment, Nena counted out two dollars (a fortune!) in nickels, dimes and quarters and knotted them in a handkerchief that she tied to the belt of my dress.

> *Don't forget to ask for a transfer when you board. Don't talk to the bus driver or to strangers. As soon as you get there, price the rides and the food. Plan what you are going to spend in advance. Be sure to save enough money for the return fare. Watch the time and take the 4:10 p.m. bus home.*

She had repeated the same directions twelve times. I knew how to go and what to do, and I would follow her instructions to the letter. I promised.

Nena finally left for work, and I went to school counting the minutes until lunch when I could set out. Before walking the half-mile to the city line, I carefully took 15 cents out of the handkerchief for the fare, got the bus to East Williston and transferred to Mineola with no difficulty.

The fairgrounds went on for blocks, the high chain-link fences surrounding them flying 4-H, Kiwanis and Rotary pennants, New York State, Nassau County and American flags from every post. Band music was coming indistinctly from a far-off grandstand, and intermittently over the buzzing of the crowds, I could hear the tinkling tunes of the merry-go-round's calliope. As I hurried from the bus stop, I peered through the fence longing for my adventure to begin. Directly down a broad unpaved lane stood a dozen white clapboard exhibition halls, and beyond and above them far down the Mid-way, a huge Ferris wheel circled in the air. Even from outside the Fair, I could sense that a great festival was taking place.

Not far from the bus stop at the entryway, schoolchildren with their mothers and teachers had massed outside two ticket booths. I joined the line and waited impatiently as it slowly moved forward. At last I got to one of the windows and gave the woman attendant a quarter. She stamped the back of my hand with ink—the mark proved that I had paid the child's admission fee. Overjoyed, I almost skipped through the turnstile waving my hand in front of a Nassau County policeman who checked it as I passed. Hooray, I had made it! I was at the Fair!

I planned my afternoon: first, following Nena's directions, I noted the prices of the food and rides. I had $1.60 left in my handkerchief. I would spend 10 cents for cotton candy, get tickets for 3 rides—they cost 35 cents apiece or 3 for $1—have a hot dog for a quarter and a drink for a dime. That would leave 15 cents for the bus. Perfect.

With my accounts in order, I headed for the exhibition halls. First, I'd visit them and the animal stalls, then look through the food concessions for a cotton candy machine. After that I'd watch the would-be sportsmen and gamblers playing games of chance, but I wouldn't spend any money there. Mommy said they were gyps. Instead, I'd go down the Mid-way to the rides and stop for a frankfurter and a soda just before I left the Fair. I'd keep an eye on the clocks in the exhibition halls or ask some nice young girl with a watch for the time. Then, I'd board the bus, get a transfer and be home before Nena walked in the door.

The first building was reserved for school displays. The children's artwork varied from school to school and included crayon and ink sketches, oil and watercolor paintings, sand sculptures, collages, pottery and Kachina Navaho and Hopi dolls carved from blocks of balsam wood. In grades 5-8 countywide, boys were obliged to take Industrial Arts and girls, Homemaking, a program that included sewing. Part of the exhibit contained boys' cutting boards, bookcases and coffee tables and girls' neatly done aprons, slips, skirts and weskits. The craftsmanship was fine.

The John Lewis Childs exhibit contained examples of the best artwork from every grade. Miss Martin had framed the 3rd Grade drawings with variously colored construction paper. I was surprised to see how professional they looked and delighted that she had framed both of my efforts in purple, my favorite color.

Satisfied that I had seen all the offerings of the schools, I next went to a building that had long tables laden with fruit and vegetables for public viewing. Judges had already awarded coveted blue, red and white ribbons to plate after plate of deserving tomatoes, squash, apples, string beans, potatoes and pumpkins—some labeled with an individual gardener's name, some with the name of the farm that had produced them. The pumpkin that took best in the show must have weighed seventy-five pounds—it was huge.

At the hall that housed baked goods, I had a grand time tasting everything with my eyes. Apple, cherry, blueberry and old-fashioned rhubarb pies were placed on tables with one slice removed to reveal the delicacy of the crust and the amount and juiciness of the filling.

I thought they looked appetizing until I spied the display of pound cakes, layer cakes and tortes towards the back of the building. The 7-layer cake that won a blue ribbon had chocolate fondant icing, mocha butter cream between the layers of yellow sponge cake and a sprinkling of finely chopped green pistachio nuts all around the base. It was beautiful. The lady who baked it really should have been proud of herself.

The next hall had dozens of quilts on display. Two older women from a church group were sitting at a table just inside the building. They were demonstrating the craft as their fellow parishioner, a younger woman, sold raffles for a red and white Log Cabin quilt on the wall behind them. People must have really liked it because she was doing a brisk business. I didn't buy a raffle, but I hung around watching the women as they swiftly stitched squares onto a quilting frame in front of them. They were so precise and quick—they made the work look easy.

There must have been more than a hundred pieces of crewel, petit point, embroidery, knitting and crochet in the Needlework hall, and scores of vases of flowers and floral arrangements—some for sale—in yet another building.

I looked at the clock. It was already 2:30 p.m. I would have hurry to the open pens beyond the exhibition halls if I wanted to see at least one competition of 4-H farm animals.

Turkeys, geese and ducks were clucking and quacking each in their own
cage as I approached the animal enclosures, but I particularly wanted to look over the Rhode Island Reds to see if any compared with Chanticleer, our proud, deep-breasted rooster at home. My mother really should have exhibited him—he would have taken first place

hands down, easily out-strutting and out-crowing Wicks Farm's blue ribbon winner.

I merely glanced at the soft-eyed dairy cows and pink piglets nuzzling an enormous reclining sow because a livestock judge was about to evaluate a group of prize female goats. Eight 4-H kids, some visibly nervous, were leading their carefully curried animals twice around a ring as a lady expert sternly examined both the children and their beasts. A sizeable audience had gathered to see how well the youngsters controlled their very lively pets.

Once the boys and girls came to a stop and had their animals stand in place, they spread the goats' back legs a bit so that the judge could compare the animals' milk bags for size. When the blue ribbon went to a spirited black and white female, the crowd applauded, and the 14-year-old who was exhibiting her flushed with pride. I even liked the red ribbon winner, a delicate white goat who obeyed her mistress' every motion. Who ever thought that goats could be cute?

But now I had to get going. I hurried towards the food concessions on my way to the rides. The crowds were getting thicker as the afternoon progressed, and many fairgoers were having a late lunch. At one large pavilion under a striped awning, older men were shucking Long Island oysters and clams and serving them on the half shell. At least twenty people stood on line. At another popular stand, two elderly men with chef's hats were hard at work grilling Italian sausage, peppers and onions for hero sandwiches. Not far from them, a fat blonde man and a skinny woman were selling steamed Polish kielbasa on a roll, and beyond that booth was a barbecued chicken concession outfitted with tables and chairs inside a large tent.

Hungry diners could buy New England clam chowder, oyster stew and homemade pea soup with Canadian bacon, French fried potatoes and deep-fried onion rings, roasted corn-on-the-cob, pizza, hot dogs and sauerkraut, sodas and beer. The aromas of the braised meats, savory soups and sizzling vegetables blended with syrupy sweet smells coming from candied apples, Belgian waffles, and caramel popcorn. A Good Humor man handed out ices, Dixie cups and Cho-Cho pops[34] to a bunch of kids. Finally, I caught sight of a cotton candy machine spinning pink fluff. I bought a bouffant cloud of it for a dime and began eating small pieces—happily getting all sticky as I headed for the Mid-way ticket booth.

I spent a dollar on three tickets and went directly to the Merry-Go-Round. I really was too big, I thought, for such baby stuff, but I loved the hurdy-gurdy music and enjoyed watching the little kids' responses to the circling motion of the carousel. The littlest children rode pretty red, black and tan stationary horses with bright saddles, and mothers with toddlers sat in swan boats painted with water lilies and roses. A five-year-old called out "Hi-yo, Silver!" imagining he was the galloping Lone Ranger as his majestic steed went up and down on its brass pole.

Nearby, a young woman held a three-year-old boy on a Pinto. When the carousel began to move and the calliope started up, he threw his head back—laughing and getting dizzy watching the painted ponies on the inside of the roof. I chose a Palomino with flaring nostrils and a golden mane. Round and round we pranced, swirls of color on a ride into wonderland. Suddenly, the music ended, the magical machine stopped and my reverie jolted to a finish.

With some regret, I jumped off the platform of the Merry-Go-Round and stood on line for the Caterpillar, twelve cars on a circular, unevenly slanted and bumpy track with a segmented canvas top that lay folded as the ride began. Couples hurried to get on as I climbed into a car big enough for two or three. When no other singles came, the attendant slammed the safety bar down across my seat and turned on the motor.

Slowly at first, the car jostled to one side, then the other, and picking up speed, the canopy overhead began to enclose and then completely cover the entire railway. Inside the belly of the beast, it was pitch black and scary as the forward speed increased, and the undulating movement up, around and to the sides accelerated. The whole machine was wiggling and whirling faster and faster, and riders were screaming as centrifugal force pressed them tightly against the backrest of the cars.

I screamed, too, holding fast to the bar. We must have gone ten times around nearly flying, over one hump, then another, before the Caterpillar came to a rest and the convertible top slowly opened. Exhilarated but half-blinded by the brightness of the sunshine, I staggered down the wooden steps behind the ride.

Across the way was another long line facing the huge spindly Ferris wheel—for me, the most frightening of all the amusements. This time when it was my turn to sit in one of the swinging seats, the operator told me to stand aside for a minute. He seated two couples as I waited, and then a woman and a teenaged girl approached. He asked if I could ride with them—he didn't like to put little kids on the wheel alone. I was somewhat offended at being called "a little kid," but the lady was gracious, and I joined her and her daughter.

As other riders took their places in the car below, we went up—coming to a sharp halt that made the seat rock back and forth. It wasn't so bad moving in mid-air and looking down when we were only three or four cars up, but as we got closer and closer to the top of the wheel, each jarring stop made me regret having eaten my cotton candy so quickly. The view was magnificent—I could look out over the whole of Mineola but looking directly down was terrifying.

The wheel began to move in earnest without interruptions, and the ground seemed to recede from us at fifty miles an hour. My heart skipped a beat as we plunged downwards. Then almost reaching the loading platform, I could breathe again. In an eye-blink, we were flying up and over, backwards and forward, again and again many times.

The jerking soon began once more as the operator unloaded a set of passengers, an action that left us stranded at the very top. We were up so high. An entire little world lay beneath our involuntarily swaying feet. Finally, after repeated stops, we approached level ground. As we waited for the operator to stabilize our car and release its safety bar, I thanked the lady and asked her for the time. It was already 3:30, and I had had a great day.

No time to watch a soldier on leave impressing his girl as he shot mechanical ducks swimming across the back of a booth jammed with pennants, stuffed animals and Kewpie dolls on a stick. No time to see fellows tossing coins at the penny pitch or throwing hoops over square columns. No time left to stare at burly middle-aged guys trying to sledge hammer a weight up a column to ring a bell or to gape at older men and women playing the roulette wheel for money.

Now I was hungry. I would eat a hot dog and drink a soda as I exited the Fair grounds on the way to the bus stop. Close by, I found a van with a fold down shelf, took out my last two quarters and waited as a man in a white kepi served five or six adults. The shelf was high, but I finally got his attention and ordered. He took my money, leaned over to hand me the frank and placed an orange soda on the shelf.

I could just reach it, but he had forgotten to give me change. I tried to get his attention, but people on line behind me were elbowing their way to the front.

"You didn't give me my change." He was serving someone down at the other end. I called out two or three times, "Please give me 15 cents change."

"Go away, kid. I'm busy. Can't you see people are waiting?"

"But you didn't give me my change."

The man moved to the far side of the van to serve other customers and ignored me. I couldn't get him to look my way, and people were pushing past me. And I wasn't big enough to make myself heard above the shelf.

Upset and running out of time to catch the bus, I began to move towards the entrance to the Fair. At the turnstiles earlier, I remembered the policeman on duty. And I knew what I should do. I'd ask the officer for fifteen cents to get home. Nena had told me that if ever I was in trouble, I should go to a cop. And if I needed money, he would loan it to me.

> *Remember, Dee Dee. Say your mother will send him back the money—return mail. Remember those words—return mail.*

I tried not to panic, but I could feel the tears beginning to well up. I choked them down. I had to get to the turnstiles, find an officer and everything would be O.K.

At 4 p.m., however, masses of people were getting off from work and coming to the Fair.

Throngs of shop girls, high school kids and County Court clerks were streaming onto the grounds as I struggled to get to the entrance. The dust from all the activity of the day seemed to be getting progressively higher as I made my way against the noisy crowd.

The people suddenly looked so big. I scanned all the unfamiliar faces. They were busy talking and didn't even notice me desperately trying to get past them. The entryway seemed so far off, the fairgoers so grotesque and gigantic.

Just as I was beginning to realize how little I was, just as I started to panic in earnest, I thought I heard a voice over the hubbub calling, Dee. Again, someone seemed to be calling, Dee. Was I imagining it? Or had I really heard my name? As workers swarmed past me, I forced my way into the center of the lane searching for the voice. And then I heard it again and knew that my mother was calling me.

I made for the voice like a homing pigeon flying straight to the safety of its coop. Stumbling beyond two talkative girls and some fresh high school boys following them, I saw Nena, still in her overalls and denim jacket. She looked so troubled. She had come straight from work.

"Oh, Mommy, Mommy, I'm so glad you're here." After all the anxiety of the past few moments, I felt relief and joy, gratitude and amazement that she had come and somehow—despite all the people—had found me. And I blurted out how the man had cheated me, but I remembered what to do—go to a policeman and borrow the fare. Suddenly, the words became all jumbled up, and the pent up tears began to flow.

> *Don't cry. Everything is all right. Let's just go home. All morning, I had a bad feeling. Finally, I told Roy. When he saw that I couldn't concentrate on work, he let me leave. And when I got here, I started calling your name as soon as I came through the turnstile. I knew that you would be making your way to the entrance, and I'd find you.*

It was true. My mother really was psychic like everyone said. We climbed on the bus, and my mind "invisibly repair'd," I fell asleep with Nena's comforting arm around me.

* * *

When I was a child, my mother was always there.

[34] A Cho-Cho pop was a delicious malt and cocoa ice cream made by Hood and Co. The ice cream was frozen in cylindrical paper cups decorated with a clown design and brown script and had a Popsicle stick inserted in the center of the lid. One rolled the cylinder between one's palms to remove the cup and inverted it. The lid of the cylinder then became a drip tray for the ice cream pop.

Part 2, Chapter 3
Casualties of War

Ah, love, let us be true
To one another! For the world, which seems
To lie before us like a land of dreams,
So various, so beautiful, so new,
Hath really neither joy, nor love, nor light,
Nor certitude, nor peace, nor help for pain;
And we are here as on a darkling plain
Swept with confused alarms of struggle and
flight,
Where ignorant armies clash by night.
—Matthew Arnold, *Dover Beach*

Not all casualties of war occur on the darkling plain of battle or end with death. The Balzacs endured the war at home or returned from it with bodies intact, but with altered and even maimed sensibilities.

Married since 1928, Joey and Anne Balzac adored their tow-headed 10-year-old, Jo Jo, but had waning affection for one another. For years, Joey had only to greet a female neighbor in the hallway of their apartment building or glance at a girl on the street, and Anne accused him of cheating on her. She read his mail, went through his pockets and flayed him verbally if he was so much as ten minutes late coming home from work or from a Rescue Company meeting at the firehouse. She carped, chided and nagged to such an extent that he had taken to referring to her humorously as his "battle ax" and introducing her as his "future ex-wife."

Whether Joe gave her cause or whether Anne's pathological jealousy drove him into another woman's arms, their marriage was all but over soon after the beginning of the war. In the early days when they were happy, he had sung "Two Sleepy People" to her; he now crooned the old standard, "Seven years with the wrong woman/ Is more than a man can stand,"[35] advancing the number of years on every wedding anniversary. He was up to "fourteen" before their relationship finally fell apart.

Anne's best friend, Marcelle Perry, was the second wife of a wealthy Yonkers manufacturer. She was tall and full-bodied, not really pretty, but her deep voice was calm and her manner reassuring. She was incapable of being a shrew.

Noble Perry was much older than Marcelle. His first wife had died leaving him with two young daughters, Penny and Virginia. At the time, Marcelle was his very competent private secretary. After the death of Mrs. Perry, Marcelle kept the grieving widower on track, running the office with remarkable efficiency, encouraging him to launch a new product line, reminding him of meetings with suppliers and sales reps, even remembering the children's birthdays and shopping for their gifts.

As time passed, Noble found that he couldn't do without Marcelle. Though he was more than twenty years her senior, they respected one another, and respect eventually turned into affection. When he asked her, she agreed to marry him. Unfailingly kind, Marcelle became more than a surrogate mother to Noble's children—they cared for her deeply, and eventually the Perrys had a son, Al.

Anne and Marcelle had been school friends in Yonkers and had stayed in touch after Marcelle married. They spoke on the phone and saw each other regularly. The Perrys entertained frequently, and Anne and Joe were often among the guests. When pretty Virginia finished high school, Anne had the bright idea of bringing Freddie Balzac to the graduation party that Marcelle had arranged for her stepdaughter. Still living at 41 Sycamore Avenue, Freddie was the same age as Virginia. They liked one another, and when Marcelle came from Yonkers to Long Island, she frequently brought Ginny along.

Though she was pleased with her matchmaking, Anne was miserable in her own marriage. She confided in Marcelle, wildly accusing Joe of constant and lascivious deceptions. Eventually, Anne's once private or semi-private incriminations began to overflow in public. Joe countered them with an increasingly embarrassed geniality. Initially sympathetic to Anne, Marcelle came to view Joe as a man more sinned against than sinning. She also found herself passionately drawn to him. As for Joe, Marcelle soon became his Rose of Sharon, Balm of Gilead and honey of Hybla all rolled into one.

The events of 1943 finally justified Anne's incessant suspicions. At a thirty- third birthday party for Joe at Koenig's Restaurant on South Tyson Avenue, he left a message for Marcelle in the bathroom under a box of tissues. Having read the note, Marcelle shredded it and hastily threw it into the toilet. Anne followed her, fished the wet and smeared but still legible pieces of the letter out of the bowl and confronted the lovers. That act signaled the end of two marriages. Joey moved out, but not before Anne made a venomous phone call to Noble Perry vilifying his wife.

Anne caused a terrible scandal–she was, after all, the injured party.

Marcelle was humiliated; she had never intended to hurt Noble or the children. As for Noble, he didn't give credence to any of the lurid things Anne had said. He cared only about Marcelle and the life they had made together. But Marcelle loved Joe in a way that she had never loved before. She went home one final time and packed.

Once Marcelle and Joe took a small, furnished apartment in Mineola, Noble realized that theirs was no casual affair. Reluctantly, he agreed to a divorce, but Anne refused to dissolve her marriage to Joe for many years. Instead, she made it her systematic business to visit their mutual friends and tell each of them just how badly she had been served.

She even came to 41 Sycamore Avenue in an unsuccessful effort to turn Nena against her brother. Beware "the lips of a strange woman," Nena thought citing Proverbs 5: 3-4, "her end is bitter as wormwood, sharp as a two-edged sword." (The passage had become one of Nena's favorites after she saw Hedy Lamar and Louis Hayward in *The Strange Woman,* based on a novel by Ben Ames Williams. Nena also read the book and noted the Biblical quotation that Williams had used for his preface and title).

Anne's next gambit was to write the local Draft Board. Since Joey was not living with her and his son, she informed the Board that he was no longer eligible for a family deferment. On one of his visits to see Jo Jo, Anne told Joe that she hoped he would be killed in the war, but if that didn't happen, she would at least have the satisfaction of seeing Marcelle and him separated.

Despite the fact that he was 33, Joe was called up late in the fall of 1943. He once again signed on as a sailor and reported to Samson Naval Training Station, Geneva, New York. On the basis of his prior enlistment when he was sixteen, the Navy promoted him from Apprentice Seaman to Seaman 1st Class. Six weeks later, he shipped from Samson to California where he trained as a radio operator on a minesweeper patrolling the South Pacific.

Before leaving San Francisco, Joey saw his sister Della and Jim Redding who had relocated from Trenton to Marin County with their two boys, Jimmy, 7 and Ross (Cookie), an infant. To Joe, Northern California seemed like a land of dreams—he loved the lay of the arroyos and canyons, the green of the valleys, the often turbulent sea. He wrote Marcelle that after the war they should leave the East and begin life anew in or around the Bay Area like Della and Jim.

Joe and Marcelle, San Francisco 1946

In late 1944, a Japanese submarine torpedoed the minesweeper, *U.S.S. Measure,* on which Joey was serving. Miraculously, he was rescued unhurt.

Upon returning to California, the Navy granted him survivor's leave. He immediately hopped a flight home on a transport plane to see Jo Jo and to be reunited with his beloved Marcelle.

In New York for the holidays, Joe didn't have to report to Camp Samson until January 19, 1945. From there, he would fly back to San Francisco to a new assignment at the Fleet Post Office. As a survivor of a torpedoed ship, he could count on remaining in California for the duration. On the basis of that certainty, he and Marcelle planned that by the spring she would join him there, find an apartment and be with him in his off-hours and forever.

Baby Peter

> *Farewell dear babe, my heart's too much content,*
> *Farewell sweet babe, the pleasure of mine eye,*
> *Farewell fair flower that for a space was lent,*
> *Then ta'en away unto eternity.*
> —Anne Bradstreet, *In Memory of my dear Grandchild*

On his last night of leave, January 18, Marcelle and Joe went to visit Mary Balzac at 41 Sycamore Avenue. They came to say good-bye and to see the children, Lenny, 4, and Baby Peter, 7 months old. Drafted into the Navy in late October 1944, Pete was also stationed at Camp

Samson. Having finished basic training, he was anticipating being shipped out in short order. Before leaving for California, Joe would be sure to see his brother and give him news of Mary and the kids.

Lenny, Mary, Pete and Baby Peter, December, 1944

Marcelle and Joe arrived at 41 Sycamore around 9 p.m. Mary had put the children to bed two hours earlier. Little Lenny, 4, was sound asleep, her thumb still in her mouth, in the yellow bedroom at the head of the stairs.

She looked so peaceful that Marcelle and Joe didn't want Mary to disturb her, but as the three adults tiptoed into the nursery alcove of the front room, the baby woke up. He saw his mother and smiled immediately. Peter was a big boy, weighing close to twenty pounds and so sweet-tempered that he was cooing as Mary picked him up and brought him downstairs. Marcelle and Joe held him and played with him, and the baby responded with hearty chuckles. He looked just like Pete. As Joey dandled Peter on his knee, Mary served cake and coffee.

Freddie came in around 10 p.m. He had been taking inventory at the Adelphi College Bookstore where he worked. He looked exhausted. He had a glass of milk and a piece of cake and chatted for a while. Though his short-lived romance with Ginny Noble had ended, he was happy for his brother. He wished Joe and Marcelle the best of luck and retired.

The couple talked about their plans and about the possibility of living in California after the war was over. With Anne still on Tyson Avenue, they didn't believe they had a future in Floral Park. Joe felt badly about leaving Jo Jo. That said, for the most part it was a touching conversation, the baby radiating genuine delight as his uncle played "So Big!" with him, Mary realizing that she might not see either Joe or Marcelle again for years.

After they left, Mary brought the baby upstairs. He was content and tired. He didn't fuss when she put him back in his crib.

She came down to wash the dessert dishes. She missed Pete and prayed that this damned war would be over soon. If only they wouldn't send him overseas! As she put the kitchen back in order, Mary listened to the 11 o'clock nightly news on the radio. A major offensive in the Ardennes Forest in Belgium had finally ended, but Allied casualties were very high, many of them boys just out of high school. And in the Pacific, American forces were in the process of liberating the

Philippines, moving from one island to another inexorably closer to the Japanese mainland. Mary was listening intently to the news when she heard strange noises above her.

Somehow she knew that something was wrong with her baby. She flew up the stairs, turned on the light and ran to Peter's crib. He was having convulsions. His face was already blue. Mary screamed for Freddie, asleep in the back bedroom.

Freddie came racing to the alcove dressed only in his shorts. The baby had stopped breathing. As Freddie desperately administered CPR, Mary called Rescue. Within minutes, Dr. Buckley and a team of firemen—fellows who knew both Joe and Pete—were in the house taking over from Freddie, one breathing for the infant, another working the baby's arms and chafing his chest. They refused to give up for over an hour, but it was no use. Baby Peter—so healthy and happy only a few hours before—never revived. At Nassau Hospital in Mineola, Dr. Buckley pronounced the infant dead at 3:25 a.m., but Mary knew he was gone before they ever got there.

Mary had been in shock, but when the reality of what had happened finally hit her, she became hysterical. Irrational guilt, grief and fear overcame her. One moment she held herself responsible for the baby's death. In the next, she sobbed that she shouldn't have had another child. A minute later, she blamed herself for not having gone upstairs earlier. She was afraid Pete would accuse her of negligence, and he would be right. He would come home to find his only son in a coffin. How could she face him?

Dr. Buckley gave her a sedative. He knew the whole Balzac family. He had attended at the birth of both Lenny and Peter, and he had seen Mary and the baby only that afternoon. An ever-conscientious mother, Mary had brought Peter to his office for the baby's first immunizations. Most women waited until their infants were two years old if they brought the children in at all.

As Mary became calmer, the doctor advised her that there would have to be an autopsy.

"No, I won't allow them to touch him!"

"Listen to me, Mary. I know how you feel, but it's the law whenever there is a sudden unexplained death."

"But I know what killed him," she cried between paroxysms of sobs. "He was having an epileptic fit just like my father. I saw it. I knew it could happen. I shouldn't have had another baby."

Papa De Turo was a severe epileptic. Claire, his only unmarried daughter, lived with him and could tell when her father was about to have a *grand mal* episode. It would start with a series of lapses; he would stare off into space in the middle of a sentence and be unaware that he had stopped speaking. Then he would be chilled and want a sweater to keep himself warm. Within 24 hours, he would have repeated violent seizures for 1 or 2 days that left him drained. After a week in bed, his confusion would pass, and he would slowly regain his strength.

Though the family contended that Papa had developed traumatic epilepsy as a result of a blow to the head when he was a young boy, secretly they were terrified lest one of their children exhibit symptoms of the disease. They knew that, in many instances, epilepsy was hereditary.

Dr. Francis Xavier Buckley was aware of all this. When Mary first conceived Lenny, she told him about her father. A fine practitioner and an adept psychologist, the good doctor had reassured her then, and he reassured her now. He knew about fears concerning babies and birth defects. He had seen perfectly healthy women refuse to get pregnant though they wanted a child and would have made good mothers. They were terrified lest some genetic defect in their family be transmitted to their infant.

"No, Mary," he answered with great compassion, "your baby wasn't epileptic. I'd stake my practice on that. And you mustn't blame yourself. Blame me, if you will. I thought it was perfectly safe to give Peter his inoculation although I knew that in very rare cases some babies have had an allergic reaction to the DPT injection. Believe me, the autopsy is a good thing. It will determine what happened and will prove to you that you did nothing wrong."

As a young man, Francis Buckley had survived an airplane crash that had all but crushed his upper spine and left him noticeably hunched over. With a large head and chest and smiling blue eyes behind rimless glasses, he was the epitome of kindness. He sympathized with Mary and genuinely liked her. An Irish Catholic and father of eight children himself, he could conceive of nothing worse than to lose a baby.

Despising the prevailing notion of child rearing, he put up a sign in his office that read: "Children should be seen and heard and listened to." He and his wife had eight rambunctious children. An indulgent father, he had difficulty denying them anything. They all were fat. He was constantly putting them on well-balanced diets only to find that they had charged candy or potato chips or ice cream at the local store. No shopkeeper would turn down Dr. Buckley's freckle-faced kids. The whole town worshipped their father.

Granted emergency leave, Pete came home within 24 hours to find Mary almost prostrate. Despite sedatives, she couldn't sleep or eat, and, try as he might to comfort her, there was neither peace nor help for her pain.

Nena and Pete made the funeral arrangements with Thomas Dalton and Sons, and once again, the Floral Park Fire Department provided an honor guard. The proceedings were piteous. Dressed in his white Christening suit, Baby Peter was laid out in front of the living room windows just like Birdie and Pepìn. At first, Pete had to restrain Mary from lifting the baby out of the tiny white coffin. She wanted to hold him in her arms just once more.

Grief compounded grief. On the second day of the funeral, Pete found Freddie weeping uncontrollably in the kitchen. Already anguished by his inability to save Baby Peter, Freddie broke up entirely when Babe Schuhmacher's brother, Gus, came to see him from across the street. Ignorant armies had clashed in Belgium, and Babe had been killed during the last days of the Battle of the Bulge.

After a Solemn Requiem Mass at St. Hedwig's, friends of the families gathered for the burial of Baby Peter at the Cemetery of the Holy Rood in Westbury. Mary was so distraught that Nena and Pete had to support her at the gravesite.

Devastated by the death of his infant son, Pete also was worried about his wife. Though his sister-in-law, Claire, had taken Lenny to stay with her and Papa during the funeral, he wondered how his wife would manage when Lenny came home. He was depending upon Nena and Freddie to look after Mary—Pete had to report to Samson at the end of the week.

Once back in camp, Pete found that his unit had already shipped out to
California. By the time the Navy arranged to get him to San Francisco, he had missed his unit a second time. It had gone on to the South Pacific. At least one of Mary's prayers was answered. Ironically, because of the death of his son, Pete Balzac never went overseas.

Fortunately, the War was seven months from its end. Throughout this period in California, Mary's letters to Pete were heart wrenching. The baby's death had all but crushed her. Pete was also troubled about 4-year-old Lenny, who always looked so worried in the photographs Mary sent.

Just as Dr. Buckley had surmised, Baby Peter had died from an allergic reaction to the diphtheria-whooping cough (pertussis)-tetanus vaccine. The thymus, a gland in the upper chest prominent in children until the end of puberty, had enlarged and cut off air to his trachea.

One night about two weeks after the burial, Mary was alone in the kitchen. Deep in thought and perhaps nodding off, she was listening to the radio when she thought she heard the baby cry. Fearing that she was losing her mind, she ran next door to Helen Rodenbostel who gave her chamomile tea to settle her nerves.

After that, she couldn't bear to stay at 41. In early February, she and Lenny went home to live with her father and sister in Jamaica.

The Recluse

Come, come away, fraile, feeble, fleshly wight,
Ne let vaine words bewitch thy manly hart,
Ne divelish thoughts dismay thy constant sprite.
In heavenly mercies hast thou not a part?
—Edmund Spencer, *The Fairie Queen*, I.ix

The Coroner's report did have a salutary effect on Mary, but nothing seemed to allay Freddie's despair.

Once before—after his Dad died in 1939—Freddie had gone into a severe depression. He was only 14 then. An honor student, he wouldn't speak or come out of his room. Neither Nena nor Bill nor Pete could get him to respond. Finally one of his teachers from Sewanhaka High School came to 41 Sycamore Avenue, went upstairs and, speaking to Freddie through the locked bedroom door, convinced him to return to classes.

The Balzacs were ever grateful to the staff at Sewanhaka. In 1936, the principal had been instrumental in getting Bill a college scholarship. Three years later, a concerned teacher kept Freddie from dropping out of school.

A few weeks after Baby Peter's burial, Freddie was coming home from work one evening when he had a run-in with crazy Mrs. Raphael, a little gray-haired woman in her early fifties. She lived on Charles Street at the south end of Sycamore Avenue. Serving in an Armored Division of the Infantry, her nineteen-year-old son, Vinnie had been killed in Belgium like Babe. At times Mrs. Raphael was lucid, but most often she walked around town addressing her boy as if he were standing next to her.

As Freddie got off the bus, Mrs. Raphael recognized him. Vinnie and he had gone to high school together and had taken some of the same courses.

"Why, Freddie Balzac," she greeted him, genuinely puzzled. There was no malice in her voice. "How is it that you're here and my Vinnie dead?"

After his encounter with Mrs. Raphael, Freddie didn't seem to be able to face anyone. Why was he alive? he asked himself. Why did Vinnie and Babe have to die? He was ashamed to have a heart condition; he was ashamed to be 4-F.

Freddie gave up his job and began sleeping all day. He wouldn't come out of his room until everyone went to bed. He raided the refrigerator in the middle of the night, took his bike out for a ride at 2 or 3 o'clock in the

morning and went god-knows-why to god-knows-where.

Freddie remained a recluse until the spring. Then one morning in May 1945, Nena came downstairs to find a note from her 20-year-old brother on the kitchen table: "I'm off on the open road. Take care of my things. I have money. Don't worry." He signed the note, "The Man Who Came to Dinner."

No one heard from Freddie again for 6 months. He ended up at Inyokern near Death Valley, California, at a government installation. He spent the spring and much of the summer working on a top-secret project that turned out to be the Atomic Bomb.

By the end of 1945, Freddie was well enough to pay Joe and Della a visit. In a happy photograph of the three of them, Joe is wearing the uniform of a San Francisco trolley car operator, a job that he held until retirement; Della is looking foxy in a men's wear striped suit and Freddie is sporting a thin, natty mustache *à la* Zachary Scott.

Joe, Della and Freddie in San Francisco, 1945

Years later, Freddie told me laughingly that he had lingered in California hoping to be discovered like Lana Turner at Schwab's Drug Store. After all, he bore a slight resemblance to Scott; he had carefully cultivated manners and gestures like those of Cary Grant, and he had a rich baritone voice. Especially when he visited Los Angeles, he was ready to perform Figaro's "*Largo al Factotum*" from Rossini's *Il Barbiere di Siviglia* with gusto and superb comic timing. Unfortunately, no talent scout appeared, and Fred gave up his youthful pretensions. Twenty years afterwards in fatherly fashion, he would sing the aria to entertain his young sons, Freddie and Billy.

The Balancing Act

She walks in beauty, like the night
Of cloudless climes and starry skies;
And all that's best of dark and bright
Meet in her aspect and her eyes:
Thus mellowed to that tender light
Which heaven to gaudy day denies.
—George Gordon, Lord Byron

Bill always associated Edna Fenty with Lord Byron's poem, "She walks in beauty like the night." She was a fair-skinned, blue-eyed brunette of medium height with a round face and regular features. At first meeting, she seemed conventionally pretty, but as people got to know her, her low and gentle voice and something regal in her carriage struck them as beautiful.

One day in 1935 when Jack was still in prison and Bill in his final year of high school, Edna and he had finished lunch and were sitting in the kitchen of the Beechhurst Avenue house. Edna's mother had just taken 3-year-old Bobby to the park. Jimmy, 8, was in school until 3 p.m.

As a post-graduate senior, Bill was considering asking Dottie D'Angelo, the very bright and fetching daughter of the local iceman, to the Prom. As Bill passed behind Edna to get a glass of milk, she began teasing him about the girl. To retaliate, Bill tipped Edna's chair back more forcefully than he had intended.

He was as surprised as Edna was when she fell into his arms. He was 19 and inexperienced; he had loved her for years. She was 30, married to a convicted and imprisoned embezzler. She was miserable and lonely. Without either of them fully realizing it, the boy she had befriended eight years before had matured into a man.

In retrospect, Nena realized that Dad and Bill had fought about Edna. Once Jack Fenty came home from jail in the spring of 1937, Dad considered it disgraceful that Bill continued to live at Beechhurst Avenue. Despite Bill's denials, Dad knew his son. The relationship between Edna and Bill was illicit even if they loved one another, Dad reminded him in Spanish. Edna was not his wife, nor with two young children did it seem that she would ever be.

Dad didn't mince words. Did Bill really intend to share that woman with her husband? *Que barbaridad!* What barbarity! Even if Edna no longer cared for Jack, she wouldn't be able to leave him. Jack could sue her for adultery and take the children away from her. Did Bill think that she would abandon her boys for him?

It could only end badly. One way or the other, Bill and she would get hurt, and they would bring ruination down on that house. Dad begged Bill—if he really loved Edna—to break off the affair and come home.

Furious with his father, Bill didn't speak to him again until Dad was on his deathbed. Bill continued living with the Fentys until December 1941 when the declaration of war delivered him from an impossible, unholy situation.

Looking back, Nena remembered that when she and Edna worked together at Bohack's during the war, she had once asked Edna whether Bill would continue to board with her and Jack when he came back from service. Nena had been surprised by Edna's immediate and sharp reply. "No," Edna had responded. "I'll never let myself in for that again."

Nena assumed that Edna was referring to the *macho* competition between Jack and Bill. In particular, my mother recalled an incident that her brother had related with glee. Jack had bought a new refrigerator for Edna and had it delivered to the Beechhurst house. The deliverymen arrived early and, finding no one at home, left the appliance at the back door. When the family and Bill returned, Jack decided to borrow a friend's hand truck in order to move the refrigerator up the three steep steps into the kitchen. Before Jack got back from his friend's house a few blocks away, Bill had improvised a lever and an incline plane with some boards from the cellar and put the refrigerator in place by himself. It amused Bill to impress Edna and to disconcert Jack.

Fourteen years Bill's senior, Jack was a slight man, debilitated by shame, alcoholism and jailhouse memories. He was no match for Bill who was ingenious, imperious and in his physical prime.

In regard to Edna and Bill, my mother's much vaunted intuition failed her completely. She so respected Edna as an older married woman and mother and so revered her brother and his sense of honor that a love affair between the two never crossed Nena's mind. Had she even once entertained the possibility, she might have come to grips with Bill's reticence about his encounter with the spiritualist, Mrs. Hurt; his protracted fascination with the monstrous Fu Manchu as an college undergraduate; his painful argument with his wise and concerned father and his precipitous enlistment in the United States Marine Corps.

Indeed, Edna and Bill were so discreet that Edna's sister, Grace, never suspected their intimacy, nor, would it seem, did Jack Fenty until after the War. From 1937 through 1941, Jack and Edna included Bill on excursions to Grace's cottage on Lake Champlain for boating weekends in the summers and to magnificent Mt. Mansfield near Stowe, Vermont for skiing during winter vacations. A natural athlete and outdoorsman, Bill taught the Fenty boys to swim and ski and to fish and hunt. Serious Jimmy and adorable Bobby looked upon Bill as a most loving, skillful and patient uncle.

Bill must have been torn—guilty for betraying a man who had treated him with inordinate kindness since childhood; hating Jack for having a legal and moral right to Edna. His own harshest judge, Bill saw himself as a "whited sepulcher," a hypocrite—a paragon of public virtue ardently pursuing private vice.

And what of Edna? What tight rope did she have to walk to continue a sham marriage for six years? What maneuvering to keep Jack unaware and Bill pacified? And during the war, had she promised to go away with Bill when he came home? All through his time in service, she wrote Bill passionate letters, signing them, "Your loving wife." Though she had told Nena that Bill would not be a boarder in her house after the war, he moved back to Beechhurst Avenue less than a month after his discharge from the Marines.

35 "Seven Years With The Wrong Woman"

Recorded by The Prairie Ramblers Written by Bob Miller

Seven Years With The Wrong Woman
Is more than a man can stand
Seven Years With The Wrong Woman
Will wreck most any good man

Seven Years With The wrong Woman
It's the same in the mountain or dale
She'll stay awake all night - tryin' to start a
fight
Then have you thrown into jail.

Seven Years With The Wrong Woman
Is punishment that is bad
Seven Years With The Wrong Woman
Will drive most any man mad.

When you've married the wrong woman
There is only one thing you can do
Just dig you a hole - then crawl in that hole
And pull the hole in after you.

Seven Years With The Wrong Woman
Put me in this dirty jail
And she got all my money
And laughs 'cause I can't get bail.

In the final day of judgment
When Gabriel starts in to blow
If I see her face - in that heavenly place
I'll ask to be sent down below.

Listen boys if you're thinkin' of marriage
Take warning to what I tell
Don't marry the wrong woman
It's worse than livin' in hell.

Seven Years With The Wrong Woman
It'll age you and turn your hair gray
They say love is blind - but search 'til you find
A face you can stand every day.

Part 2, Chapter 4
Uncommon Valor

> From this day to the ending of the world,
> But we in it shall be remembered
> We few, we happy few, we band of brothers;
> For he to-day that sheds his blood with me
> Shall be my brother
> —William Shakespeare, *Henry V, IV, iii, 61-6*

Bill loved being a Marine. He loved the rough and tumble ruggedness of military life, the values of honor, courage and commitment that inspire the Corps. At the Marine Recruit Depot at Parris Island, South Carolina, boot camp Drill Instructors claimed to break boys down and build them up again as men. After all the mental discipline that had so enrapt Bill from grade school through his undergraduate and graduate years, the sheer physicality of the training came as an overwhelming relief.

When he was inducted, Bill weighed a buff 144 lbs. After going through basic training at Parris Island, he gained 11 lbs., and it was all muscle. As a newbie Marine, he performed well earning on a scale of 1 to 5, scores of 4 for Military Efficiency and Military Bearing, 4.3 for Intelligence and 5 for Obedience and Sobriety.

When boot camp ended in late January 1942, the Corps transferred Bill to Quantico Marine Base, Virginia where he was assigned to an Engineering Battalion, 4th Marine Division. His superiors took into account the science classes, especially chemistry that he had taken at St. John's and sent him to the Engineering School at Quantico for an

8-week course in Water Distribution and Purification. He completed instruction on May 16, 1942 with a grade of "Excellent" and was recommended for promotion. Water purification was to be his specialty for the remainder of the war.

Throughout 1942, Bill and his buddies engaged in field maneuvers. They drilled, bivouacked and played war games. They charged up hills with fixed bayonets screaming "Kill! Kill!" at the top of their lungs. They ran through, over and under obstacle courses; marched with full packs double-time on rough terrain; jumped from the decks of troop transports into the ocean, knees tucked, hands cupped over groins; wriggled on their bellies under a barrage of live ammunition. During these exercises, Bill bonded intensely with his buddies, the fellows in his unit who would serve with him for the next four years. They would come to depend on one another like brothers.

Having been raised by his older sisters and guided by Edna Fenty, Bill now totally rejected petticoat government. By the time he was granted a 5-day leave after 9 months of military service, September 22-6, 1942, he had developed a fierce identity as a man among men. Along with this Corps *machismo* came an incipient misogyny—certainly in part attributable to his clandestine love affair. He particularly despised the bored married women of Beaufort, South Carolina who did their part for the war effort entertaining off-duty Leathernecks with more than tea and cookies. "Marriage?" he sneered, "the smell of Lysol behind the bathroom door."

When Bill made Private First Class in early November, 1942, his service grades had gradually gone up to 4.8 and 5 on a scale of 5. In recognition of this superior record, the Marines offered him the option of Officers' Training. At 26, he was an obvious candidate, mature in comparison to the youngsters under 20 who made up the majority of his unit. In addition, he had a college degree and credits toward a Master's. Bill nevertheless refused the opportunity preferring to stay in the ranks with his buddies as an ordinary "grunt." Having turned down Officers' Training, on November 8, 1942 Bill was transferred to the Engineering School Marine Force Training Center at Camp Lejeune, New River, North Carolina.

When the Christmas holiday approached, Bill's outfit was granted an eight day furlough, and though he divided his time equally between Sycamore and Beechhurst Avenues, both the Balzacs and the Fentys were thrilled to have him home for the holidays. All was well.

Despite the cold weather, Pete had gone all out decorating the house with strings of lights around the windows and on the roof line. 41 looked wonderfully festive with an evergreen wreath on the front door and a huge Christmas tree in front of the porch windows in the living room.

The War seemed bound to continue, and Pete wanted to make this holiday particularly memorable. He doubted that he would be home next December. He and my father hadn't been called up for service yet because they were married and had young children.

During Christmas week, the women added brightly colored bulbs and balls to the tree, Mary hanging hundreds of precisely placed strips of tinsel all over it. With a white cotton blanket and gifts of all sizes and shapes at its base, the tree was a shimmering, sparkling marvel.

On Christmas Day, Mary and Nena both cooked: fresh fruit salad to start followed by a huge golden turkey, savory stuffing, giblet gravy, Spanish rice with pimientos, twice-baked potatoes and string beans *almandines*. In addition, filling the center of the table were heaping side dishes of curled celery and carrots with black and green olives, jellied cranberry sauce garnished with thin slices of Valencia oranges and mashed turnips for Freddie. Bill officiated as head of the family, the Aunts wept to see him looking so *guapo* in his uniform, and Nena introduced her latest *pièce de résistance*: warm homemade pound cake topped with potted sliced peaches and vanilla ice cream.

The holiday flew by, and Bill reluctantly returned to Camp Lejeune on December 29. As 1943 progressed, he and the gyrenes in his outfit were honed into lean mean green fighting machines. Many were itching to face battle—at least in imagination.

Despite the rigors of being a Marine, Bill always made time for me. I wrote to him throughout the war. As a seven-year-old, I described the skating costumes that my Aunt Palma had crocheted for my Sonia Henie doll and told him about the new comic book heroine, Diana Prince. A nurse by day, she became the all-American Wonder Woman whenever needed to fight crime and corruption. I was collecting each new issue.

Bill patiently answered my letters admonishing me to look up all new words that I came across in my reading and to use them three times in sentences so that "they would be mine for life." He advised me to do more than my teachers asked and always to do my best. In the fall of 1943 at school, I had taken up the flute and developed an interest in art. Even if I thought I had little or no talent, Bill enjoined me to develop skills in every possible area as a matter of discipline and as a potential source of delight. Along with his advice, my uncle enclosed my original note corrected in red pencil.

I never took offense–Bill's words were uplifting. Ever since he had healed the robin fledgling, I looked to him as my best teacher.

Bill came home on a surprise visit for seven days near the end of spring, 1943, but something was not right. He was not on furlough. He was AWOL.

Returning voluntarily to camp on June 13, he faced a trial and was convicted. The penalty for his dereliction of duty was a reduction in salary for three months. By the end of June, his grades for Military Efficiency, Obedience, Sobriety, etc. had dropped from 4.8/5 to 3.3/5.

Seven weeks later—before Bill had satisfied the penalty for his June absence—he reappeared in Floral Park. Once again he was AWOL hiding out at the Fenty house on Beechhurst Avenue. Something was terribly wrong, but we had no idea what it was. After the War, Nena speculated that Edna had tried to end the affair in June, but Bill refused to accept any such conclusion. When she wavered again in July, he reappeared in Floral Park knowing full well that face to face she wouldn't be able to deny him.

On August 4 when Bill returned in disgrace to Camp Lejeune, his rank was reduced to Private from PFC, and he was assigned to extra patrol duty for three months. How he managed to stay out of the brig was a mystery.

Within weeks, the Marine Corps transferred Bill to Camp Pendleton, California where he was almost immediately issued a field pack for overseas duty. Whatever was going on at home, his superiors obviously believed that a radical change of scene far from the East Coast was in order.

In early September in California, Bill was assigned to Co. A, 1st Battalion, 20th Marines (Engr), 4th Marine Division. The official history of the "Fighting Fourth" reads as follows:

> Activated 25 August 1943 at Camp Pendleton, California, as Headquarters Company, 1st Battalion, 20th Marines, 4th Marine Division, Fleet Marine Force. Deployed during February 1944 to the Pacific Theater. Redesignated 31 August, as Headquarters and Service Company, 4th Engineer Battalion, 4th Marine Division, Fleet Marine Force. Participated in the Battle of Kwajalein, Battle of Saipan, Battle of Tinian and the Battle of Iwo Jima.

Rumor had it that Bill's unit was to ship out at any moment. Actually, the men of the "Fighting Fourth" continued to train intensively the entire fall, and the news of the terribly costly U. S. victories at Tarawa and Makin in the Gilbert Islands in November only increased their anxiety. Not until they boarded the *USS Callaway* in San Diego on January 10, 1944 and got their orders was some of the tension dispelled. At last, they knew their destination—the Kwajalein Atoll, Marshall Islands.

Then for a long time, we heard from Bill sporadically. Troop movements were top secret, his letters infrequent, highly censored and delayed.

We only learned after the fact that he was in the first waves to hit the beaches during the crucial battles of the Marshalls, Marianas and Volcano Islands.

On Beechhurst Avenue, Edna Fenty was beside herself. Any number of her letters had been returned undelivered. No doubt because of the activation of the 4th Marines and new designation of Bill's company, the mail took some time to catch up with him. In desperation, Edna appealed to the Navy Department for Bill's "right address as... I feel sure he is waiting for mail from home," she wrote on February 23, 1944.

By the time of Edna's letter to the Navy Department, Bill had already fought and survived the Battle of Kwajalein Atoll, the Marshall Islands (January 31-February 3, 1944).

𝔇ied some, pro patria

If in some smothering dreams, you too could pace
Behind the wagon that we flung him in,
And watch the white eyes writhing in his face
If you could hear, at every jolt, the blood
Come gargling from the froth-corrupted lungs
My friend, you would not tell with such high zest
To children ardent for some desperate glory,
The old lie: 'Dulce et decorum est
Pro patria mori.'*
—Wilfred Owen, Dulce et Decorum Est
*From Horace, "Sweet and fitting it is to die for one's country."

By fall, 1943, United States forces had their first major victory at Guadalcanal in the Solomons and were planning to island hop from Tarawa in the Gilberts to Kwajalein in the Marshalls. With each inexorable advance, they would come closer and closer to reclaiming the Philippines and threatening the Japanese mainland.

The largest coral reef atoll in the world, Kwajalein Atoll consists of 97 islets surrounding a huge lagoon that the Japanese had only barely fortified. They concentrated their 10,000 man force on the outlying islands, assuming the Americans would attack there first. Instead, after an extraordinary series of naval and air bombardments all through the months of November and December, Admiral Chester W. Nimitz, Commander in Chief of the Pacific Fleet, decided against an ocean side assault and struck through to the lagoon. On January 31 from within the lagoon, he mounted an attack on Kwajalein Island in the south and sent the 4th Marines to capture the twin islands of Roi-Namur seventy miles north. From the airfield at Roi, their primary objective, they moved on to Namur, capturing 72 Japanese out of a garrison of 3,500.

Within four days, the entire atoll was in American hands. Operation Flintlock was an unqualified success. American casualties were light in comparison to the Japanese. By the end of the fighting, only 264 of the original 10,000 defenders survived.[36]

For their efforts, the Department of the Navy issued each man a star on his Asiatic Pacific Area Service Ribbon for the Occupation of Kwajalein Atoll, Marshall Islands Operation. It was the first of many decorations that Bill was to wear proudly.

From Kwajalein Atoll and the Marshall Islands, Allied forces planned the crucially important Operation Forager, an assault on the Northern Marianas: Guam, Saipan and Tinian. Though Guam was the largest of the Marianas and had been an American territory until the Japanese invasion in December 1941, the Joint Chiefs of Staff determined to invade Saipan first. Only 1200 miles from Tokyo, Saipan and Tinian, a smaller island three miles south, would become staging areas for B-29s to bomb the Japanese mainland. Aslito airfield on Saipan and three new airstrips on Tinian were major objectives. U. S. Thunderbolts, P-47s, dropped 120 tanks of napalm for the first time in the battle for Tinian, July 24-August 1, 1944. (From Tinian a year later, two B-29s took off a few days apart armed with atomic bombs, destinations Hiroshima and Nagasaki).

A huge invading force attacked Saipan on June 15, 1944. Bill's outfit had been deployed and integrated into the V Amphibian Corps consisting of the 3rd, 4th and 5th Marine Divisions under Major General Holland (Howling Mad) Smith.

Outnumbered more than 2 to 1 by American forces and their supply lines cut, the Japanese defenders were soon down to their last ammunition and food. They feared that the fall of Saipan was only a matter of casualties and time.

Unlike the flat, near sea level islands of the Kwajalein atoll, Saipan had a varied terrain that made the fighting diverse and arduous. House by house, cave by cave, its towns, mountains and plains, swamps, reefs and cane fields demanded different military strategies; nevertheless, the carnage wreaked by Marines and Army infantry was horrific.

Nor was the Navy inactive. The Battle of the Philippine Sea began on June 19, only four days after the invasion of Saipan. The last great aircraft carrier battle of the war ended the next day with the Japanese losing 393 planes and three carriers. From then on, the U.S. Air Force bombed Tokyo with virtual impunity.

Within three weeks, U.S. forces on Saipan had backed Japanese soldiers and hundreds of natives into the northern tip of the island. In a ravine forever after dubbed "Harakiri Gulch," Japanese infantrymen clutched live grenades to their breasts and blew themselves up rather than be taken alive.

Before the invasion, Imperial soldiers had terrified the non-combatants, many of whom worked in the sugar refining factories on the island. The Americans, the Japanese said, would torture and kill them and their families if they surrendered. As a result, hundreds of civilians committed suicide by jumping from the sheer cliffs at Marpi Point at the narrow end of the island. To the horror of Army and Marine troops who tried in vain to stop them, hysterical men and women threw their babies and small children and then themselves off the high crags to be dashed on the jagged rocks below.

On the evening and night of July 6-7, 1944, Lieutenant General Yoshitsugo Saito, the Japanese commandant, gave orders to fight to the death. Preceding his men in suicide, Saito first wounded himself ceremonially with his sword and then had his adjutant shoot him in the head. Following their commander's lead, at least 3000 of Saito's sake-inspired troops sacrificed their lives in a last, desperate banzai charge. Supply lines cut, some Japanese soldiers attacked armed only with grenades or knives or sticks. To die with honor for the Emperor and the homeland was preferable to the ignominy of surrender.

The loss of Saipan was the beginning of the end. In Tokyo Premier Hideki Tojo, formerly Minister of War, resigned with his entire cabinet when the Japanese General Staff suggested that perhaps it was time to sue for peace.

> Of the 71,034 U.S. troops landed on Saipan, 3,100 were killed, 13,100 wounded or missing in action. Out of the 31,629 Japanese on Saipan, approximately 29,500 died as a result of the fighting, and only 2,100 prisoners survived. Fighting between the Japanese and the Americans was by no means completely mechanized; while ships, aircraft, artillery, and tanks inflicted the largest amount of damage to the combatants, much of the fighting was hand to hand. Besides machine guns, flame throwers, rifles, and pistols, deadly skirmishes were fought with bayonets, swords, bamboo spears, clubs, stones and fists.[37]

Protracted for 25 days, the invasion of Saipan was terrible. As Lieutenant General Holland Smith declared in August 1944, "Saipan was war such as nobody had fought before: A campaign in which men crawled, clubbed, shot, burned and bayoneted each other to death."

For their valiant efforts, the 4th Marines were awarded the Presidential Unit Ribbon, with a bar and blue enamel star for the Marianas Campaign, 16th June to 9 July, 1944. In addition they were allowed one star on their Asiatic-Pacific Campaign Ribbon.

Bill's behavior changed radically after Saipan and Tinian, and once back in Hawaii for rest and recuperation, the suppressed irascibility that he had struggled with even as a child surfaced in full force. On September 14, 1944, Bill once again was brought up on charges—this time for disobeying "a lawful command of a non-commissioned officer."

Taking into account that Bill was a seasoned veteran and survivor of the fierce fighting in the Marshalls and Marianas, a court martial convened on September 19 meted out a very light punishment—five days on bread and water in the Company brig at Oahu. As a result of this refusal to obey an order and because of his two state-side defections without leave, Bill never received a Good Conduct Medal.

A bloodier assault than the Marianas was yet to come: on February 19, 1945, American forces set into motion Operation Detachment, the battle for Iwo Jima (Japanese for "Sulfur Island"). One-third the size of Manhattan with beaches composed of shifting sulfurous ash, Iwo Jima, traditionally considered a part of Japan, lies only 660 miles from Tokyo. 2 miles wide by 4 miles long, it was one of the most brutally contested and costly pieces of real estate in the entire war.

Dominating the tiny, leg-of-lamb shaped island at its southern and wider end stands a 550' high extinct volcanic cone, Mount Suribachi. Capturing it became a primary American objective. Until the Marines secured Suribachi, the Japanese held the higher ground and commanded a view of the entire island. They could fire on any position the invaders attempted to hold. By D-Day + 4—after fighting furiously for every yard of terrain—five U.S. Marines and one Navy corpsman raised the

American flag on top of Suribachi, a moment caught and preserved in Associated Press' Joe Rosenthal's justly famous photograph.

The second objective was to take control of the airstrips from which the Japanese had been launching Kamikaze attacks on the American fleet. These runways gave U. S. forces a place for emergency landings midway between the Marianas and Japan and provided a closer base than Tinian for B-29s and their escorts engaged in bombing raids on Tokyo.

70,000 Marines, Seabees (Naval Construction Battalions) and Army infantry opposed a much smaller Japanese force estimated at 22,000 to 27,000 men. The fighting was especially difficult because the 3-day naval bombardment preceding the landing was largely ineffective. Spotters knew little about targets onshore. Adding to their predicament, the Marines had a hard time moving through heavy surf with 100-pound backpacks, and no one had counted on maneuvering up a steep slope from the beach on loose volcanic soil. When they advanced, they advanced 500 feet at a time, often engaging in hand-to-hand combat.

After Day-4 when it was clear that the Americans would win the battle, the commander of Iwo Jima, General Tadamichi Kuribayashi carefully conserved his forces, retreating by day and counter-attacking by night. Not until the very end did he authorize a banzai charge.

The battle for Iwo Jima raged for 19 days; American forces lost 6821 men, the Japanese more than 20,000. One out of every three Marines who served was killed, wounded or suffered battle fatigue. When it was over, Fleet Admiral Chester W. Nimitz commented, "Uncommon valor was a common virtue."

In February, 1945 the United States government authorized survivors of Iwo Jima to add one star to their Asiatic Pacific Ribbons. In all, Bill now had three stars representing three major battles. Additionally, for their participation, men of the 4th Engineering Battalion, 4th Marine Division received American Campaign Ribbons.

By some miracle, Bill felt, he had survived Kwajalein, Saipan, Tinian and Iwo Jima, 15 months of overseas service with respites for recuperation. Promoted to Corporal and sent back to Hawaii after Iwo, he suffered from untreated battle fatigue and survivor's guilt, but he never let his family know the severity of his distress.[38]

Homecomings

> *Died some, pro patria,*
> *Non "dulce" non "et decor"*
> *walked eye-deep in hell*
> *believing in old men's lies, then unbelieving*
> *came home, home to a lie,*
> *home to many deceits,*
> *home to old lies and new infamy*
> *—Ezra Pound, Hugh Selwyn Mauberly*

In the fall of 1945, the Marines shipped Bill home, gaunt and shaking. He returned with a chest full of campaign ribbons and medals—"lettuce," he called them.

The best man any one of us had ever known was a physical and mental wreck.

The war had changed him. Before he enlisted, he neither used tobacco drank hard liquor nor spoke immoderately; now he chain-smoked, consumed large quantities of bourbon or rye, swore obscenely and woke up screaming and sweating from terrible nightmares.

Bill at the Fenty's, 1947

In the middle of the night, Nena would get up from bed to stay with her brother. Much to my father's disgust, she'd wash Bill's face, neck and wrists with a cool washrag and then remain by his bedside soothing him, listening to him, letting him talk out his terror.

Bill would finally fall into a troubled sleep, but within an hour or two, he would awake in a panic, "eye-deep in hell," shrieking again as he relived seeing Marines using flamethrowers to immolate bunkers full of Japanese soldiers. He told Nena that he could still see their contorted faces, hear their screams as they ran out of rat holes, tunnels or caves, clothing on fire, hair ablaze. Like his buddies, some of them were little more than boys. Worse, he could still smell the sickly sweet odor of napalm on burning human flesh.

Other nights he remembered climbing over hundreds of decapitated corpses or torsos with missing limbs strewn on the beach at Saipan whose sand had turned red with blood. Between the blown-up amtracs and blasted palm trees, the bodies of the dead had bloated under the tropical sun and smelled so bad that even in his dream he woke up nauseated.

Long after Saipan officially fell, Bill recalled seeing the mutilated remains of a Marine sergeant and an Army nurse whose corpses were found off limits, each other's body parts stuffed in their mouths. Though U. S. forces declared the island secure on my mother's birthday, July 9, 1944, for months afterward, small pockets of Japanese remained in hiding.[39] Some emerged at night to forage for food; others continued to engage in guerilla warfare under cover of darkness.

The worst horror of all had occurred during a nighttime water purification detail on Iwo Jima. In charge of the patrol, Bill and his buddy had just exchanged places, Bill bringing up the rear to watch for snipers. A minute later, his buddy was blown to pieces by a landmine. The blood and brains of his friend had spattered Bill's neck and face. Had they not changed positions, Bill would have been killed.

He felt unworthy to be alive. What was he being saved for? What greater horror was in store for him? He went wild screaming and shooting at foliage. He wanted to take on the entire Japanese force and die for once and for all because he couldn't stand it anymore.

He didn't remember much after that. The medics must have sedated him. A couple of days probably passed because when he came to himself on a troop transport en route for Hawaii, the battle had ended and Iwo was secure. And then the nightmares began.

Night after night, dreaming and half in a stupor, Bill would thrash in bed crying and covering his head with his hands as imagined Japanese soldiers prodded him with bayonets. He would wake up with a start just as the cruel interrogators in his dream were about to torture him. He couldn't rid his subconscious of these delusions—repeated visions that gave him no rest.

Bill (center) and buddies in Hawaii, Stosh on right

Bill was so obviously ill that my mother and I were surprised when he moved back to the Fenty's a few weeks after returning home. Did Bill's nightmares continue there, and did Edna stay up night after night with him as Nena had?

We saw Bill perhaps once a week after he returned to Beechhurst Avenue, and from time to time, his Marine Corps buddies would visit him. By the end of 1946, no one was interested in listening to their war stories, so Bill would come over to 41 and entertain his equally haunted comrades in the dining room behind the closed pocket doors.

In particular, he looked forward to seeing Stosh, a blond Polish kid from Pittsburgh who had joined the Marines in 1941 when he was 17 years old. Three or four other fellows, Stosh and Bill would sit at the dining room table, drain a couple of bottles of Scotch and bourbon and loudly revisit terrifying scenes of battles as if to reassure themselves that their experiences were not figments of diseased imaginations.

"It was like that, right, Bill? That's how it happened, didn't it, Bill?" Stosh would ask somewhat desperately, and Bill would reassure Stosh and the others that their memories were accurate. (They all drank heavily, and to a man, none of them lived past 40).[40]

His buddies looked up to Bill. Together they had seen real life and death; they alone understood why he had turned down Officer's Training, why he couldn't go back to the Ivory Tower and complete the degree in English. His education had been a complete waste. Teaching seemed so unreal to Bill now. Kids should be learning survival skills, he claimed. They were infinitely more necessary than grammar.

After August 1945, it seemed almost impossible to disagree with Bill. The atomic bombs dropped on Hiroshima and Nagasaki initiated a terror even more devastating than the war. During the next years at least twice a week at school, the same bells rang that had been used for mock air raids. Named "Duck and Cover" drills, schoolchildren were taught to huddle beneath their polished hardwood maple desks.

Alternately, they were quickly herded into the corridors of the school away from windows until the all clear sounded.

Government agencies actively promoted building lead-lined bomb shelters. At home, many parents discussed constructing such shelters in their backyards or, at the very least, stocking emergency supplies in their cellars. At the time, few realized the nature of radiation sickness and the uselessness of these precautions and preparations.

By the end of 1945, the Armed Forces honorably discharged all the men in the family who had served. Like Della and Jim, Joe and Marcelle stayed in California, and operating a San Francisco trolley, Joe more than once was named "Employee of the Month."

Pete Balzac returned to Long Island rejoining Mary at her father's house in Jamaica, but by the spring, his sister-in-law, Claire and he were arguing bitterly. As a result, Pete and Mary moved back to 41 Sycamore Avenue with 6-year-old Lenore, late in 1946 rejoining my father, mother and me.

The Seabees discharged my father in December 1945. He had served in the South Pacific with skilled construction workers made up largely of German and Italian volunteers, almost all of whom had been in the States since early childhood. Kept behind the lines in Okinawa for reasons of security, they welded together Marston mats composed of thousands of interlocking 2-inch metal rings. Within four hours after bulldozers had cleared an area, the Seabees were able to join these mats together and lay them over any terrain to create instant runways for planes.

He was proud of his service in the Navy and of the naturalization papers conferred on him when he was sworn in. In his nineties, he still considered going through the Panama Canal on a troop ship from New York to California the most exciting experience of his life.

Happily for my father's family, brother Frank and my aunts' present and future spouses all returned intact and easily made the transition to civilian life. In every instance—unlike Bill—they came back to fiancées or wives and children or to a job they cared about.

From time to time, we heard troubling reports from Beechhurst Avenue. Bill was drinking heavily and having trouble controlling his explosive temper. Once again he was living the lie that he had gone to war to escape. Edna seemed content to leave things as they were, but Bill was almost 30 and no longer a kid. He wanted her to go away with him and start a new life.

My Hero

Faster than an airplane, more powerful than a locomotive, impervious to bullets. 'Up in the sky - look!' 'It's a giant bird!' 'It's a plane!' 'It's SUPERMAN!'... A being no larger than an ordinary man but possessed of powers and abilities never before realized on Earth... champion of the oppressed, physical marvel extraordinary who has sworn to devote his existence on Earth to helping those in need.

—First version of opening signature from "Superman on Radio" created by Robert Joffe Maxwell and Allen Ducovny, 1939

And yet, the old Bill—my personal Jack Armstrong, Dr. Kildare and Captain Midnight—could still emerge were an injustice perpetrated against any of his own.

I was 9 years old in 4th grade in the spring of 1946, a few months after Bill came home for good. That year I had Mrs. Purdy for a teacher, the only bad apple I would come across at the John Lewis Childs School. On the verge of retirement, she had utterly lost patience with the children in her class. She disgraced one or another of them for the slightest infraction making the boy or girl sit on a high stool in a front corner of the room crowned with a dunce's cap.[41]

One day after school when my mother and Helen Rodenbostel, our German next-door neighbor, had gone food shopping, I was playing kick-the-can with a bunch of the Sycamore Avenue kids. I was hiding in the Rodenbostel's side path to the street. Helen's charming husband, Cord, a skilled carpenter, had built a heavy gate made of 2 by 4s securing it with a large metal lock. He had also installed a strong spring mechanism to keep it closed. The gate stood at the Sycamore Avenue end of the narrow defile between our houses. As I peered out from behind the bushes near the gate, I could see the boy who was "It." He had captured four of my teammates and now was cautiously walking away from 41 looking for the rest of us. Spying my opportunity to free my jailed compatriots, I raced to the gate and with a quick shove pushed it open. It rebounded instantly, and before I could escape, the heavy brass lock plate caught me square on the right wrist.

I sat moaning on Helen's front stoop holding my arm and waiting for my mother to return. I wasn't crying, but my wrist was throbbing with a constant dull pain that I had never felt before. I knew that when my mother got home, she would not be very sympathetic. I was clumsy and always getting hurt. When my father got out of the Navy in December 1945, he had insisted that she give up working. With just one salary and post-war prices, they could ill afford doctor's bills.

By evening, however, the wrist and hand were badly swollen, and Nena called Bill at Fenty's and asked him to take a look at it. (Not that Bill had any particular medical expertise. My mother simply depended on him to know what to do, and he always rose to the occasion). He came over and took me upstairs to the bathroom sink. While he numbed the hand by running tepid tap water over it, he gently but firmly palpated the bones of the wrist, then wrapped it with a snug bandage that gave support and temporary relief.

He couldn't feel any displacement, Bill said to his sister, but suggested that she send me to school with the arm in a sling. If it still was giving me pain at noon, Nena should take me to see Doc Mendelsohn, the druggist who served as a non-paid diagnostician for half the town. No point in seeing Dr. Buckley—he would send us to the nearest hospital, the only facility at that time with an X-ray machine, and she would have to pay his as well as the radiologist's bill.

That night I had a difficult time sleeping, but the pain seemed to have lessened by morning. Dutifully, my mother improvised a sling with a colorful bandana, and off I went to endure the tender mercies of Mrs. Purdy.

She didn't believe I was in pain and late in the morning, despite the sling that my mother had carefully pinned in place, insisted that I write and solve a long division problem on the blackboard. I should have refused, but she had so cowed us all that, barely able to hold the chalk, I obeyed and completed the work. The throbbing then became unbearable, and for the first and only time when I was at school, tears streamed down my cheeks involuntarily as I waited in agony for the noon bell to sound.

I didn't go back to class that afternoon. Mommy was worried and took me to Mendelsohn's Pharmacy on Jericho Turnpike and Emerson Avenue. Round-faced, dark-eyed, gentle Doc Mendelsohn brought me into the back of the store, checked my hand and re-bandaged it. He couldn't tell if it was fractured—if so, Bill had done a good job setting it—but Doc didn't like the swelling. He thought my mother had better take me to Nassau Hospital in Mineola and have it X-rayed just to be sure.

All the way there on the bus, I prayed that my wrist was broken. And then I'd go back to class triumphant literally armed with a big cast. Take that, Mrs. Purdy, you old witch!

The radiology report confirmed not one, but two broken bones—a compound fracture of the radius and ulna. When I did return to John Lewis Childs the next day it seemed as if every kid in the 4th grade rallied around me to sign the cast. At the same time, they sent scornful looks in Mrs. Purdy's direction.

Far more important to me was Uncle Bill's letter that I gave to Mrs. Purdy—having first hand delivered a copy to Rena C. Hayden. In it, Bill forcefully expressed our family's outrage. He asserted that in victimizing selected students inside the classroom, Mrs. Purdy consciously encouraged attacks on them outside the school. At the beginning of the term, she merely seemed mean, a petty tyrant who demanded absolute obedience, but in insisting that a pupil write on the blackboard with a possible broken wrist, Mrs. Purdy had joined the ranks of the merciless and sadistic. Having lost all sympathy for another's pain in addition to all feeling for children, the woman clearly should not be teaching. She should retire or be forced to retire as soon as possible.

Mrs. Purdy's only defense, she later wrote on my report card, was that

"Children are often malingerers." I do not know whether Uncle Bill's letter hastened her retirement. I only know that as far as I was concerned, he was and had always been my hero. He hadn't needed to win all those campaign ribbons and citations to prove the point to me.

---

[36] Samuel Eliot Morrison, (1961) *Aleutians, Gilberts and Marshalls, June 1942-April, 1944,* History of Naval Operations in World War II, Boston: Little, Brown and Company; S.L.A. Marshall, Joseph G. Dawson (2001), *Island Victory: the Battle of Kwajalein Atoll,* University of Nebraska Press.

[37] Mark Griggs, "WWII Veterans from Ponchoula," 2nd *Marine Division in WWII, the Marianas Islands: Saipan* http://www.tarawaontheweb.org/

griggs.htm: See also Philip A. Crowl, *Campaign in the Marianas*, USA WWII Series, Washington, D.C: OCMH, 1960, III-XII; Major Carl W. Hoffman, *Saipan: the Beginning of the End,* USMC Historical Monograph and Maj. F. Stott, *Saipan under Fire,* 1945.

[38] Theodore Lidz, M. D., "Psychiatric Casualties from Guadalcanal" *Psychiatry,* 9 (1946), 193-213. In a study of the survivors of Guadalcanal, Lidz profiled the men most likely to suffer severe and protracted effects of battle fatigue (now referred to as Post-Traumatic Shock Syndrome). They either had joined service to get away from an unbearable situation at home and/or had suffered the death (or divorce or abandonment) of a parent at an early age. They feared the future, death, suicide or insanity and "blew their tops" in combat when either a buddy on whom they depended got killed or a fiancé withdrew support. The lost relationship "had finally provided these men with the needed affection they had been seeking since childhood. The loss of it renewed a pattern of insecurity, resentment, and guilt that had been established by the inconstancy or absence of parental affections" 44.

Though Bill did not serve at Guadalcanal where American soldiers were abandoned for months, his experiences both before and after the war fit the classic profile for battle fatigue.

[39] Unable to believe that Saipan had fallen and the war was over, Imperial Japanese Army Captain Sakeo Oba with 46 of his men did not surrender until December 1, 1945.

[40] Only recently did I come across a psychiatric study that examines the effects of combat on health. See Glen H. Elder, Jr., Michael J. Shanahan,

and Elizabeth Colerick Clipp, "Linking Combat and Physical Health: The Legacy of World II in Men's Lives" *The American Journal of Psychiatry*, 154, no. 3 (March 1997), 330-6. "Conclusions: Combat in World War II predicted that in the 15 years after the war, a subject would experience physical decline or death. There was no evidence that the effect of combat was more pronounced among men of different ranks, theaters of engagement, or levels of self-worth in 1940" 330.

[41] Mrs. Purdy singled out for particular scorn Donald Duester, a thin, blonde boy who spent much of the year on the dunce's stool. Ragged and deprived by severe German immigrant parents, derided in class by Mrs. Purdy and run home daily by gangs of kids bent on beating him up, by 4th grade Donald was pilfering small toys and candy from the 5 & 10 cent store on Jericho Turnpike during his lunch hour.

Donald had a talent for math and was a swift runner. Had any teacher or coach paid attention to him, he would have blossomed. Instead at the age of 15, he was caught rifling a sporting goods store and sent to reform school.

Part 2, Chapter 5
Farewell the Tranquil Mind

Othello, Act III, iii, 348

Not, I'll not, carrion comfort, Despair, not feast on thee;
Not untwist—slack they may be—these last strands of man
In me ór, most weary, cry, "I can no more." I can;
Can something, hope, wish day come, not choose not to be.
—Gerard Manley Hopkins, (*Carrion Comfort*)

Bill was having trouble holding even the least demanding of low-level jobs. Jack Fenty had recommended him for a position making boxes for Continental Can Corporation in Jamaica, and at first everything went smoothly. An attractive blonde named Caroline showed him around the plant and taught him to use the machines. She was delighted at how quickly he learned. He was her best student, she told the manager. It was a mindless job, and Bill worked satisfactorily at it for about six months.

A minor argument with Edna one morning put Bill on edge. Later at work, he lost his temper over some trifle and savagely rabbit-punched the frightened foreman. Before the job with Continental Can, Bill had had little work experience. The personnel director had hired him because he was a decorated war veteran. Regretfully, the company let him go.

After that, Pete found him work with the town, but unable to sleep at night, Bill couldn't get up in the morning, and when he arrived at the job site, he was so belligerent that no one wanted to work with him. He finally quit, much to Pete's relief. It was like having two jobs, Pete said, his own and a second 8-hour shift keeping his brother out of trouble.

A couple of months later, a beer distributor in New Hyde Park hired Bill to load cases of Budweiser on trucks. The foreman, a big guy, tended to bully the men under him and made the mistake of picking on Bill repeatedly. Eventually, the foreman foolishly goaded Bill into a fight. Bill nearly killed him. The cops came, but when they learned from other workers that the foreman had thrown the first punch, they let Bill off with a warning. Summarily fired and full of regret later when he regained control, he told Nena that the Marines had taught him how to kill, but they didn't teach him how to stop.

By 1948, Bill was done with bosses and had decided to go into business for himself. In the spring he painted the house of one of Edna's neighbors and contracted to paint the Rodenbostel's Dutch colonial, next door to 41 Sycamore Avenue. Helen Rodenbostel was a huge woman, easily 5'10' and 275 lbs., who was always on a diet, a circumstance that justified making a dinner of hot dogs and beans for her husband, Cord, and their two girls while she ate steak and a huge salad. A very talented carpenter, Cord stood 5'6" and weighed in at 145 lbs. He called Helen "his monster" and let her handle all their financial affairs rarely opposing anything she said or did.

Bill had worked hard painting the Rodenbostel's house, and soft-spoken Cord was very pleased. He often invited Bill for an ice-cold beer on his screened-in back porch at the end of the workday. When Bill had finished the job, however, Helen held up paying him what was due until Bill went back over some trim pieces. He dutifully repainted the places indicated. When she still didn't pay him—she was broke, and he would have to wait—he exploded and called her a "cheap ball buster." He came very close to her face and threatened that unless she wanted a multi-colored house, she had better get him the remaining monies. She finally settled the bill two weeks later, but their friendship was at an end.

With money in his pocket, he harried Edna daily to come away with him. They could go to California like Della and Joe and begin again, something they should have done before the war. Her son, Jimmy, was 21. He would understand, and if she couldn't leave Bobby, 16, then they could take him with them.

Edna begged Bill to wait just a little while longer and let Bobby finish high school. She couldn't just wrench him away from his school, his home, his friends, and what if he didn't want to come with them? What then? Alternately, Edna would argue that she couldn't conceive of a life without her sons. Without them, she was nothing. They had gone over the same ground a hundred times before, Bill countering with the agonized question, "What about your responsibility to me?"

Before the war when they had reached this impasse, Edna would dissolve in tears, and Bill would end up comforting her, but now, his frustration led him to despair. He was 32 years old and had nothing to show for his life, neither wife, nor child, nor home, nor profession. He had begun to think that Edna would never leave.

While he was in service, she seemed to have come to an *entente cordiale* with Jack. Or was it something more? Bill didn't dare face the possibility that while he was fighting in the South Pacific the Fenty's marriage had resumed. That way surely madness lay.

The flip side of Bill's despair was pure rage. When he couldn't stand Edna's prevarication any longer, he threatened to kill Jack or her or himself. For her part, Edna was more conflicted than ever: she did care for Bill, but she also knew that he was ill and getting worse. Increasingly she feared what he might do in a moment of desperation.

Bill was more and more resentful. Dinner at the Fenty's became a nightly ordeal. Whether the topic was political or cultural, if Jack said white, Bill said black. Constantly anxious and often ruffled, Edna would have to intercede to keep the argument between the two men from boiling over. The Fenty boys found the tension almost unbearable and agonized seeing their father continually humiliated and their mother continually upset. Living with Bill was like waiting for a dynamite keg to explode.

Bill had lost his appetite for food if not for confrontation. He picked at his meals and was losing weight. It seemed as if the only thing he wanted to do was to drink himself into oblivion. After dinner, he would sit in the living room on Edna's brand new couch and place a bottle of scotch and a full ice bucket on the leather embossed coffee table that he had bought her for Christmas. To annoy Edna and show her what a weakling her husband was, he would tempt Jack to have a highball. Bill easily out-drank Jack, who had promised Edna that he wouldn't have more than one. After the fourth, Edna would have to help her collapsing husband upstairs to bed. Bill would continue making highballs until the quart was empty or he passed out himself. When Edna objected that he was ruining her couch sleeping on it all night, he left in a huff, slamming the front door and making the windows rattle.

Many nights, he ended up at the Idle Hour Tavern on Mc Kee Street where Uncle Vincent and Popeye Martone hung out. A number of times when all three were reeling, the two older men walked Bill home to Beechhurst Avenue singing and making so much noise that the neighbors complained.

In the mornings, when Jack and Jimmy had gone off to work and Bobby had left for school, Bill was surprised to find Edna still displeased from the night before. She was increasingly reluctant, despite his insistence, to accompany him upstairs.

One night in late November 1948, Bill returned from the Idle Hour roaring drunk, and when he couldn't find the clothes hook to hang up his jacket, he punched a hole in the plaster wall and stuffed his parka and hat into it. The hole in the wall was the last straw. The next day, backed up by his whole family, Jack mustered his courage and told a seriously hung-over Bill to pack his things and get out.

And Bill did, but not before he addressed the boys directly, finally telling them in detail that their mother and he had been lovers for fourteen years, how throughout the war, she had signed her letters to him as "your loving wife." Edna begged him to stop, but brushing her and her objections aside, Bill went on. She had stayed in a loveless marriage because of them, but now that they were mature enough to know, neither their mother nor he need go on hiding, lying, pretending. She finally could get a divorce and end this charade.

Jack's face had turned white. He sank into a living room chair, his gaze fixed on his wife's face. "Edna," he said quietly. "Is that... is that what you want—a divorce?" Edna tried to control her voice, but strangled sobs punctuated the few syllables she spoke. "I don't know, I don't know, I don't know," she finally cried.

Bill gave her an ultimatum—she had one week to decide what she wanted to do. He packed his things and came back to Sycamore Avenue.

Resignation

> but once in special,
> In thin array, after a pleasant guise
> When her loose gown from her shoulders did fall,
> And she caught me in her arms long and small,
> Therewithal sweetly did me kiss
> And softly said, "Dear Heart, how like you this?"
>
> It was no dream, I lay broad waking.
> But all is turned, through my gentleness,
> Into a strange fashion of forsaking.
> —Sir Thomas Wyatt the Elder, *They Flee From Me*

The years before Bill left the Fentys' had been a happy time at 41 Sycamore Avenue. Working once again for the town, Pete came home daily for lunch. One noontime just as Nena was serving him a bowl of yellow split pea soup, they heard a horrendous boom coming from somewhere behind 41. Pete was out of his chair instantly, sprinting over the fence in one leap on his way to Martone's extra yard on Lewis Avenue. Pat Martone, a cesspool contractor, used the lot to dump extra sand, cement blocks and bricks. Pete had once worked for Pat—the explosion sounded like the detonation of a dynamite cap used to blow up bedrock for cesspool installations.

And Pete was right.

Three of Pat's young sons had been playing on the sand pile, found a cap and decided to light it. Tony, 10, had blown a hole in his neck, Robbie, 6, eventually lost an eye and Jimmy, 8, had shrapnel wounds all over his legs. The next moment from our back stoop, we saw Pete walking Tony by the neck with one hand and throwing the two younger terrified and bloody kids into the cab of Pat's pickup. Pete drove madly like the fireman he was to Mineola hospital, saving Tony from bleeding to death. As far as I know, Pete never received any public recognition for his quick thinking. He was far too modest to tell anyone, but the Martones never forgot to thank him.

And Mary slowly healed as well.

Reassured by Dr. Buckley that Baby Peter's death had been an anomaly, she overcame her terror, sustained an

Nena and Moe, Godparents, 1948
Christening of Jeanne Marie Balzac

uneventful pregnancy and delivered a beautiful little girl, Jeanne, in September 1948.

Once again there was a new baby in the house. Never was a child so welcome. Bill posed with a great broad smile holding his niece the day of her christening, and my mother and father stood up as her godparents.

Above all, we were relieved that Mary's grief seemed at an end. No one knew that she kept all of Peter's clothing in a small cardboard suitcase that she carefully unpacked on his birthday for the next 15 years. Having touched each little suit, each romper and sweater, a silver rattle, a baby fork and spoon, she would shed a few tears and then carefully refold the cache and put it away.

In late 1948, Bill's return to 41 Sycamore Avenue meant a reshuffling of rooms. My mother and father had the front room that had been Pepìn's. Bill took over the green bedroom that had always been his and only lately mine. Lenny, 8, and Jeanne sleeping in a crib shared the yellow room next to Pete and Mary who occupied the back bedroom.

I was the odd man out. My mother set up a folding bed for me in the dining room. "And what will happen if Freddie decides to come home?" I had visions of the dining room turned into a nursery, Thanksgiving dinner served against a backdrop of diaper pails, bathinettes, and army cots.

> *Don't get miffed. This sleeping arrangement is only temporary.*
> *Bill and Edna will probably be going away very soon, and then*
> *you can have the green room once again.*

I knew that the Fentys had thrown Bill out, but I was surprised one night after dinner when Nena told me to take the baby upstairs and go with Lenny to the yellow room and stay there.

> *Edna will be here in a few minutes. She and Bill are going to*
> *resolve this thing one way or the other.*

My mother's language was uncharacteristically vague. She, my father, Mary and Pete were going to their respective bedrooms to give the unhappy lovers a chance to talk privately. At the last minute, Mary and Pete decided to bring the baby and Lenny with them telling me to stay in the yellow bedroom. 41 became unexpectedly silent; all the adults closed their doors, and their discretion gave me the opportunity to tip-toe into the hallway and out to the stairs.

Seated in the dark, pressed up against the banister, I was perched just above the kitchen door. I had a full view of the foyer and the narrow hall from it to the kitchen. Within a few minutes, Edna came in from the front of the house and headed towards the kitchen door where Bill was waiting for her. She never looked up or saw me. The two of them couldn't have been more than four feet below me. I felt like a theatergoer in a darkened loge seat; below me, a great love affair was coming to a conclusion.

After a very short and low interchange, I heard Edna say sadly, "I can't. I won't." At that, Bill sprang. He had his hands around her throat, but he wasn't strangling her. He was pushing her down, saying over and over, "You must submit, you must submit."

She was lost. An inarticulate, mournful wail kept coming from her throat even as he tried to force her to the floor. Just then, the foyer door flew open, and Bobby Fenty came running in with a rifle pointed directly at Bill. I learned later that when he heard his mother cry out, Jimmy Fenty ran into the kitchen from the back door wielding a Bowie knife. Prepared to hurt Bill if necessary, her sons had accompanied Edna and armed themselves in case she needed protection.

When I saw Bobby running through the foyer, I was on my feet. I fled down the stairs and out the front door to Helen Rodenbostel's house.

"Helen, Helen! Please call the police! Someone's going to kill my Uncle Bill."

Helen was so afraid of him since their brouhaha over the house painting that she agreed to dial for me but wouldn't speak to the cops herself. Instead she handed me the receiver. It seemed to take the operator forever to get the information straight.

"Yes, yes. 41 Sycamore Avenue. Please hurry."

By the time I got back to the house, Bill was lying face down on the marbled kitchen floor. Patterned with swirls of black and red on a cream ground, the linoleum was smeared with blood, and a huge glob of what looked like liver lay close to Bill's body. Hearing his mother cry and seeing Bill menacing her, Jimmy Fenty had stabbed Bill in the small of the back.

Perhaps the trauma jolted Bill to his senses, for he immediately told Edna's boys to take their mother and go home quickly. Bill was conscious, but weak. Just before the ambulance arrived, two detectives came. They didn't believe his story that as he came down the stairs he had fallen on his knife.

My mother rode with Bill to the hospital, and for three days he was in critical condition. The knife had perforated his left kidney. The surgeon thought he could save the kidney if Bill were operated on immediately. Though Bill and Mary had never liked one another, she generously donated blood for him.

Once Bill's condition stabilized, the detectives interrogated him and the family once more. Though Bill refused to press charges, Jimmy Fenty was arrested for felonious assault with a deadly weapon. Curiously, the shock of the stabbing had sobered Bill, and during the months before the trial as he recuperated, he was silent, alcohol-free and calm. His good breeding and fine manners reasserted themselves.

When the case was tried in early 1949, Bill did everything he could to exonerate Jimmy. Bill testified that he was at fault, that the Fenty boys were only trying to protect their mother. Pressed by the prosecutor, Bill refused to answer anything about the nature of his relationship to Edna.

In support of her son, Edna was in the courtroom during the entire trial, sometimes breaking down and weeping silently. Neither the prosecution nor the defense called her to the stand. Edna could not testify; she had lost the power of speech.

The trial came to an end in late March. An Eagle Scout who had never been in trouble with the law, Jimmy Fenty was given a suspended sentence with five years' probation and set free. Three weeks after the ordeal was over, the Fentys sold their house and moved somewhere in Suffolk County. Bill never saw Edna again.

1950

When, in disgrace with fortune and in men's eyes,
I all alone beweep my outcast state,
And trouble deaf heaven with my bootless cries,
And look upon myself, and curse my fate,
Wishing me like to one more rich in hope,
Featured like him, like him with friends possessed...
With what I most enjoy contented least;
Yet in these thoughts myself almost despising,
Haply I think on thee...
—William Shakespeare, *Sonnet 29*

Nena and I and peripatetic Freddie (lately returned from California, then Boston, then Florida) loved Bill inordinately. Pete also loved his brother but kept his feelings in check in deference to Mary.

Even before the War, my father and his sister Mary feared Bill. Early in my parents' marriage when they were living in Jamaica with my paternal grandfather, my father hit my noticeably pregnant mother bruising her face and giving her a black eye.

Her in-laws who had heard the whole argument said nothing. They sprang from a culture where such male behavior was acceptable. Hadn't Papa slapped their saintly mother around when "she got out of line," and in broken English, didn't he often say of marriage, "You've got to put two feet in one shoe?"

Nena wouldn't stay with Moe in their bedroom; she stumbled downstairs and spent the night crying in the basement. Around 5 a.m. she heard the milkman as he made his rounds and opened the side door as he was leaving a couple of bottles of milk. She begged him to take her to her father's house in Floral Park. She had no money, but her Dad would pay him for his time and trouble. The deliveryman took one look at her battered face and burgeoning body and brought her all the way home.

Two weeks later, my father had calmed down. He wanted his wife back and went to Floral Park to see her. Incensed that any man would lay hands on a woman, much less a pregnant woman and his sister to boot, Bill took the wife-beater out into the back yard at 41 Sycamore, thrashed him bloody and knocked out one of his teeth. Of course, Mary and the rest of his family took their brother's part blaming Nena for "not treating him right."

But Mary's dislike of Bill became an irrational hatred only after his court trial. Months later, he had fully recovered from the kidney wound, but he hadn't found work, wasn't even looking through the want ads and no longer contributed to the upkeep of the house. He was sick physically and emotionally. He sat in the sun porch hour after hour playing his harmonica or reading Elbert Hubbard's *Scrapbook*, a collection of philosophical passages and poems that Edna had given him one happier year at Christmas. Inscribed on the flyleaf in his hand was Shakespeare's *Sonnet 29*. He hated to leave the house and would beg me to go up to Ruby's Candy Store across from the Polish Church and buy him a pack of cigarettes. Reluctantly, I'd stop whatever I was doing and go on the errand for him.

If he had money for Camels, Mary huffed indignantly, then "he could at least pay his share of the telephone bill including the tax." In the heat of an argument over charges for his calls, Bill called her and her whole family (with the exception of Jenny) ignorant, petty and cheap. As a final insult, he scornfully accused Mary of militant stupidity, and she never forgave him.[42]

Nena begged Mary not to provoke Bill. Mary responded that even if he cowed everyone else, she wasn't afraid to stand up to him. My mother was too much of a diplomat to tell Mary that courage in the face of murderous irrationality was another instance of militant stupidity.

Nena's concern was to keep Bill from hurting someone. Mary and Moe were obvious targets. Poor Pete was in the middle: he knew that the war had terribly damaged Bill, and he sympathized with his brother's hopelessness especially in regard to Edna, but Pete had little respect for anyone who didn't want to work. He also resented the threat Bill posed to Mary. In order to assuage his wife, Pete stopped speaking to his brother. Less said, less conflict, he reasoned.

All of us felt as if we were living with a time bomb. We just didn't know when it might go off.

This acrimonious and potentially dangerous situation led both Mary and my mother to make the important decision to leave 41 Sycamore Avenue to Bill and Freddy (presently working in Florida during the winter and alternating between Floral Park and Boston in the summer).

Early in 1950, my father convinced my reluctant mother that they should look for a house in northern New Jersey. With the War years excepted, he had been driving to the Presto Lock Company in Garfield since 1937, and the 2-hour commute each way was wearing him down. Every time he had broached the subject of moving before, Nena had flatly refused. It was as if in her insistence on remaining in Floral Park, she had married him in order to care more adequately for her brothers. In 1950, however, Nena finally agreed to relinquish stewardship of Freddie and Bill, an obligation that she had undertaken 23 years before.

We moved in August to a new two-bedroom cape on a high hill in Lodi, New Jersey. At last Nena and Moe had their own place, and at a distance from both their families, their marriage gradually improved.

Over the past few years, Pete and Mary had become very close to Peg and Bill Reilly, an older couple who lived at 17 Sycamore Avenue, one of the newer houses on the street. When Bill Reilly retired and wanted to move to California, Peg and he offered to sell their house to their young friends. Born in the front bedroom at 41 Sycamore, Pete left his father's house for good in early November 1950 when he was 32. He was to spend the next 43 years in his home six doors away.

Small Durance

> *O the mind, the mind has mountains; cliffs of fall*
> *Frightful, sheer, no-man-fathomed. Hold them cheap*
> *May who ne'er hung there. Nor does long our small*
> *Durance deal with that steep or deep. Here! creep,*
> *Wretch, under a comfort serves in a whirlwind: all*
> *Life death does end and each day dies with sleep.*
> —Gerard Manley Hopkins, *(No Worst, There Is None)*

First Nena, now Pete, Freddie thought, as the last truckload of Mary's furniture left 41. Jesus! The Balzacs are abandoning ship.

He wouldn't do that. Bill needed his support. He had come from Boston at the end of October. By that time, with neither Pete nor Mary speaking to Bill, things were tense. Though Freddie should have been heading south, he would stay through the holidays and try to talk his brother into coming to Vero Beach, Florida before the cold weather really set in. The change of scene, the warm weather, the sea would be good for Bill's physical and mental health.

At 18, Bill had been a powerful swimmer, sleek and swift like an otter. Often in the summer when Freddie was still living with Vincent and visiting 41 on the weekends, the Balzacs would pile into John Porth's car and go to the North Shore. At Bar Beach as a 10-year-old, Freddie had so admired his brother's skill in the water that Bill offered to teach him the Australian Crawl. The boy was an apt pupil, and Bill, a talented teacher.

Eventually, Freddie wanted to swim out to the huge rock offshore where his brother and sister sunned themselves. At first Nena was apprehensive about allowing her little brother to go into deep water, but swimming at Freddie's side, Bill made sure that the kid wasn't getting winded, and even if he did tire, Bill could easily tow Freddie to the beach. As Freddie looked back on those days, his siblings had struck a nice balance: Nena protected him, and Bill allowed him to dare.

Freddie had fond memories of those sun and salt-water summers. With a similar regimen in Florida, Freddie was sure that Bill could get his health back. If Bill weren't exhausted all the time, he wouldn't be so irascible. Good food, hard work and frequent exercise, preferably in the ocean, would solve Bill's problems with sleeping. That was a first step, Freddie reasoned.

Once in Vero Beach, the "Gateway to the Tropics," Andy Di Pietro would be sure to look after them. If Andy couldn't employ the Balzac brothers at his foundry, he knew everyone in Vero and would help Freddie and Bill find work.

The Di Pietros were an Italian-American family originally from Boston who had taken a liking to Freddie a few years before. Coming back from California, Fred had found a job in a hotel dining room in Boston.

He met Dom Di Pietro, a street-wise snowbird who was a waiter there in the summer and an ironworker in Florida in the winter. When cold weather began to grip the Northeast, Dom invited Freddie to come down to Vero where Dom's father, Andy, owned an ornamental iron works.

What did the Di Pietros know about heart defects? Andy put Freddie to work as a welder. Though it was a hot and heavy job, Freddie learned to pace himself and never had a weak spell. Coincidentally, he learned a trade. In the summer of 1950 when the slack season in Florida came, Dom and Fred returned to Boston, but by the fall, with Nena living in New Jersey and Pete about to move into his new home, Freddie had come back to Floral Park to be with Bill.

Now the brothers' immediate problem was to prepare 41 Sycamore Avenue for the cold of late November and December. Neither Bill nor Freddie wanted to spend what little money they had for coal. Fortuitously, a few weeks before, a windstorm had blown down a number of trees, and armed with an axe and a saw, Bill had collected a considerable pile of wood in the side yard by the cellar door. Cut into 2' lengths, the logs could be burned in the furnace for fuel. Bill was using a section of a tree trunk as a chopping block, and Freddie was helping by dragging one large branch at a time to the block and then stacking the pieces Bill had cut.

Bill hadn't slept much the night before and was working himself into a lather. There was no hurry, but he was over-exerting himself out of sheer irritability. Since he was doing the majority of the work, he expected Freddie to keep up with him.

"Hey, get the goddamned lead out! Let's go here! Move it!"

When Bill was annoyed, there was no way to satisfy him. It was best not to say anything, Freddie decided. He turned his back on his brother who didn't approve of the way Freddie was stacking the wood. When Bill continued barking orders, Freddie quipped humorously, "Hey, I'm not trying out for the Marines, and you're not my D.I."

The next thing Freddie knew Bill had thrown a good-sized log at him, and if Freddie hadn't heard a whistling sound, turned and jumped aside, it would have hit him hard in the back of the head. The blow could have killed him. Instead the log glanced Freddie's cheek. Stunned more than hurt, Freddie took one long look at his brother, then stripped off his work gloves and went into the house. By the time Bill came in to apologize, Freddie was already packed. Bill begged him to stay. Sorry to have lost his temper, Bill promised that it wouldn't happen again. Freddie didn't respond. He just picked up his suitcase and left.

Alone, abandoned, cut off from Fred and Nena, Joe and Della, with Pete close by but not speaking to him, Bill's physical and mental condition steadily deteriorated.

[42] Mary so despised Bill and his education that years later she made Lenny, an Honor student, take secretarial courses in high school and encouraged Jeanne to become a hairdresser. "My daughters are not going to college," she declared defiantly, "to become arrogant like Bill."

Part 2, Chapter 6
Broad Day's Midnight

A night flowing with birds, a ragged moon,
And in broad day the midnight come again!
A man goes far to find out what he is—
Death of the self in a long, tearless night,
All natural shapes blazing unnatural light.

Dark, dark my light, and darker my desire.
My soul, like some heat-maddened summer fly,
Keeps buzzing at the sill. Which I is I?
- Theodore Roethke, *In A Dark Time*

The week before Christmas 1950, as Bill strode up the street headed for Ruby's Candy Store to buy cigarettes, he seemed to hear the three witches gossiping about him, whispering behind their starched lace curtains. That's who they reminded him of, the three witches from *Macbeth*. As soon as Helen Rodenbostel, Tante Paula Hartmann and Ruth Martone spied him coming their way, they began catcalling, chanting his name over and over like some obscene litany. They were driving him crazy. "Bill Balzac, Bill Balzac, Bill Balzac," they raved. "Balzac's a fairy, a fairy, a fairy."

The women thought he couldn't hear the hateful things they were saying about him, but he could. He was sure that all the neighbors had begun talking about him. They had begun harassing him in the summer after Nena moved to New Jersey. At first he tried to tell himself that his mind was playing tricks on him, that no one was speaking, but now as winter came on, he heard their clanging, ringing voices practically every time he left home. Some nights, he couldn't get to sleep because the shrikes had gotten into the house somehow, and he could hear them buzzing like a swarm of demented bees inside the walls at 41.

Ever since Bill finished painting the Rodenbostel's house two years before, he had nothing but scorn for his German neighbors. Helen was always gossiping with Paula Hartmann, who lived with her husband, Fritz, at 35 Sycamore Avenue, two houses down from 41. That Paula was a prying old bitch! She insisted that all the children on the block call her "Tante Paula"—as if anyone would ever want her to be their aunt! Bill laughed bitterly at that thought.

Didn't that nosey Paula lure little Lenny with cookies? Then with the two of them seated on Paula's stoop, she would pump the kid for information. Bill sucked his teeth in disgust. Because of that rotten scandalmonger, Mary had taught Lenny at 2 years old to say, "I mustn't repeat," the child's very first sentence.

"Look there," Tante Paula pointed at him as he passed. "There he goes, that homo drunk. He never dated anyone nor took a wife because he was queer. That's why he liked the Marines so much—all those young boys."

Helen was even nastier than Paula. "He called us Nazis and didn't like living next door to us. Well, we didn't like living next door to a *schwartze.* For years he passed for white, but we knew better."

Paula responded looking down her long nose, "He's a killer—even the Marines said so—and the professor at his university called him a throwback to a primitive African tribesman."

In the next yard, though the temperature was near freezing, Ruth Martone made believe that she had come outdoors to hang up the wash. Actually she couldn't resist adding her two cents worth to the evil sisters' diatribe. "Can you believe it? That's Bill Balzac, the swaggering Marine coward-hero. How come he returned, and his buddy's rotting on some gook island?"

"Just look at him!" She curled her lip in scorn. "They call me a drunk, but
at least I'm clean." She sniffed under her arms but wasn't altogether pleased by her own aroma. "He's filthy. Now that he isn't bedding that holier-than-thou Fenty woman, he doesn't wash, shave or cut his hair. He smells worse than a latrine, and it looks like he hasn't had a bath or a decent night's sleep in a month of Sundays."

Bill hurried to the corner of Hitchcock Avenue to get away from their gibes and walked quickly to Depan Avenue and Jericho. He entered Ruby's Candy Store and bought cigarettes, nervously lighting one before he left. He decided to stop at the Idle Hour until it got dark and have a couple of beers to calm down. If he could just sneak home without the women seeing him! And then he wouldn't have to listen to their spite.

Thank God, the neighbors must have been eating supper because he didn't hear a peep out of any of the women as he passed by. Reaching

41, he entered by the side door, then went into the kitchen. He had brought the mattress down from his bedroom and placed it under the window. In very cold weather, it was impossible to sleep in his frigid upstairs bedroom. To save money, he banked the furnace maintaining a temperature of 60° throughout the house and ignited a small kerosene heater in the kitchen as needed.

He was chilled and terribly tired. He lay down in his clothes, pulled the blankets up and gratefully wrapped them around his body. He was just nodding off when a large blinding searchlight began sweeping the first floor of the house. Unless they turned it off, he'd never get to sleep.

He got up to look out. He was shocked. The light was coming from Estelle Sommers' dining room bay window across the empty lot next to 41. He had never had any trouble with Estelle and John. She and Bill had gone to Sewanhaka together long before she ever met John Sommers. Why were they doing this to him?

Bill put on his trench coat and stormed over to the Sommers' house. He banged furiously on the front door. After a moment or two, timid, bespectacled Estelle put on the porch light and peered into the darkness. Her face lit up when she saw him. She had always admired Bill in high school. He was such a good student, so bright and clear. In math class, he had once explained quadratic equations to her, and she had never had difficulties with them again. As valedictorian, he had delivered an eloquent graduation address. Despite the Depression, he spoke to the aspirations of all his fellow students. He was their Paraclete urging them on.

"Why, Bill," Estelle said in surprise. "Please come in," and she held the door open wide. "Whatever is the matter?" Just looking at him, she could see that he was in distress. "Come in and have a cup of tea with me." Assuming that Bill had come to talk to her husband, an insurance agent, she added, "John is at the store with the children, but they'll be back in a couple of minutes."

No, he hadn't come to see John, and he didn't want tea. He needed to get some sleep. He wanted her and John to stop shining that light into the kitchen at 41. It was coming directly from her dining room.

"But Bill," Estelle replied, shaking her head sadly from side to side, "I swear to you there's no searchlight here. Come see for yourself." She was so sincere and spoke to him so gently that Bill was disarmed. He followed her into the dining room where John had put up a big Christmas tree only that afternoon. Estelle, John Jr. and little Ronnie had had a grand time decorating it. On its very top, the Sommers had placed a large illuminated star.

Was that the light Bill had seen? Estelle asked. Bill was so embarrassed he couldn't speak. Realizing that something was seriously wrong, Estelle insisted on removing the star from the tree. "No. No. I'll take it away. There," she said solicitously unscrewing the bulb within the star, "the light is gone. You'll be able to sleep now."

Estelle was staring hard at him from behind her glasses, but before Bill could take offense, she asked him if he had eaten—she, John and the boys had finished dinner only an hour before. She would fix a dish for him.

Bill thanked her for her kindness, but he wasn't hungry. He was so ashamed, so sorry to have bothered her. He just wanted to go home and get some rest.

Christmas, 1950

Yet each man kills the thing he loves,
By each let this be heard,
Some do it with a bitter look,
Some with a flattering word.

Some kill their love when they are young,
And some when they are old;
Some strangle with the hands of Lust,
Some with the hands of Gold:
The kindest use a knife, because
The dead so soon grow cold.

Some do the deed with many tears,
And some without a sigh:
For each man kills the thing he loves,
Yet each man does not die.
—Oscar Wilde, *The Ballad of Reading Gaol*

Helen Broderick called Pete on Christmas Eve. She and her husband, Smitty, a New York City cop, had lived on Sycamore Avenue in the 1930s. Childless, she had watched the entire Balzac brood grow up. Now in her late 60s, retired from nursing and widowed, she lived in Queens

Village. Over the years she and Nena had stayed in touch largely by notes in Christmas and Easter cards. Pete and Bill would stop and see her every now and then, and when Helen was in Floral Park, she was always made to feel welcome at 41.

Because of the holiday, Pete wasn't surprised to hear Helen's raspy voice. But she wasn't telephoning to wish him a Merry Christmas. In her no-nonsense way, she didn't bother with the usual pleasantries.

"Pete," she said tersely, "You'd better go down to 41. Bill went crazy last night and says he destroyed it. For whatever reason, he's ended up on my doorstep, and he's very sick. I can handle him, but I thought you'd want to know about the house."

Except for Bill, everyone—including the Aunts—had been invited for the first Christmas dinner at Pete's new house. There would be nine plus the baby at the table, eating and exchanging gifts. We, the New Jersey contingent, were looking forward to the holiday and started out early so that Nena could help Mary with the cooking and serving.

As Nena was making the gravy for the turkey and Mary and I were setting the table, my mother remarked on the closed Venetian blinds in the living room and dining room. It was a bright, if chill, day. She suggested that the sunshine would make the house look more festive. Mary confessed that she kept the downstairs blinds closed at all times.

She was afraid for herself and the children whenever Pete went to work or was out. She thought that Bill was looking in her windows.

She had instructed Lenny not to speak to him should the child see him when getting on or off the school bus. At all other times, Mary made Lenny and the baby play in the backyard; the front was off limits. My mother was troubled—it was hurtful to forbid Lenny to say hello to her uncle—but she didn't pursue the conversation further because the Aunts had just entered the house. Pete had returned from Brooklyn where he had gone to pick them up.

Nena took one look at her brother's face and knew that he was upset. Pete had been sick ever since he had gone down to 41 the night before to find water pouring out the side door. The cellar was flooded, but he was able to reach the cut-off valve, turn the water off and pump it out. The gas line had also ruptured, so he capped it, then called the emergency telephone number at Jamaica Power and Gas to cut off service to the house. As for the ground floor and upstairs, he couldn't describe the devastation—Nena would have to go down and see it for herself.

Pete was sick not only over the destruction of the house but over the months of work that restoring it would take. He would and could do all the repairs in odd hours after work and on the weekends, but only on one condition: once fixed, the house was to be rented. Bill was never to live there again. Not until my mother saw 41 for herself did she agree to her younger brother's demand.

Mary immediately began to question what all this work was going to cost. Would the house insurance pay anything when they learned that one of the owners had vandalized his own family's property? Who was going to pay the taxes? Why should Pete always be stuck with fixing everything?

My mother volunteered to come from Jersey and do whatever she could to clean the place up. Mary's heated response to that offer was that <u>she</u> wouldn't lift a finger to help. She had spent enough years cleaning a house that six people owned but only one seemed to be responsible for whenever something went wrong. It was just ridiculous. Pete saw Nena flinch, but she didn't say a word. Surely, not only Pete, but she also had expended energy—for many more years than Mary had—taking care of 41.

Stridently, Mary began once more to question who was going to pay the final gas, electric and water bills. Pete exploded. He wouldn't allow his wife to badger his sister. "Goddamn it, Mary. It's none of your business. Shut the hell up."

At home the day before, my mother had cooked Spanish rice and beans for Bill and had brought them from Lodi in an insulated bag. Her intention had been to have dinner at Pete's, then visit with her outcast brother at 41 while he ate the food she had prepared for him. Instead, after Christmas dinner, heavy-hearted Nena and I walked together to the deserted house at 41 Sycamore Avenue. Mary and my father refused to have anything more to do with the disaster.

We went in through the side door, entered the kitchen and gasped. The porcelain sink had been ripped off its legs and broken in pieces. The floor-to-ceiling wooden cabinets lay overturned, hacked to bits, glass from the top windows shattered and strewn all over the floor.

A month of newspapers covered a filthy mattress thrown under the window. Near it lay two tattered and dirty blankets that were so thin they couldn't have kept anyone warm. There were hundreds of deep cuts, probably knife marks, in the wall opposite the mattress. Bill must have lain in bed and repeatedly practiced his throw.

In the dining room, Bill had used an axe or a sledgehammer to smash the few pieces of furniture left when Mary and Pete moved out. Debris from old chairs and end tables, newspapers and magazines, broken china and glassware littered the dining room and living room floors making it difficult to recognize the scene of so many happier holidays.

Bill had pulled the pocket doors off their tracks and thrown them onto a pile in the center of the living room. Beneath the doors lay Dad's splintered and upended bookcase. Numerous volumes of the *Harvard Classics* and *Book of Knowledge,* that had been so precious to Pepìn, lay ripped and splayed on the floor. The whole downstairs smelled of mildew and neglect, and the walls radiated a penetrating cold.

Upstairs a few intact bureaus were jammed up against the windows so that no light could penetrate nor anyone see in. Beds frames were broken, their mattresses slashed. In the bathroom, an odor of decay from broken pipes and half-dried puddles of water assailed us. The cast iron, claw-footed tub had been pulled off its cement footing and lay on top of the cracked sink and broken toilet.

Speechless, we went back downstairs to the cellar. A giant hand seemed to have mangled the overhead copper piping; a giant arm had stove in the furnace. Our beloved house was in ruins.

The Madhouse

The wild winds weep,
And the night is a-cold;
Come hither, Sleep,
And my griefs enfold

Like a fiend in a cloud
With howling woe,
After the night I do croud,
And with night will go
For light doth seize my brain
With frantic pain.
—William Blake, *Mad Song*

The two weeks after Christmas were anxious ones for my mother. Helen Broderick had told Pete that she didn't want anyone to call until Bill felt better. Finally on January 6, 1951, Helen got in touch with Pete and Nena.

On Christmas Eve when Bill rang Helen's doorbell, he was so gaunt and unkempt that at first she didn't recognize him. He tried to tell her what had happened to him and what he had done to the house, but he broke down.

She realized that he was exhausted—whatever his recent problems, they would wait. "When did you eat last"? He couldn't remember. For the moment what he needed, Helen realized, was to have some nourishing food and get some rest. She brought him a clean bathrobe that had belonged to Smitty and talked him into taking a shower while she prepared dinner for them both. While he was showering, she threw his dirty clothes in the washing machine, set the table and ladled out a hearty bowl of New England clam chowder for each of them. She started to serve him some left over roast beef and vegetables, but he was already full.

After eating he asked for a drink to steady his nerves. Instead, she brought him warm sweetened milk and a sleeping pill. "You don't need alcohol right now. You need rest." She made up a bed for him on the couch, got him to lie down and turned off all the lights except one in the kitchen. When she came back ten minutes later to check on him, Bill was already asleep. He didn't wake up until 1 p.m. the next day.

Despite her diminutive stature, Helen Broderick was a powerful woman. Standing no more than 5'1" and weighing about 105 lbs., she was as stringy, intelligent and tough as the Dowager Empress of China. She exhaled authority, and as a head nurse with many years' experience, expected compliance and deserved respect.

By the time she clipped Bill's hair and shaved him with a straight razor the next afternoon, he had begun to look like the Bill Balzac she had known for more than twenty years. She told him straight out that she wanted to help him, but she meant to pry. If he wasn't ready to talk honestly to her, he had better leave and not waste her time. Bill accepted that stricture and did talk to her—about Edna, the war, the nightmares, the knifing, the inability to work and the desire to kill.

Had he not destroyed the house, she concluded, he would have murdered somebody. After two weeks of rest and good nutrition, he was able to concede that he had been hearing voices and having hallucinations. Finally lucid after months of neglecting himself, he fully realized that his neighbors—Helen Rodenbostel, Tante Paula and Ruth Martone—were innocent. They had not been whispering obscenities about him nor taunting him whenever he passed by their houses. With Helen's help, he was able to face the implications of those delusions.

Helen had seen cases of battle fatigue before. For some men, though they never forget the horrors of battle, over time they are able to relegate the images to a back burner of the mind partially because their resumed civilian life claims their full attention. For others, depending upon their background and sensitivity, the morbid effects of warfare—depression, insomnia, nightmares, irritability, uncontrollable rage—just do not go away. Medication and psychotherapy can benefit those so afflicted. She explained and Bill agreed: he needed professional help.

On January 6, Bill and Helen went together to Bellevue Hospital in New York City where he voluntarily signed himself in as a mental patient. The most famous psychiatric facility in the country, Bellevue served as a diagnostic center. It did not have the space to treat patients who sought help there and could only keep them for a short time. Over a period of two weeks, psychiatrists on the staff would observe, evaluate and then send Bill to another facility for treatment. Not until he was relocated could he have visitors.

The preliminary diagnosis stated that Bill was suffering from paranoia-schizophrenia. Nena and Pete were horrified, bewildered and relieved all at the same time. Insanity was the terror they had dared not name much less think about, and without any prior experience with mental illness, they lacked information about methods of treatment and long term prognoses. Bill was in Bellevue—the very name frightened my mother; nevertheless she blessed Helen Broderick for convincing Bill to seek help there.

For his part, Pete was grateful that Mary and the kids could resume a normal life. Mary could open the blinds, the kids could finally play in their front yard and Pete could stop worrying about his wife and children when he was away from the house. Despite Mary's overreaction, he had never believed that his brother would harm the children. Bill loved Lenny and, like all of us, had joyously welcomed Jeanne's birth; nevertheless, Pete had feared that his children might witness an ugly confrontation between his wife and his brother, especially if Mary caught Bill peering in one of her windows.

In late January 1951, Bill was sent from Bellevue to the Kings Park Psychiatric Center in Suffolk County, Long Island. A huge hospital at the time, Kings Park housed over 8,500 patients, its population peaking in 1954 at 9300. In order to deal with so many inmates, the over-taxed staff relied on medicating them heavily, and in many cases, administering multiple courses of electric or insulin shock therapy.

Frontal lobotomies were routinely performed on the most violent patients. Though these therapies are largely discontinued nowadays, at the time thousands of inmates were subjected to them. In particular, transcranial electroshock induced a 2 to 3 minute convulsion akin to an epileptic seizure and produced retrograde amnesia including a loss of memory of the treatment itself. Having forgotten what was troubling them at least for a time, many disturbed persons were enabled to return to ordinary life.

From the very first, Bill despised Kings Park, and his complaints were constant and numerous. Though the reception rooms for visitors and their families were clean, the wards were not. Rats and roaches were everywhere, Bill claimed, but worst of all, patients, many of whom were elderly and incontinent, were neglected, and at night, in particular, the inmates had to put up with the nauseating stench coming from adults' unchanged diapers. In comparison to other inmates, he was normal; in fact, the behavior of some patients was so bizarre that just watching and having to be with them would make a sane man crazy.

During the week, the food was so bad that he lived on orange juice, milk and bread and butter waiting for Saturday when Nena would bring him rice and beans or sliced *pernil*, pork shoulder, with oven baked potatoes and onions.

And as far as care was concerned, how much could doctors accomplish when they only saw patients for 45 minutes per week? To top that off, he had had an interview with a woman doctor wearing a short skirt who kept crossing and uncrossing her legs. He couldn't decide if she was teasing him or testing his sexual responsiveness. Sometimes he wondered who was loonier—the patients or the staff?

Clearly, Bill was armored against any therapy given him, and we had difficulty deciding whether what he described was true or an exaggeration. And almost from the outset, Bill wanted to get out of the hospital, but having signed himself in, it wasn't so easy to be released. A medical review board would determine when he was well enough to go home.

My mother went to see Bill every week never missing a visiting day, a fact that Bill boasted about to other patients. She caught a bus from Lodi to New York's Port Authority on 42nd Street, then took the subway down to Penn Station and the Long Island Railroad train from there to Kings Park. On a good day, it took her over three hours each way. Seriously ill with diabetes, the trip exhausted Nena. Bringing Bill his favorite foods and trying to satisfy his ever-increasing demands for psychiatric literature, she spent about three days every week attending to her brother's needs.

Between shopping for special foods and cooking them, running to libraries to get the article or book Bill wanted, and having to rest for most of the day after her trip to Kings Park, Nena was frazzled, a state that both concerned and angered Moe. Wasn't that why they had moved from Floral Park? To get away from her brothers at long last? After a nine-month respite, he felt that she was right back where she had started.

Nena could manage the physical claims on her energy, but assuming total responsibility for Bill's treatment was almost more than she could bear. Admitted to Bellevue and considered *non compos mentis*, Bill had signed papers naming her his legal guardian.

Sometime in late February when she arrived at Kings Park and requested to see her brother, she found instead that a staff doctor urgently wanted to see her. He ushered her into his office, prefacing his comments by telling her that she couldn't see her brother that day. Two days before, Bill had become agitated when another inmate had taken his magazine. The attendants had had to restrain him with a straight jacket, and for the time being, Bill had been transferred to a floor for violent and uncooperative patients. The doctors and staff had reviewed Bill's behavior and concluded that medication alone was not an adequate therapy for him. They necessarily looked to her for permission to administer electric shock treatments to her brother.

Nena refused until she was able to see Bill the next week. He begged her not to sign the papers. Mad or not mad, he was formidable, and she wavered, not knowing what to do. I was 14 at the time and often went with her to see Bill. Nena naturally turned to me for advice, and I can remember saying, "Mommy, if you want Uncle Bill to get better, do what the doctors say."

Poor, guilty Nena signed, and poor, angry Bill underwent 38 electric shock treatments, three times a week over a period of almost four months. By May, he had lost 40 pounds and his teeth had literally rotted in his head, but he certainly was more docile. He no longer had nightmares—memory routes seemed to have been erased—and he didn't mention Edna any more.

Though to Nena, Bill seemed befuddled and weakened by the therapy, his doctors were pleased with his progress. They had turned a brilliant and violent psychotic into a stolid and submissive automaton. My mother was in anguish not knowing when or if Bill would come back to himself. What had she done?

Over his six-month stay at Kings Park, Bill learned how to satisfy his doctors, and at the end of the summer, the hospital's medical board released him in my mother's custody with the proviso that he not leave the state.

Bill needed care. Where was she to take him if not home with her to Lodi, New Jersey? And this time, it wasn't Moe living in her family's house, but Bill Balzac living under Moe's roof.

Part 2, Chapter 7
Turn About

After great pain, a formal feeling comes—
The Nerves sit ceremonious, like Tombs—
This is the Hour of Lead—
Remembered, if outlived,
As freezing persons, recollect the Snow—
First—Chill—then Stupor—then the letting go–
—Emily Dickinson, (341)

Nena wrote Freddie frequently in Florida and kept him informed about Bill's condition. She knew that Freddie was concerned, but he never called or wrote back. Any number of times, confused about what she should do in regards to Bill, she had wanted to confer with Freddie. Finally, just before Bill was to be released from the hospital, she decided to call Andy Di Pietro in Vero Beach. If Freddie had left Florida, perhaps Andy had a contact number.

Andy's response was curt and to the point. He requested that she send all future updates about Bill to him. Freddie had gone into such a terrible depression as a result of her letters that he was only beginning to come out of it now. He had been unable to eat, sleep, work, speak or be with people, and for weeks, Dom had maintained a suicide watch over his friend. Having left Bill to face his demons alone, Freddie's guilt had overwhelmed him.

Nena apologized abjectly to Andy. Admonished by a stranger for insensitivity, she had not realized how fragile her younger brother was.

I do not know how Nena managed. Essentially, she was alone—Pete didn't want to hear about Bill's sufferings; Freddie couldn't be told and my father adamantly opposed her continuing involvement in Bill's welfare.

Nevertheless, somehow she got Moe to agree to house her brother—just until Bill got on his feet. In addition, as the foreman of the Polishing Department, he was able to get Bill a job at Presto Lock. And my father did try to be a Good Samaritan, however ill-suited he was for the role.

Bill was emaciated, tired and silent. He slept on a folding cot in the living room. Though I was more than willing, my father would not allow me to give up my room to Bill. Wisely, my mother didn't challenge Moe about this decision. A subtle tactician, she permitted Moe to win the skirmishes as long as she won the war.

And Moe waged guerilla warfare against an all-but-defeated, long-standing enemy. Since my father couldn't rid himself of Bill, Moe did any number of petty things, like run the vacuum early on Saturday mornings so that Bill couldn't sleep or turn off the radio when Bill obviously had tuned into a Spanish music station and was listening.

I also had to be very careful not to show affection for my uncle. If Bill were talking to me about my high school Ancient History course (about which he had forgotten nothing), my father would interrupt and send me on an unnecessary errand. In as many ways as he could, my father demonstrated that Bill was not welcome.

Bill never objected, and for the better part of six months, I wasn't sure whether he even noticed. He said little and did little more than sleep and eat and go to work. He was an emotionless robot, and it broke Nena's heart and mine to see him so diminished.

After 5 months, Bill had regained some of his strength and much of the weight he had lost. Though he was still very quiet, he seemed more self-assured. He told my mother at Thanksgiving that he had been saving his money for the past few months to rent a place of his own. Passaic had many rooming houses and commuting from there by bus to Presto Lock in Garfield would be easy. Eventually, he would find a small apartment. What he didn't tell her was that, using his sick day allowance to take off from work, he was also looking for another job. On days that Bill begged off going to work, my father believed him and told everyone at Presto that his brother-in-law wasn't feeling well.

When Bill did give notice at the plant, my father was incensed, though he didn't dare say a word in his brother-in-law's presence. Moe had gone out on a limb to get Bill the position, and now Bill didn't want it. Moe fumed bitterly. He should have known better. That Bill was quitting made my father look bad. After this fiasco, he maintained, the bosses at Presto Lock wouldn't pay any attention to his suggestions or recommendations for a long time.

Nena took the full brunt of my father's seething resentment. Would Moe really lose prestige at work, she wondered, or was he just angry that Bill had asserted himself? By taking another job, Bill evaded being under my father's thumb at least for 8 hours of the day.

Christmas morning, 1951, started out splendidly. My mother was making pancakes for the four of us when Bill made her stop and open two huge presents in the living room. He had bought her a Duncan Phyfe mahogany coffee table with a tooled leather insert, much like the one he had bought Edna a few years before. To go on it, he had picked out a 2' high cut glass vase at one of the best gift shops in Passaic.

My mother loved his presents, both of them in exquisite taste and very expensive. He had gone out of his way to thank her for standing by him.

I can't remember what Bill bought me that year, but it was probably one of the invaluable reference books that he said I would need for college, most likely *Bartlett's Familiar Quotations.* He had already given me a leather-bound Kings James Bible when I graduated grammar school and a *Webster's Collegiate Dictionary* for one of my birthdays. His intention was to set me up with the beginnings of a desktop reference library.

We were reseated at the kitchen table when Bill handed my father his present, a couple of pairs of warm socks. Though he had wrapped my mother's presents and mine beautifully with Christmas paper and bows, my father's gift was wrapped in toilet paper. Moe thanked Bill for the socks and as an afterthought somewhat quizzically asked, "What kind of paper was that?"

It was as if Bill had been waiting for six months to answer that question. He replied, "They were wrapped in toilet paper because you're a prick."

My father turned white. He threw the socks at Bill and ordered him out of the house. My mother got in between the two of them, but Bill was laughing merrily. He was already packed and happy to leave. Christmas had ended for us, but no doubt about it, the old Bill was back.

Better to marry than to burn

> *Come, my Celia, let us prove,*
> *While we can, the sports of love,*
> *Time will not be ours forever,*
> *He, at length, our good will sever;*
> *Suns that set may rise again;*
> *But if once we lose this light,*
> *'Tis with us perpetual night.*
> —Ben Jonson, *Volpone*, III.vii

For the next four or five months, Bill stayed in touch with my mother by phone. On a visit to Queens Village to see Helen Broderick, he decided to look up Caroline, the girl from Continental Can who had trained him on a box-making machine.

Within a few weeks, Bill and Caroline were off to California. Almost immediately, reports from Della and Joe about the two were not good. Caroline had landed a job right away; Bill wasn't as fortunate. He stayed at home and brooded. On Caroline's paydays, he took her check and returned only enough money to her for a soft drink at lunch and round-trip bus fare. When she objected, he beat her up.

Finally, he landed a job in a food-processing factory, and the couple seemed to be getting along better. Caroline bided her time and kept quiet, fearful of another black eye. On one of her paydays, she received her check, came home early, collected her things and was gone before Bill returned from work.

Bill remained in California for almost two years, hanging out at Joey's on weekends until they had a fistfight in the yard. Bill bloodied Joe's nose and alienated a most even-tempered friend and brother. Then Bill moved in with Della for a time, but when he began contending with Jim Redding, Della threw Bill out. There was no anger on her part; she simply wouldn't allow anyone to show disrespect toward her husband. Bill didn't take offense, and though they could not live together, he and Della remained close.

Bill was in California when Jim Redding was killed in a freak accident in 1952. An electrical lineman, Jim was working on a scaffold to rewire a government building. One of the ropes holding the scaffold broke, and a plank from the flooring swung and hit him in the head. He died instantly, leaving Della, 40, a widow with two sons, Jimmy, 15, and Cookie, 10. Bill supported his sister emotionally during and after the burial, and she was always grateful to him for his thoughtfulness, especially to her boys.

Nena worried that Bill was getting sick again. His treatment of Caroline and his brother Joe seemed to indicate an uncontainable irascibility, but despite his unwarranted displeasure with Jim Redding at times, Bill had come through for Della after her husband's death and behaved selflessly when the situation called for his help. If only he could control his temper!

By mid 1953, the romance of California had worn thin, and Bill was ready to come back to the East Coast. Though Pete had refurbished 41 Sycamore Avenue, Bill didn't ask or want to return to Floral Park. Instead, he found a small apartment in Passaic and resumed the factory job he had formerly held.

Freddie came from Florida to stay with Bill briefly in late 1953. To be near his brother, he had taken a job as a welder with a local firm that made and installed fire escapes and ornamental railings. Like Della, Fred recognized that he couldn't live with Bill, but they did enjoy each other's company. Just before Thanksgiving, Fred rented a studio in the neighborhood. The two bachelors usually had dinner together on Thursday nights, sometimes even taking in a movie, and they called each other with reasonable frequency. Freddie promised himself that he would never again walk out on Bill.

Over the Labor Day weekend, 1954, Fred turned 30. It was a clarion call—he realized that he didn't want to traipse around the country anymore. He wanted to put roots down, he told Pete and Mary, and not be such a will-o'-the-wisp.

Mary happened to repeat this conversation when she went to Bellerose to visit her sister, Jenny. A few years before, Jenny's daughter, Ann, had married Hank Ascuitto, a quiet, blonde Italian-American who happened to have an unmarried sister. Ann and Hank introduced Ida Ascuitto to Freddie, and they began dating.

Normal life seemed to be reasserting itself. Relieved, Nena took a deep breath—God was in his heaven, and all seemed right with the world.

A few weeks before Christmas 1954, Uncle Gena Balzac, his wife, Titi, and Cousin Pepìn, Gena's son, flew in from Puerto Rico. Gena was the half-brother of Pepìn, Fidela and Rosa. Gena immediately got in touch with Pete who contacted Nena, Freddie and the Aunts. Nena telephoned Bill who, with a little practice, spoke Spanish well enough and was glad to serve as a guide for his aunt, uncle and cousin around Long Island.

In order to entertain our Puerto Rican relatives, all animosities were forgotten. Almost four years had passed since Bill had been sick—it was time to let bygones be bygones, Nena argued persuasively. Mary, Pete and Moe began speaking once again to Bill, and on his best behavior, he was invited to 17 Sycamore Avenue for the first time.

Mary and my mother made a big dinner in honor of Uncle Gena and his family. With his shock of white hair, copper-colored skin and round face, Gena reminded Nena of her father, and though Bill's Spanish was rusty, he got on famously with Cousin Pepìn.

Gena's visit to Floral Park was delightful but brief. He had come to New York to be admitted to the Columbia-Presbyterian Hospital for a

Dee, Mary, Bill, Lenny and Belisa, 1954

checkup. Like his brother, Pepìn, and my mother, Gena was diabetic.

With his father under treatment and his mother visiting the Aunts, Cousin Pepìn (whom my mother dubbed "Sporting Life" because he loved to party) was free to steal away to the Barrio where he seemed to know everyone. He took Bill along on these amatory excursions. In Spanish Harlem, Pepìn had countless *amigos* and *compadres* from Mayaguez and San Juan. Though they were Neuorican shopkeepers, many of them still did business with Balzac and Company. But Pepìn wasn't here to sell coffee and cane sugar to *bodegas* and *restaurantes*.

For the next two weeks, he and Bill were guests at wild Advent parties and at numerous holiday dinners where they danced all night and drank too much. Not surprisingly, Bill's Spanish improved markedly.

It was fiesta time, and Pepìn, 40, was overweight, humorous and surprisingly graceful on the dance floor. He was indefatigable and wicked gyrating to samba, mambo, merengue, rumba, and tango rhythms—amusing his partners, on-lookers and cousin. With a pudgy face and pitted skin, Pepìn resembled Babe Ruth, and in his insatiable womanizing, he acted like King Farouk. He loved women, and women loved him because he was generous, well-heeled and comical.

While Cousin Pepìn was in New York, he decided that his new mission in life was to find a girl for Bill. His Yankee cousin, his *primo,* was 38 years old and unmarried—Pepìn understood completely—no wonder Bill was depressed.

To this end, Pepìn lined up a bevy of eligible Puerto Rican females, much to his cousin's embarrassment. One of them, however, did strike Bill's fancy. Her name was Belisa, and they were married in six weeks.

At 35, Belisa was a sweet, gentle, unsophisticated woman originally from Arecibo, not far from Mayaguez, who had no family in New York and had never been married. She was neat and clean, had a pretty face and an amiable manner. Nena liked her instantly and prayed that Bill would be good to her. Maybe Pepìn was right. Maybe this marriage was exactly what her brother needed: a woman who adored him and wanted to make a home.

Invited to Pete's house for Easter dinner 1955, Bill and Belisa were good company, telling funny stories about wayward Cousin Pepìn and his amatory encounters. Whenever he was in New York, Pepìn seemed to develop amnesia. He forgot he had a wife and children at home in Mayagüez.

𝕳ail and 𝕱arewell

For thee, O now a silent soul, my brother,
Take at my hands this garland, and farewell
There lies not any troublous thing before,
Nor sight nor sound to war against thee more,
For whom all winds are quiet as the sun,
All waters as the shore.
—Algernon Charles Swinburne, *Ave Atque Vale*
(Hail and Farewell)

In January 1956, two years after Bill met Belisa, Freddie married Ida Ascuitto. Pete served as Fred's best man and, heavier than he had ever been, Bill was an usher.

In the spring of that year, I was a sophomore at New York University. My mother had taken a part-time job working evenings at Mike's Bakery in Lodi, two blocks from our house. Super responsible, Nena never missed work. My father hated to talk on the phone, so I used to call my mother at the bakery every Thursday night. I would let my parents know if I would be home for the weekend or if I would be staying in the city to study for an exam or to finish a paper.

When I called as usual in mid-April, Mike's son, Victor, answered. I was surprised—Victor worked days and was never in the shop in the evening. I greeted him and asked for my mother. After some hesitation, he said, "She's not here. Don't get upset, but something has happened to your uncle." He had no other information. I immediately assumed that Freddie–prone to weak spells and married less than three months—was ill or hurt in an accident.

The only thing to do was to call Floral Park, but I had spent all but a dime of the money I had on the phone call to Mike's Bakery. I dialed the operator and put through a collect call to 17 Sycamore Avenue. Lenny, 14, answered, but upon hearing a child's voice, the operator wasn't going to connect us. "Please, it's a matter of life and death."

Finally Lenny was allowed to speak. "Dee Dee, Uncle Bill is dead." She was weeping. "He and Belisa moved to Philadelphia four days ago. Last night Uncle Bill had a heart attack. Your parents and mine are in Philadelphia to help Belisa with the funeral arrangements and to bring his body back to Floral Park."

I couldn't believe it. Bill had been at the house and seemed perfectly healthy when I was leaving for school less than two weeks before. We had a heated discussion about the French writer, André Gide. I had been a Gide fan since 1953 when I saw the play, *The Immoralist*, based on his novel. The Broadway production starred Louis Jourdan, Geraldine Page and a new comer, James Dean. Despite Bill's moral reservations about the merit of Gide's work, we had ended our talk happily, and he had very generously given me $15 in case I needed anything at school.

When I finally reached my mother on the phone the next night, she was sobbing.

Oh, Dee, Bill's dead, and you and I have killed him.

She assumed that the shock treatments he endured at the Kings Park Psychiatric Facility had weakened his heart prematurely. She had signed for them, and I had encouraged her to do so. It took at least a year before I learned and explained to her that Bill had died of a coronary infarction as a result of overwork. In a fit of rage and despair, he had carried a refrigerator up three flights of stairs and set up an entire apartment. His death had nothing to do with the shock treatments, which, if they had affected his heart, would have caused heart failure, a gradual and progressive disease.

Bill had precipitously decided to move to Pennsylvania, moreover, because of a terrible fight with Nena. On Monday of the week he and his wife relocated, Nena had phoned Belisa, as she often did, just to say hello, but Belisa was sick in bed. Bill had beaten her with a cane leaving welts across her thighs and calves. She was in such pain that she couldn't walk. Deeply troubled, my mother said she would pick up an analgesic at the drugstore and come for a short visit.

She took the bus to Passaic and went directly to her brother's first floor apartment to find Belisa in bed applying cold compresses to thick, red ridges marking her swollen and painful legs. Nena dressed Belisa's wounds with the analgesic providing the poor girl with some relief.

Belisa explained that Bill had been drinking heavily on the weekends for some months now. He would start in a good mood, sometimes fixing a highball for her, but he seemed unable to quit until he had drained the entire bottle of Jack Daniels. Then he would become mean pinching her or pulling her around the room by her hair, sneering that she was a bad cook and a rotten housekeeper. Worst of all, he accused her of being with other men when he was at work.

The prior weekend, Belisa had tried to get Bill to stop drinking early before he got mean, but he became furious. "Don't you tell me what to do," he screamed. Then he took the cane and beat her until he tired.

My mother feared for Belisa, but she dared not say that Bill had been in an insane asylum and was dangerous.

> *When he is in that mood, you mustn't talk back to him,* Nena advised Belisa. *You must remain silent and stay away from him as much as possible, so that he has no excuse to take his anger out on you.*

Having made tea and a little lunch for Belisa, my downcast mother left for home.

Bill was a devil. Unknown to his wife or sister, he had stayed home from work and hidden in the cellar. He knew that my mother often called Belisa after the weekend and suspected that Belisa would complain about him. He overheard every cautionary word that his sister had said.

He was livid, walking the five miles from Passaic to Lodi and getting to our house only minutes after Nena arrived home by bus. She was just hanging up her coat when he pushed open the unlocked kitchen door. His face was black with rage.

She had betrayed him, he snarled, and as far as he was concerned, they were no longer sister and brother. He was moving away from her and his entire family "who had been fucking him up for years."

Under ordinary circumstances, my mother would have pacified her brother, but his unjust accusation outraged her. Nena was so angry that she forgot her fear of riling him and shouted right back. And for once Bill listened.

> How *can* you blame the family? We've been walking on eggs for years not to upset you, and we've exhausted ourselves trying to help you. A misbegotten love affair, an inconceivably brutal War and your own stubborn refusal to use your education in and out of the Marines have ruined you.

> But nothing justifies beating Belisa. She's not to blame for your mistakes—she's an innocent. You used to defend women. What has happened that you've turned into a drunken sadist worse than Uncle Vincent? It's a miracle your neighbors didn't call the cops. Had they seen her legs, they would have locked you up and thrown away the key.

> And don't flatter yourself. You're nothing like Marcus Aurelius or Epictetus either—a combination of Fu Manchu and Mr. Hyde *is* more like it.

Bill was so taken back by Nena's vituperation that he was speechless. Trembling and silent, he turned on his heel and left. Regretfully, Nena locked the door behind him and watched him walk away—not knowing that she would never see him again.

Early the next morning, Bill rented a U-Haul truck and made half-crippled Belisa pack everything they owned. They drove to Philadelphia, stopped at a realtor's office and took the first rental they saw, a three-room, third floor apartment. Using straps, Bill carried all their furniture on his back—including the refrigerator—up three flights of stairs. By the third morning after they moved, everything was in place, even the pictures on the wall.

Soon after going to bed that night, Bill developed chest pains. Belisa wanted to call a doctor, but Bill wouldn't allow her to do so. Doctors were too expensive, he told her, yet only recently he had given me $15, the amount a physician would have probably charged for a house visit.

Instead, he had Belisa warm some liniment on the stove and rub it on his chest. When the pain didn't subside, he growled at her, "You stupid thing!"

Those were last words. Bill's eyes rolled back and closed. Belisa ran to the next door apartment to ask someone to call an ambulance. It came quickly, but the paramedics could do nothing for Bill. He was already dead.

Bewildered and in anguish, Belisa called my mother who contacted Pete and Mary. They volunteered to go with my parents to retrieve the body. Then Nena got in touch with Freddie now living with his bride in a garden apartment in New Milford.

"My poor brother," Fred cried brokenly. "My poor brother is finally out of his torment."

Part 2, Chapter 8
Nena and the Movies

> Wherein lies happiness? In that which becks
> Our ready minds to fellowship divine,
> A fellowship with essence; till we shine,
> Full alchemized, and free of space.
> —John Keats, *Endymion*

My mother survived the taxing responsibilities forced on her by her immediate family and the catastrophes in the world at large by escaping them as often as she could. She proudly and openly professed her *modus vivendi: she lived to eat, sleep and go to the movies.*

I do not know when her rich fantasy life began, but I do know that it was already in full force when I was born. She took me at six weeks old with a bottle of warmed formula to see Alfred Hitchcock's *Sabotage* (1936) with Sylvia Sidney, one of her favorite actresses. I drank the entire contents of the bottle, she said, and slept soundly all through the thriller. Undeterred by a baby, then by a toddler, then by a pre-school child, Nena Balzac took me to the movies two or three times a week. Sometimes before entering the theatre, she would buy a pastrami sandwich and a cherry smash from the nearby deli and eat her lunch in the dark. By the time I was three or four, she shared these movie meals with me. I had to take care not to crinkle the paper as I unwrapped my food, lest I annoy a nearby hungry but less provisioned member of the audience. On such occasions, smelling of caraway seeds, warm, brined meat and garlic from half-done pickles, the back five rows around us were as aromatic as a kosher restaurant.

Floral Park was well situated for an avid moviegoer. When my mother had seen the double bill at the Floral, we could always hop on the bus and go one mile west to see two different flicks at the Bellerose Theatre. Three miles west on the bus brought us to the Queens Theatre where my Uncle George worked as a movie projectionist. If we had exhausted these venues, there was always the Park Theatre in New Hyde Park, less than a half mile east of Sycamore Avenue and within walking distance. All the local movie houses changed programs on Mondays and Thursdays, a schedule that provided 16 different films per week within striking range.

The Park Theater featured re-runs from the 1930s. I was four years old when we went to see Greta Garbo in *Camille,* originally released in 1937. I sobbed convulsively when that beautiful creature coughs her way into oblivion reclining on a chaise longue, camellias strewn on the bodice and waist of her white gown.

My mother begged me not to be so distraught:

> *Dee Dee, Dee Dee,* she pleaded. *It's only a movie. Please stop crying. If you make noise, they'll throw us out.*

After viewing *Camille,* my mother had no argument from me when she wanted to rinse my hair. She would fashion my shampoo-laden tresses into an upsweep, hand me a mirror and tell me that I looked just like *Greta Garbage.* Ah, vanity, thy name is woman—no matter how young!

I submitted meekly to full pots of water dumped over my head, my eyes protected with a wash cloth. I could endure anything, if that's what it took to resemble the divine G. G.

From 1st grade on, once or twice a week, I would join my mother after school at the Floral Theater by 3:00 p.m. or if she told me to meet her in Bellerose or Queens, I would take the bus and be there by 3:30 at the latest. She would have arrived in time for the first show at 1:30 and paid for her ticket as well as for mine. All the theater managers knew us for miles around. When I arrived at the appointed place, an usher would automatically take me to her seat. Nena would have seen the first movie, and the coming attractions or newsreel would be on.

In Floral Park during the intermission before the second feature began, the ticket taker allowed us to leave the theater and go next store to Meiers' Ice Cream Parlor. It was an unforgettable old-fashioned confectionery with dark wooden booths next to the windows, marble-topped tables and wire chairs in the center of the room and black-cushioned stools banded in chrome in front of the long soda fountain. Covered with one-inch square black and white mosaic tiles, even the floor bespoke an earlier epoch.

White-haired, round-faced and jovial, Mr. Meiers made his own fragrant hand-dipped chocolates, fruit-shaped marzipan, tan and dark brown caramels, red and black licorice and rock candy on a stick. His shop smelled deliciously of vanilla beans, almond extract and various fruit syrups. Vats of homemade cherry, peach, pistachio and butter pecan ice cream sat next to containers of blackberry, raspberry, orange and lemon sherbet in a glass-covered refrigerated display case. The place and its white-aproned proprietor belonged in a Norman Rockwell illustration.

My grandfather had frequented the store, and Mr. Meiers recalled making Pepìn his favorite pineapple ice cream sodas. Now a third generation of Balzacs was sampling his wares. Greeting Mr. Meiers warmly, my mother often ordered a black and white ice cream soda or a peach Sundae, and I would have a frappe—a dish of golden vanilla ice cream topped with walnuts in simple syrup. (According to Mr. Meiers, a Sundae consisted of two scoops of ice cream, a choice of fruit, nut or syrup toppings, whipped cream and a Maraschino cherry. A frappe—no doubt for those watching their waistlines—had only one scoop and a topping and was otherwise nude. I didn't like whipped cream and was quite content with the less expensive frappe). Having had our treat, my mother and I would then return to the movie house, show our ticket stubs and re-enter for the second film.

I would stay until 6:00 p.m. to see the complete program, but Nena would rush all the way home when the second movie ended to make supper and, most importantly, to empty the water tray under the icebox. Every third morning from spring through autumn, hard-working Mr. D'Angelo would deliver a huge block of ice and place it in the top of the icebox. It would melt and drip down into a shallow tray beneath the cooler. In warm weather, this basin had to be emptied three times a day. If Nena didn't get home before the blasted tray overflowed, the water would make a big white stain on the linoleum, and my father would know that she had been spending his hard-earned money at the movies again.

We didn't have a refrigerator until after the war. Having lost his linoleum litmus test, after 1946 my father's only recourse was to check if any beer or milk bottles stored on the porch were missing, returned for their deposits to pay the price of admission to one of the nearby theaters. Had a significant number disappeared since he left for work, he would have proof that my mother had been out "gallivanting." And he would often catch my mother in a lie. Thanks to some forgotten film script, she had a sharp quip when he nosed around the back porch searching for evidence that she had been to the movies:

> *Watch out*, she'd say to anyone listening, *Shell-Shocked Holmes is on the prowl again.*

My father didn't dislike films; he just disliked addictions and deceptions. In fact, perhaps once every month on the weekend, he took us to the Valencia Theatre in Jamaica, a Moorish palace built in 1929 with graceful fountains in matching marble pools on either side of the lobby. The wide ledges of the pools were designed so that moviegoers could sit on them to watch schools of goldfish swimming through coral labyrinths, past seaweed and water lilies. The lobby and orchestra were carpeted with thick red velvet rugs that matched the proscenium and side exit curtains, and gold-leaf ornaments and sconces adorned the boxes on either side of the second floor loge. Upstairs, the Ladies' Lounge could have graced a castle. It was appointed with beveled mirrors, crystal chandeliers and thickly cushioned divans that sighed when one sank into them.

During the intermission between films at the Valencia, the floor of the orchestra pit would open as if by witchcraft, and a huge organ would slowly rise, the lady organist already seated and playing a medley of popular tunes. Some nights she chose all George Gershwin or Irving Berlin or George M. Cohan songs to demonstrate her keyboard expertise. Then as the organ mysteriously disappeared down into the pit, ushers would pass a slotted canister from row to row collecting money for polio research or for a patriotic cause.

Best of all, the high domed ceiling of the theater looked like a glorious night sky. Projected stars twinkled on it, and clouds drifted by. I hated musicals and slapstick, but it didn't matter to me if the Valencia was showing a soppy Nelson Eddy-Jeannette MacDonald operetta (my mother adored such stuff) or an Abbott and Costello comedy (which suited my father's taste). I would just lean back in my plush seat and watch the magically moving heavens.

On holidays, my father sometimes drove us to New York City: to the Apollo Theater in Harlem for a stage show, more often to the films and live performances at the Radio City Music Hall, the Paramount, the Capitol or the Roxy. We watched Cab Calloway furiously shuffle, scuffle, stomp and do repeated toe stands and splits on a table. His hair would fall down over his eyes as he reduced himself to a state of total exhaustion. We admired the elegant Lena Horne singing "Stormy Weather" in her fine, slow drawling way and loved the precision of the Rockette's dance routines. We heard Xavier Cugat, Louis Armstrong, Kay Kyser, Tommy Dorsey and Desi Arnez with their orchestras. Dinah Washington, Marilyn Maxwell, and Lucille Ball were just a few of the headliners I can remember from these wonderful excursions.

My father would have been furious, however, had he known that because of the movies, Nena often made me skip school. On the average, I missed 15-20 days a year, only two or three of them because I was sick. When I was in 2nd grade, under the rubric "Hygiene" on my report card, the school nurse, Miss Marshall scrawled that I was an inveterate liar. It wasn't true.

"Put the blame on Nena," someone should have told Nurse Hangnail. I couldn't really explain that my mother frequently begged me to stay home from school and keep her company on a trip to the city to see a brand new Humphrey Bogart or Gary Cooper or Cary Grant film.

> *Please, Dee, stay home. We'll go to New York, take in a movie and stage show and then eat at the 'Chinks'.*

I liked school, loved my teacher, Miss Lynch, and really didn't want to miss yet another day. Eventually, I would succumb to the bribe—I adored Chinese food—and Nena would prevail. We would have a grand time—especially if I didn't slip up and inadvertently reveal where we had been when my father came home.

The next morning, looking healthier than Charles Atlas, Nena sent me back to school armed with her note explaining my absence. I had to report to the nurse's office and give the excuse to the school nurse before I could be readmitted to class. In her beautiful hand, my mother would have written, "Yesterday Diane had a blinding headache" (or a sore throat or diarrhea or any other minor ailment that Nena hadn't recently employed). No wonder the nurse disliked me. She thought that I was faking these illnesses and convincing my poor Mommy to allow me to play hooky.

In 1944, probably during the Christmas vacation while my mother was working for Sperry's in Lake Success, my Aunt Jenny made the mistake of inviting me to a film in Manhattan. My aunt, her daughters Ann, 13, Joanie, 11, and I were headed to some fantasy suitable for children when I spied a Broadway marquee advertising *The Lodger* with Laird Cregar, a great "heavy" of the era.

Outside the theater, the posters plastered on either side of the ticket booth showed the towering Cregar making his menacing way through the dense fog of 19th century London. In jagged black letters at the top of each poster was the question: "Is the new Lodger in the neighborhood Jack the Ripper?"

I was ecstatic. I insisted on going to this movie—Merle Oberon, George Sanders and Laird Cregar—could anything *be* better?

I was my mother's daughter. Nena had made me into such a film buff by the time I was 8 that I refused to move from the spot. Adamant, I caused a scene, practically having an apoplectic-epileptic fit in the middle of Times Square. My embarrassed aunt caved in, and we went to see *The Lodger.* Or at least she and I did. My cousins spent most of the next 84 minutes with their hands over their eyes screaming during the best parts. Though Aunt Jenny continued to treat me with great kindness, after that junket, she never invited me to the movies again.

Two years later when I was in 5th grade, my teacher got the flu, and a substitute, Miss Duryea, took her place. Making mischief, some of the boys threw spitballs around the room and acted up when her back was turned. Miss Duryea, who usually worked as an administrative assistant in the office, punished everyone by keeping the class after school. At 2:50 p.m. when the day normally ended, I explained that I had to meet my mother at the theater in Queens Village, but Miss Duryea was angry at the world. I sat down and was absolutely silent and respectful hoping she would relent in time.

3 o'clock came, then 3:05, then 3:15. I approached the teacher's desk again. She wasn't interested in hearing anything I had to say, but I couldn't wait any longer. If I missed the 3:20 bus, my mother would be beside herself, frantic about what had happened to me. I told the highly indignant substitute that I was leaving and that I was sorry to upset her, but if I didn't arrive in Queens by 3:45, I would upset my mother more. The class gasped as I walked out. The next day, despite Nena's note of explanation, I spent much of the morning and afternoon outside Rena C. Hayden's office standing and looking at the wallpaper, my comeuppance for obeying my mother.

My concern for Nena was not feigned. Diagnosed a diabetic like her father, his brother Uncle Gena and most probably her Balzac grandmother, only recently she had spent 16 days in the hospital. Like Pepìn, she had developed an enormous thirst and appetite; nonetheless, she was losing weight and feeling tired all the time. She recognized the symptoms and changed her diet to eliminate sugar, but her condition was severe. Not until she developed diplopia, double vision, did she seek medical attention.

She made an appointment to see Dr. Sigmund Schoenfeld, a brilliant German-Jewish refugee, and together one evening in 1946, she and I walked along a dark country lane in New Hyde Park to his office. This time she didn't bring me along merely for company. She was seeing two sets of headlights on every car and needed me to guide her out of the way of on-coming traffic.

Dr. Schoenfeld hospitalized her immediately and prescribed daily shots of insulin. She was 32, seriously ill, and I would not allow anything to distress her if I could help it. I didn't tell Miss Duryea or Mrs. Hayden why I was so concerned about my mother—it wasn't their business.

Partially as a result of her illness, Nena's physical strength diminished, but as she aged, her naturally sharp wit became more acute, honed by her proclivity to remember dialogue. Unbeknownst to them, many of the best scriptwriters in Hollywood wrote some of her repartee.

Even before she developed diabetes, when life seemed overwhelming and consulting the kind spirits afforded no relief, she had fallen back on lines from *Gone with the Wind* (1939). Scarlet O'Hara Balzac would wring her hands and opine, *I'll think about it tomorrow*, or, if really disturbed, she would take her cue from Rhett Butler: *Frankly, my dear, I don't give a damn.*

In *Gaslight* (1944), Ingrid Bergman won her first Academy Award portraying a terrified young wife at the mercy of her demonic husband, Charles Boyer, who tries to convince her that she is going mad. Did Nena invent the verb "to gaslight" meaning "to cause someone to believe they were going mad"? Or was the term a New York neologism derived from that popular film?

That same year, Nena saw Tallulah Bankhead for the first time in *Lifeboat* (1944). For months afterwards, my mother addressed members of the household as *dahling* in lieu of their given names. Some years later, whenever she was annoyed, everyone within range was *estúpido*, the verbal whiplash Rita Hayworth uses to dismiss everyone except Glenn Ford in *The Loves of Carmen* (1948). Some Monty Wooley or Clifton Webb film supplied my mother with the alternate phrase, *pusillanimous poltroon*.

Nena's most pointed jab resulted from Rosalind Russell's character study of an aging actress in *The Velvet Touch (1948)*. Nena withered any man who was *giving her static* by eyeing him significantly down and up and down again. Then echoing Russell, Nena would retort,

Don't look now, but your ego's showing.

Not all Nena's cinematic borrowings were "thrusts home" to the heart *à la Cyrano de Bergerac (1950)*. As a young child, she called me her *Rosebud*, but unlike *Citizen Kane* (1941), she promised never to lose me. As a teenager, she repeatedly woke me with *Rise and shine, Morning Glory*, a rallying cry that she lifted from Tennessee William's *The Glass Menagerie* (1950). Once when I was about 13, she sweetly reassured me that *I was pretty enough for all normal purposes*. Many years later in college, I read Thornton Wilder and realized Nena had quoted a line from *Our Town*, remembered from the film of 1940.

Nena not only cited scripts without giving attribution, she read the novels on which many of them were based. If a first-run or re-issued film provoked her interest, she sent me with her card to the Floral Park Library for the book, play or short story from which the screenplay was drawn. She contended that the book was almost invariably better than the movie if only because of length. How thrilled she was to discover a second generation of Earnshaws and Lintons when she obtained *Wuthering Heights* from the library and realized that the cinematic version only covered the first half of the novel! Whether as a result of seeing the film or reading the book, when I developed a crush on a boy who worked in the delicatessen on Jericho Turnpike, she teased me mixing references,

Oh Heathcliff, Heathcliff! Wherefore art thou, Heathcliff?

By 1947 following Nena's lead, Aunt Mary and I became voracious and indiscriminate readers. Mary had never read anything more taxing than *Reader's Digest* before she came to live at 41. Inspired by the movies, we three happily occupied ourselves with Charlotte Brontë's *Jane Eyre*, Ernest Hemingway's *For Whom the Bells Toll*, John Steinbeck's *Grapes of Wrath* and F. Scott Fitzgerald's *The Great Gatsby*. In 1947 we also read Franz Werfel's *Song of Bernadette* and Kathleen Windsor's (then scandalous) *Forever Amber* back to back and never skipped a page of either tome. Bernadette, a poor French girl in the 1800s, repeatedly sees and hears the Virgin Mary. In contrast, Amber makes her way from gutter to royal court in 17th century England leap-frogging over the bodies of 27 or 28 lovers. Inspired by the first and titillated by the second, I doubt that we ever compared the moral values of these very diverse heroines.

My mother's ongoing interest in spiritualism made R. A. Dick's *The Ghost and Mrs. Muir* and Robert Nathan's *Portrait of Jennie* must-reads. The widowed Mrs. Muir is attracted to the portrait of a dead ship's captain. At odd moments, his spirit appears and counsels her.

Robert Nathan's novel has a similar theme but is even more improbable. Having drowned in a boating accident, Jennie appears first as a child, then as a young woman to an artist who is finally reunited with her at the lighthouse where she died.

The best film in this genre was Noel Coward's *Blithe Spirit* (1945) based on his comedy of the same name. A spiritualist has to be called in to reveal that a dead first wife is jealously tormenting her newly remarried husband. Both the film and the play had us howling with laughter in the movie house and again at home.

Because Nena loved cinematic treatments of historical periods, we added Pearl Buck's *The Good Earth,* Victor Hugo's *Hunchback of Notre Dame* and Mika Waltari's *The Egyptian* to our reading list, among many others. Classic English or American literature, sacred or profane novels, ghostly tales, historical fiction, claptrap—we devoured anything that had been made into an arresting movie and could be had at the Floral Park or Jamaica Libraries (where Mary still was a member).

As a result, when I was 12, I failed the 7th grade Literature Achievement Test miserably, and for good reason. When other girls were poring over *The Secret Garden,* Dorothy Macardle's *The Uninvited* had held me spellbound; when my peers were reading *Pollyanna,* I was absorbed by Daphne du Maurier's *Rebecca* and who would pick up *Lassie Comes*

Home with Arthur Conan Doyle's *The Hound of the Baskervilles* at hand? My kind teacher, Miss Sara Levy, who knew from my book reports some (and only <u>some</u>) of the novels I had enjoyed, comforted me by saying, "Don't worry about it, Diane. You'll read the books mentioned on the exam someday to your children." And so I did.

When I was in college at New York University busy with papers and labs, I no longer had time to accompany my mother to the Radio City Music Hall or some other first-run New York theater. So she would come into the city by herself, see the early morning show and meet me for lunch downtown.

One spring day in my senior year, I knew that something was terribly wrong when Nena didn't show up at our favorite restaurant in Greenwich Village. From the time I was very young, we had had an agreement that I would stay where we had planned to meet until she came. I waited from 1 until 3:30 p.m. with increasing apprehension until she finally appeared at The Jumble Shop eatery on 8th Street.

She had rushed so in the morning to catch the bus that she hadn't taken time to have a proper breakfast. And once in the city, she had hurried to the Radio City Music Hall to make the first show. A few hours later as she exited the theater, she had a severe diabetic reaction. On the corner of 50th Street and Sixth Avenue, she went into a cold sweat and became faint. Feeling too shaky to cross the street, she held on to a lamppost as she desperately fumbled in her pocketbook to find a LifeSaver candy.

A policeman who had been directing traffic saw her and thought she was drunk. Her straw hat had tilted, and her hair was in disarray. He could see that she was wobbly. She called to him weakly, and he approached with some annoyance until she gasped that she was diabetic and needed a drink of orange juice. Could he walk her to the Whelan's lunch counter across the street? Abashed, he not only helped her but also got her express service and stayed with her until she felt better. And then he cautioned her: "Lady, you must get an identification bracelet or necklace for your own safety. I was ready to run you in."

After 1950 when we moved to New Jersey, my mother wasn't able to see as many films as she had living in Floral Park, but her love affair with the movies never ended. They served as mini-vacations from the rigors of her life. Through them, she sojourned in the land of the imagination.

Films also provided a primary reading list for Nena's self-designed continuing education. She saw them in the same way that Pepìn had looked to the New York Public Library: they were her People's University. Nena never missed an Orson Welles or Lawrence Olivier production of a Shakespearean play and gleaned an extensive, if popularized, knowledge of history seeing period pieces and reading the original texts. Her acquaintance with classical music largely derived from the playing of pianist José Iturbi and violinist Isaac Stern, of opera from the arias of Deanna Durbin, Katherine Grayson, Marilyn Horne, Mario Lanza and Lauritz Melchior. They all appeared in or were heard on the sound tracks of films. She was enthralled by the *études* and *concerti* of Chopin, portrayed by Cornel Wilde in *A Song to Remember* (1945), as well as the scores of *Intermezzo* (1939) and *Humoresque* (1946) in which respectively Leslie Howard and John Garfield play the parts of gifted violinists.

Movies sharpened Nena's verbal acuity, developed her taste and helped create her eccentric and endearing personality. Her being's heart and home was in a darkened theater in the rich company of Bette Davis, Katherine Hepburn, Spencer Tracy, Paul Muni and other *novas* of the silver screen.

Part 2, Chapter 9
American Idyll: Summers in Floral Park[43]

Sumer is ycomen in,
Loude sing cuckou!
Groweth seed and bloweth meed,°   *meadow blossoms*
And springth the wode° now.   *wood*
Sing cuckou!
—The Cuckoo Song (Traditional)

Perhaps childhood always seems idyllic in retrospect, but in the summers of the 40s and 50s, Floral Park, New York (pop. 16,000) took on the aura of a quintessential American village. Though they couldn't have put the feeling into words, the children, in particular, sensed the realm of myth permeating every day events around them.

Long established rituals marked each month. The season unofficially began at the end of May with the solemn commemorations of Memorial Day and the opening of the beaches. June meant the end of school followed closely by the 4th of July with its thrilling fireworks. In August, everyone looked forward to the first Saturday of the month, the date of the annual Firemen's Tournament, as much an embodiment of Americana as Model-T Fords, baseball games and Aunt Em's apple pies.

For a week or so before Memorial Day, war veterans sold red paper poppies along Jericho Turnpike outside the A&P, Bohack's and Woolworth's Five-and-Ten Cent Store. Every family bought them. (Francis Xavier Buckley, M.D. purchased eight). At the John Lewis

Childs School, Miss Sara R. Levy, a gifted 7th grade teacher, explained the symbol by reading to her class Lieut.-Col. John Mc Crae's poem commemorating the dead of World War I:

> In Flanders fields the poppies blow
> Between the crosses, row on row,
> That mark our place
> If ye break faith with us who die
> We shall not sleep, though poppies grow
> In Flanders fields.

With a deeper respect for the nation's sacrifice, Miss Levy's students pinned the paper flowers on their white shirts and blouses for the holiday. (When Dee recited these verses, Tia Fidela's eyes filled with tears remembering her gallant Doughboy, Edmundo, who died "over there" in World War I).

To most of the children, however, Memorial Day seemed to exist for its grand parade. Early in the morning, mothers and aunts carried beach chairs to Plainview or Tulip Avenue along the parade route. (Tante Paula reserved a place for herself right in front of Bohack's). As the crowds gathered, little kids on fathers' shoulders could hear strains of martial music.

Hawkers were still selling brightly colored balloons when the first marchers came in sight. Twirlers threw their batons high up into the air and effortlessly caught them. High-stepping majorettes blew their whistles and with a swing of their short satin skirts turned sharply to signal the players. Drummers beat out the roll call. In response, school bands from Floral Park and neighboring towns performed "Tiger Rag" and "When the Saints Come Marching In" and "The Washington Post March." Hands down, the townspeople clapped most for John Philip Souza's "The Stars and Stripes Forever", the high-pitched piccolo obbligato trilling above the melody. Then an Irish-American fife corps with green and black uniforms piped "Danny Boy." (Diminutive Mrs. Jones thought of Galway with a sigh).

Interspersed between the musical groups, the town's organizations paraded past the throngs lining the sidewalks. The Veterans of Foreign Wars walked smartly, with kepis rakishly angled on their heads, and the Ladies' Auxiliary stepped in time, one edge of their capes thrown back over their shoulders. (Rena C. Hayden marched proudly in the front row). Teenaged girls whirled pom-poms, and Sewanhaka High School's Rockettes, kicking in unison, preceded the members of the Lion's Club and Rotary. The Campfire Girls followed close behind, as did the Brownies and Cub Scouts, the Girl Scouts and Boy Scouts. The Masons, the Order of the Eastern Star, young men of DeMolay and Rainbow Girls kept their rows straight. And parading school-age children from Floral Park-Bellerose, St. Hedwig's, Our Lady of Victory and John Lewis Childs grinned self-consciously as they passed admiring families, neighbors and friends. (Approaching Tyson Avenue, young Ronnie Sommers smiled toothlessly as he waved to his mother, Estelle).

As soon as the police force and the volunteer firemen appeared in close order formation (Pete Balzac looked grand in his navy uniform), some of the crowd headed for parade's end, the Memorial Park near Our Lady of Victory Church. There they listened to the prayers of the clergy and the speeches of the mayor and other dignitaries. (It was going to be a fine day, Reverend Ralph M. Durr mused after he delivered the Invocation). Every year, Mrs. Mendelsohn, the operatically trained wife of "Doc" Mendelsohn, the kindly druggist, sang "The Star Spangled Banner" as townspeople stood at attention, hands over hearts.

The end of May also signaled the opening of the beaches. The children didn't mind trudging through the sand, loaded down with jugs of homemade lemonade and huge bags of sandwiches, burdened by blankets, towels and gaily-striped beach umbrellas. (Dr. Buckley's kids couldn't wait to get into the water). Almost all the boys and girls of Floral Park were swimmers. They considered the ocean, lakes, bays and Sound their birthright and early on developed a healthy regard for the water's delights and dangers.

On warm weekends in June, some village families trekked to the Rockaways where the sea was so rough at times that often one had to jump the huge waves holding on to ropes strung between wharf pylons. (About to be married, Cousin Ann still adored the surf). Initially, the water was numbingly cold, but with all the screaming and diving through the breakers, the boys and girls soon warmed up and had to be half-dragged back to the blanket for lunch. Though they were hungry enough, eating almost seemed like a punishment. Their parents demanded that after lunch the youngsters sit on the blanket or make sand castles for at least 30 minutes before they went back into the water. Otherwise, the children were told, they might develop leg or stomach cramps. (If he didn't eat, he wouldn't have to rest, Jimmy Martone decided).

Others families headed east preferring the less crowded Jones Beach with its brick walkways and pavilions. (As Ida Balzac stood on line for an ice cream cone, she admired the splendid clock tower and formally landscaped gardens). The waves there never seemed as violent as at the Rockaways, but when the wind was up, swimmers knew enough to be wary of a wicked undertow. On such days, families with small children opted for Zack's Bay or for the heavily pebbled North Shore sites at Bar Beach or Cold Spring Harbor where the water was serene. (Maudie Porth much preferred the Sound).

The days in June lengthened perceptibly. In their classrooms during the week, the children squirmed with the heat, finding it more and more difficult to concentrate on seemingly endless review work. At last, toward the end of the month, exams finished and school let out. "No more teachers, no more books," the younger kids chanted on the playgrounds. (Miss Dorothy Lynch, a capable 2nd grade teacher, was looking forward to the vacation).

The desire for liberation was so strong that it even affected older students on graduation day. The girls, all in white dresses with wrist corsages, and the boys, scrubbed, combed and in dark suits, fidgeted as they lined up outdoors in front of the J.L.C.S. Auditorium. The long-standing photographer of school events, harried Mr. Lenskold, could barely get the 8th graders to stand still for their final class picture. A rite of passage, a first step towards adulthood, was taking place.

For the 4th of July, most of the houses and businesses and all the public buildings proudly displayed Old Glory. (Even Ruby's Candy Store had patriotic buntings draped over the front door). Mothers dressed little boys in white shirts and navy blue short pants and little girls in white summer dresses with red, white and blue ribbons in their hair. In the afternoon, the kids played with sparklers, but the highlight of the holiday was the nighttime display of fireworks at the municipal playground.

Not everyone filed into the extra bleachers put up there specially for viewing the pyrotechnics. Some folks climbed up on the slightly pitched roofs of the Long Island Railroad storage sheds that stood on the far side of the tracks across from the park. They had the best, if not the most legal seats in town. (Fred Balzac held his little niece, Jeanne, on his lap).

The show began around 9:30 at night, men from the Fire Department in attendance while a representative from Grucci, the Long Island fireworks firm, set off twenty or more skyrockets, at timed intervals, in every color imaginable. ("How lovely!" Mrs. Fleischer exclaimed). Great booms and flashes of light rent the black night, and from small explosions emerged what looked like long red threads or green waterfalls or a hundred silver shooting stars. Again and again, came the thundering thud, and again and again, like tinted diamonds or Rapunzel's golden hair, a dazzling spray illuminated the heavens and then slowly fell to extinction.

Toward the end of the program, individual sallies detonated three or four times, each new burst of sound trailing a different colored flare. (In the bleachers, Mr. Meiers had closed up the Ice Cream Parlor for the night and was thoroughly enjoying the show). The children covered their ears but strained to see the too-soon-dissipating beauty that followed the deafening shocks. ("Those were Roman candles," Dottie and Jo Jo Balzac explained to their kids).

Finally, many rapid blasts assaulted the ears of young and old, and what came forth then was lovelier than all that had gone before: the entire sky lit up first red, then white, then blue. Just as those shells died out, the display climaxed with a magnificent representation of the nation's flag, its fireworks' Stars and Stripes appearing to sway and flutter in mid air. ("Sharming, just sharming," Cord Rodenbostel said with a Plattdeutsch accent to his wife, Helen). As complete darkness and silence once again prevailed, the kids were proud of their country, were proud to be Americans.

In August, the village itself embodied that pride. For decades, every year the all-volunteer Floral Park Fire Department played host to more than thirty tournament teams from Nassau and Suffolk. Enormous crowds gathered; everyone knew a fireman, and almost everyone came to root for a hometown team. The men of the Department who didn't participate in the contests set up food tables and huge barbecues, grilling hundreds of pounds of hot dogs and hamburgers, selling thousands of cans of ice-cold beer and soda. (Though the sun was broiling, Mary Balzac felt refreshed as she drank a can of ice cold Hires Root Beer). Other firemen had been working for days designing programs and tickets, ordering food and chairs, setting up the P.A. system and comfort stations and testing targets and equipment for the various competitions. Still others erected a twenty-foot high, platformed arch across Raff Avenue or Floral Boulevard that figured centrally in tests of the firemen's skill and speed.

There were three events that no one wanted to miss: the Motor Hose, the 3-Man Ladder and the invariably comic Old Fashioned Bucket Brigade. In the first contest, teams arrived in screeching fire trucks, fellows jumping off the running boards, grabbing the hose and racing to attach it to a hydrant. Their fastest man ran with the heavy nozzle and, throwing himself down on the ground, aimed for the red target at the side of the road. If he hit the bull's-eye quickly, the crowd roared its approval. (Home from the sea, Vinnie Rapetti cheered louder than anyone).

"Good time for Saint James," the voice on the P.A. system blared.

Pete Balzac and Freddy Pepe at a Fireman's Picnic

Sometimes, however, the lead man, perfectly placed, aimed the nozzle but had no water supply. His teammates at the hydrant had fumbled getting the cumbersome hose attached.

Then the voice on the P.A. system droned, "No go for the Wildcats."

The 3-Man Ladder competition took agility and daring. (Even sour Mrs. Gertrude Purdy had to concede that). Again a fire truck came to a screaming stop, and two men, the footers, lifted the long, unwieldy ladder off the truck and tried to place it against the 20-foot high arch. A third man was already scaling the ladder, sometimes before the footers had stabilized it. He raced to touch the platform of the arch. Precise placement of the ladder, balance and speed were all. If the ladder tipped, the climber had to jump off, and he could get hurt. "62 seconds for the Teddy Boys of Oyster Bay," the announcer intoned.

The children's favorite contest was the Old Fashioned Bucket Brigade. A line of eleven firemen filled and passed buckets of water up the ladder to a final man whose job was to fill a 50 gallon barrel on the arch's platform. The men moved so fast that they almost threw the buckets at one another. (Laughing, Lenny Balzac jumped back to avoid getting splashed). Of course, many got drenched, slipping and sliding helter-skelter. The crowd roared. "1 minute 50 wet seconds for the Floral Park Doodle Bugs," announced the official.

After the winning teams received their trophies, participants scattered all over the village to change into dress uniforms for the Fireman's Parade. And though their marching was hardly as crisp as it had been on Memorial Day, very happy companies paraded up Jericho, with fire engines, trucks and Chiefs' cars shining brilliantly, sirens blaring in the late afternoon sun. At the very end of the parade, the gorgeous Miss Rheingold sat on top of a Cadillac convertible waving and blowing kisses to the cheering crowd. (Sipping frothy beers, Uncle Vincent and his side-kick, Popeye Martone thought the girl was pretty enough, but they drooled over the car).

And then one cool morning in late August (Nena Balzac claimed it was the first day of fall) as women hung their clean wash on the backyard clotheslines, they became aware of a distinct earth smell, neither acrid nor sweet, emanating from the damp black and rich soil. That familiar odor was a signal. Whether one shopped in Floral Park or at Gertz' Department Store in Jamaica or at Arnold Constable's in Hempstead, it was time to buy school clothes. (Peering in Bluma's Children's Store window, Ruth Martone admired a plaid Cinderella Frock for her daughter, Patsy Ann).

All its gay parades and giddy splendors concluded, summer had silently slipped away.

The Mink and the Motorcycle

Jack Sprat could eat no fat
His wife could eat no lean
And so betwixt the two of them
They licked the platter clean.

Jack ate all the lean,
Joan ate all the fat.
The bone they picked it clean,
Then gave it to the cat.
—Traditional Nursery Rhyme

In late 1959, Pete and Mary had been married for twenty turbulent years, and as marriages went those days, it wasn't a total disaster. Mary had even talked Pete into renewing their vows in a church ceremony to celebrate their anniversary. To top it off, she bought them both new rings.

Pete had never worn a wedding band before. When they got married in 1939, the Depression was just beginning to ease. Like most of the young people in America at that time, he just didn't have the money. It was also the first time since his wedding that Pete had entered a church other than to celebrate someone's baptism or marriage or mourn a friend's or relative's death. Nevertheless, led to the altar, Pete rolled his eyes, shook his head in disbelief and said, "I do" once more.

Mary's Catholicism amounted to making *baccalá* (cod, Italian style) and fish cakes on Fridays during Lent and attending Mass at the Polish Church fairly frequently on Sundays now that the girls were grown. Notwithstanding Pete's reluctance and abashed countenance, she was thrilled by the ceremony.

Afterward her sister, Jenny, planned a modest party for the two of them. The entire De Turo clan and the Balzacs gathered at Jennie's house in Bellerose. Freddie, Ida and their baby boy were also there, always included at such festivities since Ida was the sister of Jenny's son-in-law.

The cellar was decked out with cardboard wedding bells and white and silver crepe paper pinned to the ceiling and encircling the support posts. A large sheet cake, coffee urn, cups, saucers and plates lay in readiness on the table.

As we all gathered downstairs, Jenny's oldest daughter, Ruth, detained Pete and Mary upstairs, so that they might make a delayed entrance. Deftly, she provided Mary with a veil improvised from an old lace curtain and gave her a bouquet of artificial flowers to hold. Two of Jenny's grandchildren held the ends of Mary's train, and at a sign from Ruth, her sister, Ann, put on the record player. Trying not to smirk, the happy couple came down the stairs slowly and with appropriate solemnity in time to Mendelsohn's "Wedding March."

Everyone roared with laughter. Ida leaned over towards Fred: "This is one family," she whispered, "that doesn't need liquor to have a good time."

Lenny and Jeanne stood on either side at the bottom of the stairs. As Mary and Pete stepped into the room, their daughters conducted them to two high-backed rattan chairs and handed a beautifully wrapped gift to Mary and an identical one to Pete. The bride read the accompanying card: "To Mary and Pete, In acknowledgment of your twenty years together. Love, Your Daughters." Mary and Pete ripped off the paper to find two small white boxes. Inside, Lenny and Jeanne had placed two hand-sewn satin Purple Hearts.

Despite the universal recognition that theirs was not a marriage made in heaven, Mary and Pete complemented one another, however roughly. Mary was noted as a good and thrifty housekeeper. She made her own slipcovers, was ingenious about disguising leftovers, and still called a well-maintained vegetable patch "the Victory Garden." Her major marital problem was checking Pete's more extravagant impulses. Because of her, their house was more than half paid off, and they had a snug little savings account to insure a pleasant retirement. Because of Pete's more expansive outlook on life, they had two cars, a piece of property in Florida and, of late, some wonderful vacation memories that include cruising around the Caribbean and touring California.

But in a marriage like theirs, things were not always a bed of roses: Mary's thriftiness sometimes clashed head on with Pete's bon vivant lack of restraint. I vividly recall an incident that erupted into a feud a few months after their remarriage.

On the spur of the moment, one bright August day, I decided to drop by 17 Sycamore Avenue. To my surprise, instead of the normal cheery welcome that I almost always could expect, a grim-faced Aunt Mary greeted me.

"You might as well know it right now, Dee. Your Uncle Pete and I aren't on speaking terms. And I'd appreciate it if you would stay for supper. That way you can pass him the mashed potatoes and peas, and I won't be obliged to have anything to do with him."

I smiled to myself remembering other quarrels they had had and the reconciliations that inevitably followed. But my Aunt Mary was obviously very upset, so I tried to sound sympathetic.

"Oh, Mary, what has he done now?" I asked consolingly.

"Look, Dee, I've known for twenty years that marriage doesn't work out like a June Allison-Van Johnson movie. Nobody gets married and lives happily ever after. But this time I just can't forgive him. He's lost his head over some Harley-Davidson."

I immediately had an image of some voluptuous blonde pursuing my Uncle Pete. "That can't be true, Aunt Mary! How do you know her name?"

She groaned. "No, Dee, you don't understand. I'm in competition, all right, but it's not with another woman. Harley-Davidson," she fumed in total exasperation, "is a <u>motorbike</u>! At his age too! He has a married daughter! At forty-six, he's worse than an adolescent."

"Ever since he bought it, he's come home from work, grabbed the paste wax and chamois and gone right back outside. All through the house you can hear him purring and crooning over that silly contraption as he shines it up. He seems to have forgotten the bike accident he had when he was eighteen—he broke both arms, and his brothers had to help him in the bathroom for the next six weeks."

"Moreover, he had no right to dip into our savings to pay for a bike. He never even told me about it. Well, this time I won't stand for it. If he can have whatever he wants, I can too. I'm going to buy a mink coat."

Just then I heard the low roar of a motorcycle pulling into the driveway.

"There's Second-Childhood Pete now," she murmured bitterly.

Before turning off the ignition, Uncle Pete deliberately revved the bike loudly, four or five times, until all the windows in the house shook.

"You see what I mean? He's doing that on purpose just to annoy me," she stormed. "You can greet him. I'm going to my room."

And with that, she turned on her heel and disappeared up the stairs.

I didn't wait for Pete to enter the house. I ran out the back porch door, and behold! There was Uncle Pete, resplendent in a black leather jacket and a massive red and white crash helmet. And standing behind him was a huge, gleaming red motorcycle complete with every accessory known to man.

"Hi, honey!" he said with a sheepish grin on his face. "How do you like my new toy?"

All the pride of ownership shone in his eyes as he wiped off a splatter on the mudguard.

"It's gorgeous, Uncle Pete," I responded admiringly.

Running his fingers through his tousled curly hair, he said, "Come on, Dee. Let's go have a beer on the front stoop, and later I'll take you for a spin around the block."

We sat on the cool brick steps sipping our beers.

"What made you decide to buy a motorcycle, Uncle Pete?"

"Well, I've always liked 'em. You've heard about the one I had when I was eighteen. I had a pretty bad crash with it, but these days," he chuckled, "I'm not as wild as I used to be. Actually I bought this one to go to work with. It's impossible to find a parking space for the Buick in the mornings. With this baby, I just zip in at five to 8:00, and there's always room for it one step away from the job."

"Aunt Mary is pretty angry about it, Uncle Pete. She's threatening to go out and buy a fur coat."

"Well, I wish she would! She's been talking about that damn' coat for years. If it weren't for me, she'd never spend a dime on herself. She'd get no pleasure out of life at all! Anyway, she'll come around when she sees how much we're saving on gas."

I did my duty as a loyal niece and stayed for supper, passing the peas to the Great Stone Face on my left and the potatoes to Ma Barker on my right.

And despite Aunt Mary's scowl, Pete and I went for a nifty motorcycle ride around the block afterward.

* * *

Fearing that Aunt Mary might have taken my defection to heart, I hesitated before visiting them again. Instead, about two weeks later, I made a phone call to Aunt Jenny in Bellerose, one mile away.

"How are things at 17 Sycamore Avenue?" I queried after catching up on the rest of the family's news. "Is it safe to go there?"

Aunt Jenny just laughed. "A couple of days after your visit, the two of them made up in the morning and came to see me in the afternoon. And Dee Dee, it was quite a sight."

At Pete's urging, Mary had gone out and bought herself a mink stole. (Full-length coats, she decided when she saw their price tags, were just too impractical). While Mary was shopping, Pete dropped by the cycle shop and got her a fur-covered crash helmet and goggles.

Aunt Jenny was in the yard as they rode up to her house, Pete piloting the bike as if 168th Street were the Indianapolis Speedway—Mary, helmeted and begoggled, behind him. She was clutching his middle with all her might, the tails of her new mink stole flying gaily in the wind.

[43] "Summers in Floral Park" was published in *The Gateway*, the Floral Park newspaper, under the title "Summers of Yesteryear: When the Living Was Easy," Vol. LXXVIII No. 43, Wednesday, July 14, 2004, 1, 6-7.

Part 2, Chapter 10
Anniversaries

God pity them both! and pity us all,
Who vainly the dreams of youth recall;

For of all sad words of tongue or pen,
The saddest are these: 'It might have been!
—John Greenleaf Whittier, *Maud Miller*

I was an only child, and I wouldn't have known any more than most kids did about their conception had I not once innocently asked why no one ever sent my mother anniversary cards. And I didn't know about my mother's second pregnancy until Nena came near to dying.

Nena was pretty upset, somewhat unreasonably, about the anniversary cards. As I thought about it later, my aunts' lapses of memory seemed more a matter of good taste than a sign of disaffection. Not that her in-laws had any real love for Nena, or she for them, for that matter. In fact, the only reason Nena told me at all was to beat them to the punch. (To their credit, not one of them ever indicated by so much as a raised eyebrow that I was, as Nena euphemistically put it, a 'love child').

Or maybe Nena was only feigning annoyance at not receiving the cards. She had obviously wanted to tell me for some time, and her neglected August wedding anniversary gave her the perfect opportunity.

We were sitting over coffee in the red and white kitchen of the old Dutch Colonial at 41 Sycamore Avenue. We had just finished putting up string beans and peeling potatoes for supper. The meat loaf was already in the oven, and we were alone. To me, this peaceful hour, before my father and uncles got home from work was always the best part of the day. Over coffee, with supper started and the day's work finished, Nena often became expansive—gossiping, telling stories and sharing confidences.

Those were hard days, Dee. You wouldn't understand about that now, but it was the Depression, 1936. I had been going out for five years with an Irish fellow named Johnny O'Neill. And oh, how I loved him! Many an evening when he was broke, he'd bring over some of his sister's records. We'd wind up the victrola in the parlor and do all the popular dances and some of the old ones, too–the Peabody, the Black Bottom, the Tango. What a great dancer! He was so graceful and handsome, Dee, with big blue eyes and black curly eyebrows. And he was such a gentleman. But we couldn't get married–he didn't have a steady job, and he wouldn't consider asking me until he had some prospects.

And then one day, your Uncle Pete brought your father home. He was good-looking, too—dark and rough, sort of. He didn't talk much, and he didn't know how to dance. But he took me out a couple of times, and then he began hanging around the house every night. And he was no gentleman. We used to go to Lake Success in his old, battered Studebaker. It was a warm spring, and the lake was silver-smooth, and though it was private property, we used to sneak past the gatehouse and go swimming. Even at night, the water was crystal clear, and you could see straight to the bottom. And all around the banks, the trees were in that parsley stage, when everything is yellow-green and newborn.

When I found out, I cried and cried. I cried for my mother, I cried for myself and I cried for my lost Johnny O'Neill.

I tried everything before I told your father. We had an Irish neighbor who lived across the street—Kitty Bradley—the one who touched up my hair for me after my mother died. One day she saw me looking pretty down in the mouth and asked me into her kitchen for a cup of tea. And there I was, in trouble, dissolved in tears, motherless, with Kitty Bradley's freckled arms holding me close. She got me quinine pills and told me to take mustard sitz baths.

Nena paused, and the sound that issued from her throat seemed midway between a chuckle and a sigh.

Nobody could get into the bathroom. God, I must have stayed in the tub for half that spring.

If it had been up to your father, we would have been married right away. He was so happy; he wanted me to meet his family, especially Aunt Jennie and Uncle George. He wanted to introduce me to his father. But I kept saying 'no', hoping against hope that it was an hysterical pregnancy. I read about that happening once to an English queen.

Then August came, and I couldn't say 'no' any longer. So Jenny and George took us to South Jamaica, bought me a cheap ring and stood up for us before a justice of the peace. And that was my wedding. No trousseau. No white-tiered cake. No bridal gown. And no anniversary cards.

"But didn't you want me ever?"

Oh, Dee, don't think that. Once you were here to stay, no baby was ever wanted more. When I was alone, I talked to you and played with you, poking first one bulge here and then, when you moved, poking it there. I wanted you to be musical, so I listened faithfully to the opera on the radio every Saturday and borrowed every Verdi and Puccini record in the library. I wanted you to be bright, so I hauled home tons of books of poetry and read them until your father got worried that they were too heavy for me to carry. After all those months, I wouldn't have been surprised if, instead of crying at birth, you had sung an aria from <u>Madame Butterfly</u> or recited "The Road not Taken." I thought you would be a boy. I never dreamed of having a little girl, but there you were, a red-cheeked, dark haired Eskimo, with perfect hands and perfect feet and with that extra bit of bone behind your ears common to everyone in my family. That's how I knew you were mine.

* * *

We had time, nothing but time, that final winter when I came home from graduate school over the Christmas vacation. Nena was recovering from an infection in her index finger. She had never had an infection before. It was nasty—probably caused by a piece of steel wool she used for scouring pots that had penetrated the side of the nail. The doctor had cut all the way around the top of the finger—a fish mouth incision, he called it. Her whole hand still hurt, so I cooked, cleaned up, helped with the shopping. I wrote notes for her, too, but mostly, we just talked.

Nena wanted to talk about death.

> *Don't wince at that word. I'm not afraid to die. I'm too tired to be afraid. They say when people die, their life flashes before their eyes. Somehow, I don't think that will happen to me. No, I'll be thinking of your brother.*

Brother? What brother?

The word hung in the air between us.

> *It happened at the beginning of the War. You were only five. As the Depression eased, we had gotten on our feet, moved into an apartment building in Brooklyn, and then the War changed everything overnight. Your father was fired from his job. His patriotic boss called him an enemy alien. Can you imagine that? Your dad was only four months old in 1914 when his mother got off the boat. Your grandfather always had a notion of someday taking all his children back to Italy. He never got citizen papers for himself and never encouraged Jenny or your father or your Aunt Palma to apply. Before the war, you*

didn't have to be a citizen. Jenny used to go to the post office every January, fill out a form for each of them, and that was that.

Suddenly there was no money for food, and we couldn't pay the rent. Your father wouldn't go on relief–he would rather have died.

Living across the hall was a crude, loud, brash Jewish woman named Mae Goldsmith. She was one of those women who knew where you could buy anything you needed wholesale, who came into your apartment to chat and immediately made you rearrange all the furniture in your living room. She managed to mind her friends' business, your business and her own—and she was good at it, too—without batting an eye.

Mae had a heart as big as a baseball field. She found us homework. We made up little red and green laundry tickets, one hundred to the packet. When that job petered out, she got us another one, addressing thousands of envelopes. That's when I got pregnant again. Your father never knew. The pressure of another mouth to feed would have broken him. As it was, he was constantly flying into rages over little things that wouldn't normally have bothered him.

I would go to the butcher shop and get free lamb or beef bones for a broth. With a handful of elbow macaroni, ten cents' worth of vegetables and lots of bread, I could make a cheap meal. You called it 'bone supper,' and you hated it. You *wouldn't eat. With your elbow on the table and your cheek propped up on your hand, you would push the carrots back and forth with your spoon until your father screamed at you.*

Funny, Dee, that was in August too, a particularly hot, humid August, and once again, I couldn't wait any longer. It was Mae, of course, who helped. She loaned me money that she didn't have. She took me to a shabby dentist's office and brought me home by cab. She fed me chicken soup, and she felt as bad as I did that I had lost my son.

Nena closed her eyes. She was getting tired. I was about to leave the room when my mother looked up for a minute and addressing no one in particular said:

I would have called him Johnny.

The Death of Nena

And I, my mind in turmoil, how I longed
To embrace my mother's spirit, dead as she was!
Three times I rushed toward her, desperate to hold her,
Three times she fluttered through my fingers, sifting away
Like a shadow, dissolving like a dream, and each time
The grief cut to the heart, sharper, yes, and I,
I cried out to her
"Mother—why not wait for me? How I long to hold you!
Homer: *The Odyssey*, Book XI, trans. Robert Fagles

Why does all bad news start with a phone call?

In late January 1960, I was working on an English graduate paper for a second year class at the Johns Hopkins University in Baltimore. My small
apartment was a mess—dirty dishes in the sink, papers all over the table,
books everywhere.

The phone rang. It was my father. He may have spoken three sentences: "Your mother is in the hospital. She's in a coma. You'd better come home." My response was just as laconic—"I'll be on the next train to New York."

I packed hurriedly, then ran down the street to the rooming house where Aldo Fortuna, another English graduate student, was living. The minute I told him that my father had called, he understood. No Italian father calls unless something is terribly wrong. I gave Aldo the keys to my apartment, told him to eat anything in the refrigerator, gave him $5 that I had borrowed to repay another student. I also asked Aldo to see the Chairman of the Department to inform him that I was suddenly called home and to ask for an extension of the due date on the paper. Aldo promised to take care of everything and walked me to the Baltimore train station ten blocks away. It was the worst walk of my life. I was afraid that Nena was already dead and that my father hadn't told me.

It took an age to arrive at Pennsylvania Station in New York City, another century to reach the Port Authority Building on 42ⁿᵈ Street, and an eon to get the bus from there to Lodi. I arrived home around 1 a.m.

My father had waited up for me. On the prior Friday in the middle of the night, he recounted, my mother had gotten up from bed to use the bathroom. She groped for the hall light and flipped the switch on, but the hallway was still pitch black. My father found her in the hall on her hands and knees crying,

Moe, Moe, help me. I'm blind.

Nena had been in the hospital for a week. My father hadn't let me know because he was sure that she just had a cold. In actuality, she had a severe respiratory virus that had thrown off her sugar-insulin equilibrium, and the doctors were having a difficult time stabilizing her. They called her a "brittle diabetic." On arrival at the hospital, Nena's blood sugar was 640. A normal reading ranges between 100-120. To bring her blood sugar down, the medical team had given her a large dose of insulin, but it was too large—it had thrown her into insulin shock. Then they gave her glucose to raise the blood sugar, but her blood pressure skyrocketed, and she developed dropsy as her kidneys failed. To eliminate the edema, they were treating her with diuretics, and the kidney function was slowly normalizing, but her blood pressure still hadn't come down. When she went into a coma, my father called me in Baltimore.

When I saw Nena first thing in the morning, she was still comatose, in an oxygen tent, tubes everywhere. She was breathing hard, and her lips were cracked.

My father and I each took twelve-hour shifts at Nena's bedside, talking to her, holding her hand, moisturizing her lips with Vaseline ointment. We were certain that she could hear us. Sometimes one of my father's sisters or my Cousin Ann relieved us during the day, or Tia Rosa's son, Cousin Bill (he of the black, never-to-be-red-again, hair) stayed while we went home to sleep. Ida and Freddie came as soon as he was off work. Mary helped, but Pete couldn't bear to see his sister ill and stayed downstairs in the waiting room.

Nena finally regained consciousness on a Wednesday, a week after she had gone into the coma. Though parched and hoarse, she could speak in monosyllables and was fully aware of her surroundings and condition. Her blood pressure was still too high, and in the afternoon she had three small strokes. In the midst of the seizures, she asked me as her face twitched involuntarily,

I'm having a stroke, aren't I?

Then she began coming in and out of consciousness. At one point she called out,

Shigemitsu is here.

Why was she dreaming about Japan's wartime Foreign Minister? Had she remembered that he had signed the instrument of surrender in September 1945, or was she recalling the war crimes tribunal that sentenced him to seven years in prison? In her delirium, she began thrashing about, and a nurse and I tied her hands loosely to the side rails of the bed with a soft bandage. She needed to rest. As I restrained her, she looked up at me and said,

You're a hard woman, Diane.

Later that afternoon, she had settled down and was once again fully conscious. She had stopped flailing about, and we were able to remove the restraints from her wrists. When the neurologist came in to examine her, he poked her foot with a pointed instrument. "How many times am I sticking you, Nena?" She was annoyed.

Three times, stupid, she replied.

My mother was not usually rude, and her sharp response made my father think that she was recovering. Though she had suffered little obvious damage and was in no pain, her reply was an example of cerebral irritability, a common effect of stroke.

I had been checking her vital signs and knew that she wasn't "out of the woods" as my father had so happily declared. Her pulse was wildly erratic, ranging from 85 beats per minute to 160. Her heart was fibrillating. I tried to prepare my father, but he wouldn't listen. "She's going to be fine," he argued. "Her mind is so clear. You heard her. She's come out of the coma, and she's going to be fine."

By Wednesday night, she was conscious and could speak hoarsely between labored breaths.

Please take me home, she pleaded more than once. *I want to die in my own bed.*

"Please, Mommy, you know that we can't take you home. The hospital has equipment that you need."

"Don't talk like that, Nena. You are going to get well," my father told her.

Her response was to ask for a priest. Nena had never been religious. Though baptized, she hadn't made her Holy Communion and Confirmation. As far as I knew, she had never attended Sunday Mass; nevertheless, a Catholic priest came and administered Last Rites at her request.

When he left, she asked us to pray for her. Ann and Mary were present, and the three of us recited "The Lord's Prayer" and "Hail Mary, Full of Grace" over and over until she fell back into an exhausted sleep.

Cousin Bill stayed with her that night allowing my father and me to go home and rest. I don't think I ever adequately thanked him for all his kindnesses to my mother. (After the funeral, I never saw him again. Tia Fidela had died in 1956 five months after Bill, and Aunt Rosa and Cousin Bill returned to Puerto Rico sometime in the early 1960s).

On Thursday evening after Freddie arrived, Nena broke our hearts utterly and forever. She turned to my father and asked him to get her a pineapple ice cream soda, Pepín's favorite confection but one that she never ordered when she was well. Only Freddie and I recognized that at the very end of her life she was determined to die just as her father had twenty-one years before. She was consciously repeating his last request and, by so doing, telling the two of us that she was acquiescing to death. Verily, verily, man is a symbol-making animal.

My father willingly trotted downstairs to the coffee shop to do her bidding, but he didn't understand. When he returned with the soda in a paper cup, my mother took two sips and, like Pepìn, was too tired to drink more.

She remained conscious Friday morning until 10 a.m. when her breathing became markedly labored. She was in no pain, but she was very tired. An hour later, we saw the blood leave her feet and heard the brief rattle of her last throe.

So died Nena Balzac, weaver of tales, preserver of the past, mother and surrogate mother, avid moviegoer, kindest of kind spirits.

Envoi

Long have you timidly waded, holding a plank by the shore,
Now I will you to be a bold swimmer,
To jump off in the midst of the sea,
and rise again and nod to me and shout,
and laughingly dash with your hair
—Walt Whitman, *"Song of Myself"* (1855), 1227-30

We are essentially peoples of the sea: the Balzacs from Puerto Rico, the Lopez from Jamaica, and their issue from Long Island. My mother and all her brothers were strong swimmers. My parents first put me into the water at Rockaway Beach when I was eight months old. Over the next several years, I took to it so completely that my father began calling me a water rat and had to threaten that he would drag me out of the surf if I didn't come back to the blanket to eat. Summers meant going to the shore; on very hot nights, sleeping on the beach with the waves pounding and casting up fine spray in the scary pitch-black darkness.

Many years later, I was detained in the desolate Mid-West for the better part of a year. One day, in a desultory mood while my students took a quiz, I watched from a classroom balcony as University custodians spread fertilizer on the scant patches of campus grass. Suddenly I got a whiff of phosphate salts—they smelled like the Atlantic—and I knew that I had to go home.

So if I invoke the metaphor of the sea, I'm not reaching for a poetic image; I'm trying to hone in on the essence of all these lives. These sketches seem to me to mirror the movement of the waves depositing and reclaiming bright fragments of shells on the battered shore.

𝔉inis

March 25, 2011

_____